Human and Social Biology

for CSEC®

Trevor Alleyne • Mervin Brown

Richard Fosbery • Camille Mitchell

A Caribbean Examinations Council® *Study Guide*

Great Clarendon Street, Oxford, OX2 6DP, United Kingdom

Oxford University Press is a department of the University of Oxford.
It furthers the University's objective of excellence in research, scholarship,
and education by publishing worldwide. Oxford is a registered trade mark of
Oxford University Press in the UK and in certain other countries

First published by Nelson Thornes Ltd in 2013
This edition published by Oxford University Press in 2015

British Library Cataloguing in Publication Data
Data available

978-1-4085-2083-3

5

Printed and bound by CPI Group (UK) Ltd, Croydon, CR0 4YY

Acknowledgements

Cover photograph: Mark Lyndersay, Lyndersay Digital, Trinidad
www.lyndersaydigital.com
Illustrations: Barking Dog, GreenGate Publishing Services and Wearset Ltd
Page make-up: Wearset Ltd, Boldon, Tyne and Wear

Although we have made every effort to trace and contact all
copyright holders before publication this has not been possible in all
cases. If notified, the publisher will rectify any errors or omissions at
the earliest opportunity.

The manufacturer's authorised representative in the EU for product
safety is Oxford University Press España S.A. of El Parque Empresarial
San Fernando de Henares, Avenida de Castilla, 2 – 28830 Madrid
(www.oup.es/en or product.safety@oup.com).
OUP España S.A. also acts as importer into Spain of products
made by the manufacturer.

Contents

Contents

This Study Guide has been developed exclusively with the Caribbean Examinations Council (CXC®) to be used as an additional resource by candidates, both in and out of school, following the Caribbean Secondary Education Certificate (CSEC®) programme.

It has been prepared by a team with expertise in the CSEC® syllabus, teaching and examination. The contents are designed to support learning by providing tools to help you achieve your best in Human and Social Biology and the features included make it easier for you to master the key concepts and requirements of the syllabus. *Do remember to refer to your syllabus for full guidance on the course requirements and examination format!*

Inside this Study Guide is an interactive CD, which includes electronic activities to assist you in developing good examination techniques:

On Your Marks activities provide sample examination-style short answer and essay type questions, with example candidate answers and feedback from an examiner to show where answers could be improved. These activities will build your understanding, skill level and confidence in answering examination questions.

Test Yourself activities are specifically designed to provide experience of multiple-choice examination questions and helpful feedback will refer you to sections inside the Study Guide so that you can revise problem areas.

This unique combination of focused syllabus content and interactive examination practice will provide you with invaluable support to help you reach your full potential in CSEC® Human and Social Biology.

Throughout the Study Guide there are hints, explanations and suggestions. There is also a section at the beginning that is designed to help you use this book to revise thoroughly and effectively. The final chapter is designed to help you prepare for your exams by giving you advice on how to answer the questions in Paper 1 and Paper 2.

As you work through your CSEC® Human and Social Biology course, read through any notes that you take during your lessons. While doing this you should read your textbook, this Study Guide and any other relevant information you can find. For example, when you study the sections on health and the environment you may find that newspapers and leaflets from doctors and pharmacies have useful information. The internet is also a good source of up-to-date information.

When you finish a topic, answer the summary questions at the end of each section. You will notice that many of these start by asking for definitions of the terms relevant to each topic. This is to prompt you to use the glossary, which is on the CD. Try all the practice exam questions that are at the end of each unit. Use the answers, which are also on the CD, to check your answers. Do not look at the answers until you have tried all the questions for each section. The questions at the end of each unit only test the topics in that unit. In the examination you will find that each question may test more than one unit. Key words have been highlighted throughout the text in blue. Definitions of these key words can be found in the glossary on the CD.

The suggestions on how to revise will help you to make your own revision notes, which you can use in the weeks before the exams.

You will find many Caribbean examples in the sections relating to Modules 1 and 3. These come from the Caribbean in its widest sense – all those countries within the Caribbean basin and bordering the Caribbean Sea, not just the countries that take CXC® examinations. You can expect questions in your examination that will be set in Caribbean contexts and you should use regional and local examples in your answers.

How to revise

This Study Guide is designed to help you with your learning. Below are some effective techniques to help you do this. Try them and find out which techniques work best for you.

Make learning and revision notes

Learning notes: Divide the syllabus into sections and spend more time on the topics you find difficult. Make your own notes to help you learn. Try writing the information in a variety of different ways using prose, bullet points, tables and graphic organisers. See the next section for ideas about how to do this.

Revision notes: These should be shorter than your learning notes and easier to use in the days leading up to the exams. Make these for the topics that you find especially difficult. You could write them on cards and carry them around with you. You could put them on a computer or a mobile device, so it is easier to edit them as you revise.

Draw diagrams

Find all the topics that require diagrams. Copy them from your textbook or this Study Guide. Add some labels. Turn over the diagram and try redrawing it from memory. Then check your diagram. Do this until you have perfect diagrams. As you may be asked to draw diagrams in the exam it is a good idea to practise making them. The 'Study focus' feature below gives some simple rules for drawing diagrams.

In this Study Guide you are asked to annotate diagrams, which allows you to put a lot of information on one piece of paper. An annotation is a note that gives further information about an aspect of your diagram.

Make your own glossary

Human and Social Biology has so many words to learn! All of the terms that we think you should know are in blue in the text. They are also listed in the glossary on the CD, so look at this now. If you use other books, dictionaries or the internet you will find different definitions of these terms. Start making a glossary of your own and incorporate links to your textbook and this Study Guide. Make some vocabulary tests for yourself to make sure you know the meaning of the terms.

Make tables

Comparison tables

As you work through the Study Guide you will see that there are instructions to make tables to compare different structures or processes. When making these tables, always use an extra column for the features that you are comparing. Here is an example (from section 4.4):

Features	Red blood cells	White blood cells	
		Phagocytes	Lymphocytes
Nucleus	✗	✓	✓
Contains haemoglobin	✓	✗	✗
Function	Transports oxygen	Engulfs bacteria	Secretes antibodies

Summary tables

Get large sheets of paper and make up tables to summarise everything that you need to know about topics, such as specialised cells. You could put all the information on a spreadsheet, so it is easy to update and sort.

KEY POINTS

- Learning notes are made from different sources and should be longer and more detailed than revision notes.
- Revision notes are brief notes that concentrate on topics you find difficult.
- Diagrams and drawings should be made using sharp lines. They should be labelled using straight lines made with a ruler.
- Tables can be made to compare structures and processes – they should always have a column headed **'Features'**. Summary tables are good for organising information for topics such as drugs and diseases.

Graphic organisers make it easy to see how ideas fit together. Spider diagrams and flow chart diagrams are two examples.

Spider and flow chart diagrams

Here is an example of a spider diagram from Unit 1. You can make diagrams like this for each of the topics throughout the book. They make good aids to revision as they link together all the points you need to remember. Spider diagrams are a good way to plan your answers to the essay questions in Paper 2. See 12.3.

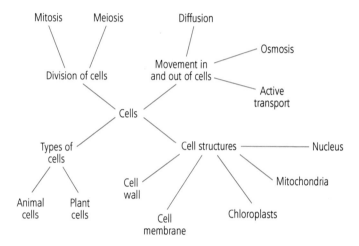

STUDY FOCUS

As you work your way through this Study Guide try making many spider diagrams and flow chart diagrams.

Flow chart diagrams

These are a good way to show processes that occur as a sequence or as a cycle; they are also good for showing the procedure to follow in a practical. You often see these drawn with boxes and arrows.

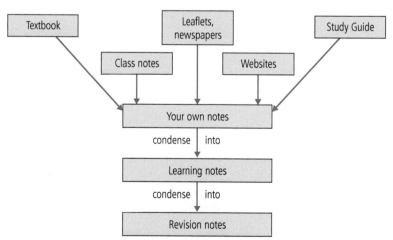

A flow chart diagram about revision

Flow chart diagrams are also good for showing how aspects of the blood, such as its temperature and glucose concentration, are regulated. Complex processes, such as sewage treatment, can also be shown this way. The thinking involved in making graphic organisers is good for revision. The final product is always worth keeping even if it doesn't look very good. It will help you remember how you made it.

Presenting and analysing data

See 2.8, 3.6, 10.12, 12.2 and 12.3 for further information about presenting data as graphs, charts and diagrams. You will need to practise analysing, presenting and interpreting data. Use the structured practice exam questions in this book to help you develop these important skills.

Revision should not be a lonely experience. Find others to revise with and give yourselves tasks to do. For example, you can write tests for each other.

Don't leave revision to the last minute. Each time you finish a section of the syllabus make sure you organise your notes and make some revision notes for yourself. You can come back to them later and improve them and make links to other parts of the syllabus. Keep your learning and revision notes organised in a folder and/or start a folder on your computer.

KEY POINTS

- Spider diagrams are good for organising your knowledge and showing the links between topics.
- Flow chart diagrams are a good way to summarise information about sequences and cycles.
- More complex diagrams can include diagrams, labels and annotations (notes).

1 Living organisms and the environment

1.1

Characteristics of living organisms

Figure 1.1.1 | What do we use this food for once we have eaten it?

There are seven characteristics of living organisms. These life processes are shared by all living organisms. They are nutrition, respiration, growth, excretion, movement, irritability or sensitivity and reproduction.

Nutrition

Nutrition is the process of obtaining food. Organisms gain energy and substances that they use for growth, to repair their bodies and to replace worn out parts. Nutrients are compounds that may be large and complex, such as carbohydrates, proteins and vitamins, or small and simple, such as **minerals**, e.g. iron and calcium.

Green plants use **photosynthesis** to capture energy from sunlight and use it to turn the simple compounds carbon dioxide and water into simple sugars. Plants convert the simple sugars into complex compounds such as starch, **cellulose** and **proteins**. Plants use minerals that they absorb from the soil to make proteins and other complex compounds, such as the green pigment **chlorophyll**.

Animals do not carry out photosynthesis. They eat plants or other animals to gain the energy and nutrients that they need. The process of taking in food is **ingestion**. The food is digested, absorbed into the blood and then assimilated by cells for growth and repair. Food that is not digested and absorbed is egested in faeces.

Respiration

All living organisms respire to release energy from complex chemical compounds. **Respiration** involves chemical reactions that occur in all living cells. **Aerobic respiration** requires oxygen and is summarised in this word equation:

glucose + oxygen → carbon dioxide + water + energy released

Respiration can also occur without oxygen, as it does in our muscles when we run very fast. This type of respiration is **anaerobic respiration**.

Living things use energy for the other characteristics of life.

Excretion

All living organisms produce waste substances as a result of **metabolism**. Metabolism is all the chemical reactions that occur in an organism. Respiration plays an important role in metabolism. **Excretion** is the removal of waste substances from the body. Animals breathe out carbon dioxide and other waste substances leave the body in the urine. Plants excrete carbon dioxide produced from their respiration at night, but during the day they use it in photosynthesis.

Growth

Growth is a permanent increase in the size of an organism. It can involve an increase in the number of cells, the size of cells or both. It always involves making more complex chemicals, such as proteins. Plants carry on growing throughout their lives. Animals stop growing when they reach a certain size. Measuring the increase in length or dry mass of an organism is a good way to find out how much an organism has grown.

Irritability (sensitivity)

Living organisms detect or sense changes in their environment. A change like this is a **stimulus** (plural = stimuli). **Irritability**, also known as **sensitivity**, is the ability to detect these stimuli and respond to them. Animals have sensory cells and sense organs for detecting the stimuli of light, sound, touch, pressure and chemicals in the air and in food. The movement of the sun is a stimulus. Plants respond to this by moving their leaves to face the light. The flowers of some plants open in the morning and close at night.

Movement

Organisms move into new areas or to change position.

Plants move slowly when they grow. Their roots move down into the soil and their leaves and stems move up towards the light.

Most animals are able to move their whole bodies to obtain their food or to avoid being caught by predators. Some animals remain fixed to one place throughout their lives, but they are able to move parts, such as the tentacles on a sea anemone.

Reproduction

Organisms reproduce to make new individuals. **Sexual reproduction** involves two parent organisms producing gametes (sex cells) which fuse to give rise to the next generation. **Asexual reproduction** involves one parent having offspring that are often identical to each other and to the parent. There are no gametes produced.

Figure 1.1.2 How many characteristics of life are involved in shooting a basket?

1.2 Animal and plant cells

Animal and plant cells

At the end of this topic you should be able to:

- describe the structure of animal and plant cells as seen with a light microscope
- list the similarities and differences between animal and plant cells
- list the functions of the main cell structures
- describe the structure of microbes: viruses, bacteria and fungi.

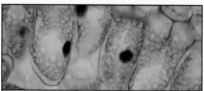

Figure 1.2.2 Plant cells, such as these palisade mesophyll cells from a leaf, have a fixed shape because they are surrounded by a cell wall

Cell structure

Cells are sometimes called the 'units of life' as all organisms are made of cells. All cells share some features in common although there are significant differences between the different types. The photographs show typical animal and plant cells that you may see through a microscope.

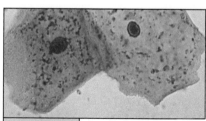

Figure 1.2.1 You can see the cell membrane, cytoplasm and nucleus in these human cheek cells taken from the lining of the mouth as they have been stained with a blue stain

Animal and plant cell structure

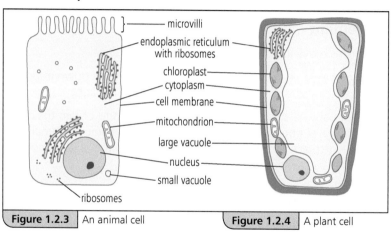

microvilli
endoplasmic reticulum with ribosomes
chloroplast
cytoplasm
cell membrane
mitochondrion
large vacuole
nucleus
small vacuole
ribosomes

Figure 1.2.3 An animal cell

Figure 1.2.4 A plant cell

Functions of cell structures

Cell structure	Functions
Cell wall (bacteria, plants and fungi)	• Stops cells from bursting when they are full of water • Gives fixed shapes to cells • Allows water and dissolved substances to pass through freely (freely permeable)
Cell membrane	• Forms a barrier between cells and their surroundings • Keeps contents of cells inside • Partially permeable (see 1.4)
Nucleus	• Contains the chromosomes (see 9.1) • Controls all activities inside cells • Controls how cells develop
Cytoplasm	• Place where many chemical reactions take place, e.g. respiration and making proteins for cells
Mitochondrion	• Carries out the reactions of aerobic respiration
Endoplasmic reticulum	• Network of membranes for attachment of ribosomes and transport of the proteins that they make
Ribosome	• Makes proteins from **amino acids**
Chloroplast (plants only)	• Carries out photosynthesis • Stores starch
Vacuole	• *Plants* – large and full of water to maintain shape and 'firmness' of cells • *Animals* – small and stores enzymes for digestion within cells

Microbes

Microbes or microorganisms are bacteria, fungi and viruses.

Bacteria

Each **bacterium** is made of one cell and is described as **unicellular**. The cell has a cell wall and a cell membrane. The genetic material is in the cytoplasm as there is no nucleus. The cytoplasm contains ribosomes to make proteins, but there are no other structures.

Fungi

Yeast is a **fungus** that is also unicellular. Unlike bacteria, each yeast cell has a nucleus, mitochondria, endoplasmic reticulum, ribosomes and a large vacuole. In many ways yeasts are like plant cells except that they have no chloroplasts. Figure 1.2.6 shows a mould fungus. Many of these do not have separate cells at all. The long thin threads are not subdivided into cells but instead contain all the structures in one long 'tube'.

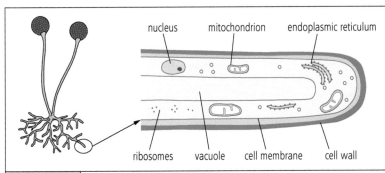

| **Figure 1.2.6** | The cell structure of a mould fungus |

Viruses

All **viruses** are **parasites**. They invade organisms and reproduce inside their cells. Viruses do not have cells. They have a central core composed of genetic material (**DNA** or **RNA**) surrounded by a protein coat or capsule. Some of them are surrounded by a cell membrane from their host cell.

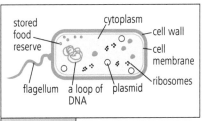

| **Figure 1.2.5** | A bacterial cell |

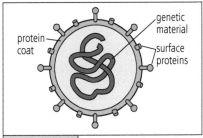

| **Figure 1.2.7** | Viruses come in a variety of shapes, but they all have genetic material enclosed in a protein capsule |

STUDY FOCUS

Before you answer question 3, make sure you read the section on page 3 about making comparison tables.

KEY POINTS

1 Organisms are made of cells, known as 'units of life'.

2 Animal and plant cells have cell membranes, nuclei, cytoplasm, mitochondria, endoplasmic reticulum and ribosomes.

3 Plant cells have cell walls, chloroplasts and large, central vacuoles. Animal cells do not have these.

4 Bacteria and fungi have cells similar to plant cells, but bacteria do not have nuclei and fungi do not have chloroplasts.

5 Viruses do not have cells. They are made of genetic material enclosed in a protein coat.

SUMMARY QUESTIONS

1 What is a cell?

2 State four structures that are found in both plant and animal cells.

3 Make a table comparing the cells of animals, plants, bacteria and fungi.

4 Explain why viruses are totally unlike the cells shown in this topic.

5 Make models of plant and animal cells using card, paper, modelling clay and any other common materials you can find. Find drawings of different types of virus and use them to make models to show their different shapes.

Specialised cells

At the end of this topic you should be able to:

• identify different types of human cells

• explain the importance of cell specialisation.

Humans, like most animals and plants have bodies made of many cells that work together. We are **multicellular**. This means that the bodies' functions are divided between different groups of cells.

Epithelial cells

Epithelial cells are found on the surfaces of organisms, for example, the outer layer of our skin. They also line internal structures, such as the trachea and lungs.

Ciliated epithelial cells form the lining of the air passages in the lungs (trachea and bronchi) and in the fallopian tubes in the female reproductive system. These cells have tiny hair-like **cilia** that beat back and forth to create a current in the fluid next to their surfaces.

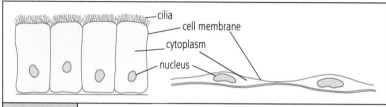

Figure 1.3.1 | Ciliated cells from the human trachea and squamous cells from the alveoli

In the lungs, cilia move the mucus that traps dust and pathogens up to the nose and throat. In the fallopian tubes, cilia move the egg from the ovary to the uterus.

Squamous cells are very thin cells. They form the outer layer of the skin and line the tiny air pockets in the lungs and the arteries and veins. Squamous cells form the walls of blood capillaries. The cells in Figure 1.2.1 on page 8 are squamous cells from the lining of the mouth.

Nerve cells

Most nerve cells have long thin extensions that transmit nerve impulses over great distances in the body. Some nerve cells, like the one in the photograph (Figure 1.3.2), have short extensions that connect nerve cells together. There are many of these in the brain and the spinal cord.

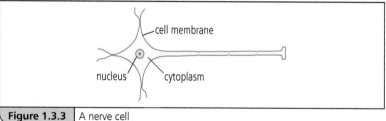

Figure 1.3.3 | A nerve cell

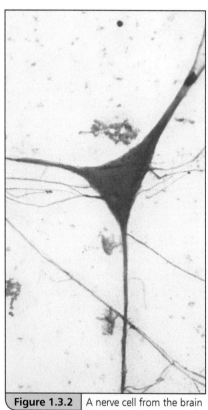

Figure 1.3.2 | A nerve cell from the brain

Muscle cells

The cells that make up muscles in our gut, reproductive system and in arteries and veins, are long thin cells, which each have a single nucleus. They all have protein filaments that move to shorten the muscles, when they contract to bring about movement.

Organisation of cells

Most cells are organised into **tissues**. Ciliated cells are arranged into thin sheets that line the trachea. The trachea is an example of an **organ** that is composed of different tissues that work together for one major function or functions. The trachea together with the lungs forms the gas exchange system. An **organ system** comprises several organs that work together for one major function of the body.

The idea that cells specialise in certain functions is known as **division of labour**. Most specialised cells carry out one function for the body and rely on other cells and tissues to provide the substances that they need and to take away and excrete their waste products. The body maintains constant conditions, such as temperature and pH, so that cells work efficiently.

Gamete cells

Two types of cell in the human body are not organised into tissues. These are the reproductive cells or **gametes** that are produced by the reproductive system. Egg cells are produced in the ovaries and sperm cells are produced in the testes. There is more about them in 8.1 and 8.2.

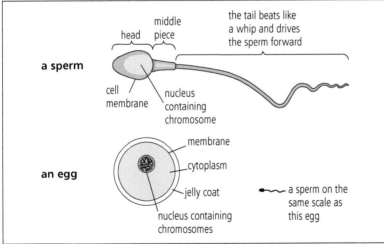

Figure 1.3.5 | Human eggs and sperm cells are specialised for their roles in reproduction

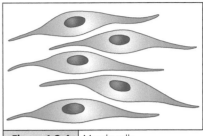

Figure 1.3.4 | Muscle cells

SUMMARY QUESTIONS

1 Define the following terms: *multicellular*, *specialised*, *tissue*, *organ*, *organ system* and *division of labour*.

2 Make some learning notes on all the specialised cells in this topic. See page 2 to help you make these notes.

STUDY FOCUS

Permeable means that substances can pass through. Cellulose cell walls are described as fully or freely permeable as all substances can pass through. Impermeable means that no substance can pass through. Partially permeable means some substances can pass through but others cannot. These terms are used throughout this study guide. Make sure you know what they mean and can use them correctly.

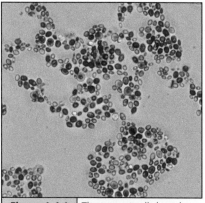

Figure 1.4.1 These yeast cells have been placed in a blue dye which has diffused into them

Cells cannot exist in isolation from their surroundings; they need to take in substances and get rid of their waste. Cell membranes surround the cytoplasm allowing some substances to enter but keeping others out. This is why they are described as **partially permeable membranes**.

Diffusion

Diffusion is the movement of molecules from a place where there is a high concentration to a place where there is a low concentration. The difference between the concentrations is the **concentration gradient**. Oxygen is needed by mitochondria for aerobic respiration. The concentration of oxygen within our cells is very low as it is used up all the time. The concentration outside the cell in the tissue fluid is much higher. Molecules of oxygen move about randomly and over time more pass through the membrane into the cell than pass out.

Osmosis

Osmosis is the diffusion of water molecules from a place with a low concentration of solutes (a dilute solution) to a place with a higher concentration of solutes (a more concentrated solution) across a partially permeable membrane.

Blood consists of cells suspended in a solution of salts, glucose and proteins called plasma. This diagram shows what happens to red blood cells when drops of blood are put into three different solutions.

Figure 1.4.2 Red blood cells in different solutions
  A Tap water
  B A salt solution that has about the same concentration as blood plasma
  C A solution with a concentration of salt greater than that of blood plasma.

In **A**, the water goes red, but it is not cloudy and there are no red blood cells when examined under a microscope. Water has moved by osmosis through the partially permeable membrane around each red blood cell. So much water has entered that the membrane has burst. In **B**, the liquid becomes cloudy red. When examined under a microscope the red blood cells in this liquid are normal. In **C**, water moves out of the cells by osmosis, the cells decrease in volume and become crinkly.

Plant cells behave differently because they have a cell wall. When plant cells are put into water, they absorb water by osmosis. The vacuole fills with water and pushes against the cell wall making the cell **turgid**. When placed into a solution with a high concentration of solutes, water leaves the cell by osmosis and the vacuole shrinks pulling the cytoplasm and the cell membrane away from the cell wall. This is called **plasmolysis** and the cells are described as **flaccid**. Water moves from cell to cell by osmosis when the cell contents have different concentrations.

Active transport

Active transport is the movement of ions or molecules in or out of a cell through the cell membrane against a concentration gradient, using energy released during respiration.

When moving *into* the cell, the molecule or ion from the surroundings combines with a **carrier protein**. Respiration provides the energy for the carrier protein to change its shape to move the ion (e.g. potassium ion) or molecule (e.g. glucose) to the inside of the membrane. After releasing the molecule or ion, the carrier protein changes back to its original shape. Active transport occurs in almost all cells.

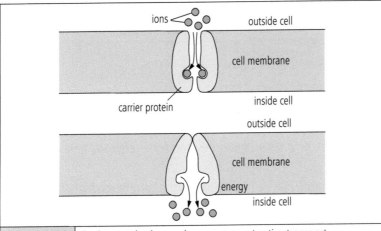

| Figure 1.4.4 | Carrier proteins in membranes carry out active transport |

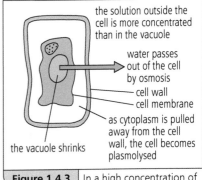

| Figure 1.4.3 | In a high concentration of solutes, plant cells become plasmolysed like this |

EXAM TIP

You should always write about water molecules, not water particles. You should also write about high and low concentrations, or concentrated and dilute solutions, never about 'strong' and 'weak' solutions.

SUMMARY QUESTIONS

1 Write definitions of the following terms: *diffusion, concentration gradient, partially permeable membrane, osmosis* and *active transport*.

2 Make a table to show the similarities and differences between diffusion, osmosis and active transport. Remember to include a column to show the features that you are comparing.

3 Explain why it is important that the concentration of the blood plasma does not become too low or too high.

4 Describe how active transport occurs to move a molecule out of a cell.

5 Make a spider diagram or a concept map to summarise what you know about movement across cell membranes.

KEY POINTS

1 Substances move into and out of cells by diffusion, osmosis and active transport.

2 Diffusion is the movement of molecules down a concentration gradient.

3 Osmosis is the diffusion of water molecules from a solution with a low concentration of solutes (dilute solution) to a solution with a high concentration of solutes (concentrated solution).

4 Active transport is the movement of molecules and ions across a cell membrane against a concentration gradient using energy from respiration.

Photosynthesis

Figure 1.5.1 Light is the energy source for these plants and indirectly for all other organisms

Plants produce oxygen which we need for our respiration. They also use carbon dioxide and water to make a huge number of different substances that are in the foods we eat. They make it possible for us to exist on earth.

The process of photosynthesis occurs in chloroplasts. These cell structures contain the green pigment chlorophyll. This absorbs light energy to drive chemical reactions which use carbon dioxide and water to make sugars. This process is summarised in this word equation:

$$\text{carbon dioxide} + \text{water} \xrightarrow{\text{light energy and chlorophyll}} \text{glucose} + \text{oxygen}$$

The glucose that is produced is used to make:

- sucrose for transport around the plant
- cellulose for making cell walls
- starch for storing energy to be used in respiration at night
- fats for making cell membranes and for energy storage, e.g. in seeds.

By combining sugars with nitrogen from nitrate ions, plants can make amino acids and then use them to make proteins, such as enzymes (see 2.6). Plants also make substances that we call **vitamins**.

Plants use the oxygen they make for their own aerobic respiration (see 3.4). However, they cannot use it all and much diffuses out of leaves into the atmosphere for other organisms, such as us, to use.

Testing leaves for starch

Testing leaves for starch shows that a plant has been photosynthesising. Much of the sugar produced in photosynthesis is converted into starch. Iodine solution is used to detect the presence of starch. The green chlorophyll must be removed first to see the colour change with iodine solution.

1 Put a leaf into boiling water for one minute. This destroys membranes so you can extract the chlorophyll.

2 If you use a Bunsen burner to boil the water, turn it off.

3 Put the leaf into a test tube of **ethanol**. The chlorophyll dissolves into the ethanol.

Stand the test tube in a beaker of hot water for about 10 minutes.

4 Wash the leaf in cold water. This removes the ethanol and rehydrates the leaf which softens it and makes it easy to spread out.

5 Spread the leaf out flat on a white surface and put iodine solution on it.

If the leaf goes blue-black, starch is present. If it stays a light yellow-brown colour there is no starch.

If you test a leaf from a plant that has been in a dark place for about a week you will find that it has no starch in it. The plant is destarched. All the starch has been converted to sugars and used in respiration. Destarched plants are used to show that light is necessary for photosynthesis (see summary question 4).

You can use the same procedure to test variegated leaves (like those in the photograph) for starch.

Photosynthesis occurs only in the green areas where chlorophyll is present. Chlorophyll is only present in chloroplasts (see 1.2).

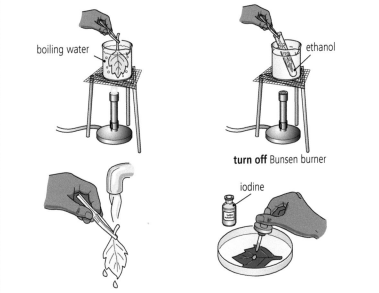

Figure 1.5.2 Testing a leaf for starch

Figure 1.5.3 Variegated hibiscus leaves

SUMMARY QUESTIONS

1 Define the terms *photosynthesis*, *chlorophyll* and *chloroplast*.

2 Write out the word equation for photosynthesis. Indicate on your equation the two raw materials, the source of energy and the two products.

3 Describe what happens to the products of photosynthesis.

4 Some leaves on a destarched plant were covered with black paper. The plant was put in the light for two days. When tested with iodine solution, the leaves that were covered were a yellow-brown colour; the uncovered leaves were black. Explain these results.

5 State and explain the results you would expect if you tested a variegated leaf for starch.

6 A leaf cell is photosynthesising on a warm, sunny day. Explain how this cell obtains the carbon dioxide and water it requires. (Use 1.4 to help you.)

7 Explain why our existence on earth relies entirely on plants.

KEY POINTS

1 Photosynthesis is the conversion of carbon dioxide and water to sugars using light as a source of energy.

2 Photosynthesis occurs in chloroplasts.

3 The green pigment chlorophyll in chloroplasts absorbs light.

4 The sugar produced in photosynthesis is converted to starch for storage, sucrose for transport and cellulose for cell walls. Some is combined with nitrogen to make amino acids and proteins.

15

Food chains

At the end of this topic you should be able to:

- state that all organisms, including humans, rely on plants for food
- define the terms *herbivore, carnivore, omnivore, producer, consumer* and *food chain*.
- draw food chains to show the flow of energy
- name and identify the trophic levels in food chains
- explain that the energy available to organisms decreases along food chains.

Figure 1.6.1 A mixed farm: grass consumed by this cow is converted to meat and milk for humans

Plants produce sugars in photosynthesis. Plants use these sugars to produce a wide range of other chemicals, such as fats and proteins. This is why plants are known as **producers**.

The feeding relationships on a small farm are written as **food chains**:

grasses → cattle → humans
crop plants → humans

The arrows show the direction in which food and energy flows. In these food chains the grasses and the crops are the producers, the cattle are **herbivores** and we are **omnivores** as we eat both plant food and food derived from animals. On the farm cats and dogs only eat food from animals. They are **carnivores**.

The different feeding levels in a food chain are called **trophic levels**. Plants are producers, animals are **consumers**. Herbivores are **primary consumers** and carnivores are **secondary consumers**. Omnivores feed at two or more trophic levels. Most humans are omnivores.

Food chains on land rarely have more than four trophic levels. Aquatic food chains are in the sea (marine) and in ponds, rivers and lakes (freshwater).

Marine food chains are often longer than those on land and in freshwater because the producers are tiny algae and the primary and secondary consumers are small animals.

A marine food chain:

algae (growing on coral reef) → parrotfish → grouper

A freshwater food chain:

phytoplankton → zooplankton → guppies → killifish
(tiny algae)   (small animals)

Energy losses in food chains

Energy flow through food chains is relatively inefficient. At best, plants absorb only 2–5% of the light energy that reaches their leaves.

At each level of the food chain energy is lost through respiration and other metabolic processes as heat to the atmosphere, faeces, urine and undigestible remains.

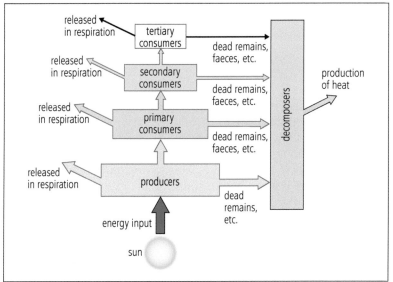

Figure 1.6.3 | Energy losses from food chains mean that there is very little energy available to animals in the top trophic level

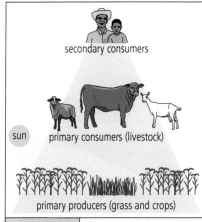

Figure 1.6.2 | This pyramid shows that not much energy is available to animals at the top of the pyramid

When farmers grow crops, such as rice, for human consumption all of the energy in the grain is available to us as primary consumers.

Livestock farmers may grow fodder crops, such as Guinea grass and cowpea, for grazing their animals. Animals, such as pigs, cattle and chickens, respire, move about and keep warm. They transfer 90% of the energy they consume to their surroundings. If we reduce the number of trophic levels in the food chain by eating only plant foods, such as rice, more people at the end of the food chain can be fed. This is because we are cutting down the 90% 'wastage' of energy by livestock at the primary consumer level.

People in many countries may have diets that consist of food of plant origin with some meat or fish. In wealthier countries, many people have a more varied diet that includes more meat.

The human population is increasing. If farmers are to provide enough food for everyone our diet may have to change to one that includes more plant foods and less meat.

SUMMARY QUESTIONS

1 Define the following: *herbivore, carnivore, omnivore, food chain, trophic level, producer, consumer, primary consumer, secondary consumer* and *tertiary consumer*.

2 Explain why there are rarely more than four trophic levels in many food chains.

3 'Humans gain their food energy directly and indirectly from plants.' Explain this statement.

4 Draw three food chains to show how humans can be primary consumers, secondary consumers or tertiary consumers.

5 Explain why a diet rich in animal produce is inefficient in terms of energy.

KEY POINTS

1 All organisms rely on photosynthesis in green plants for their energy intake.

2 Herbivores eat plant matter, carnivores eat animals, omnivores eat plant and animal food.

3 Food chains show the feeding relationships between organisms. Producers are green plants while consumers are animals that feed as herbivores, carnivores or omnivores.

4 The arrows in a food chain show the direction of energy flow.

5 Energy is lost from each trophic level in the form of heat as a result of movement and respiration, or in food material that is egested and metabolic wastes that are excreted.

6 About 10% of the energy entering a consumer trophic level is available to the next trophic level.

The carbon cycle

At the end of this topic you should be able to:

- state the importance of carbon dioxide as a raw material for photosynthesis
- state that carbon dioxide is released in combustion, respiration and decomposition
- state examples of carbon compounds that are released during combustion
- explain how the element carbon is cycled.

Carbon is the basis of life on earth. It is the element found in all the chemical compounds made by organisms, such as carbohydrates, proteins, fats and nucleic acids (e.g. DNA). There is a very large quantity of carbon on the earth, but this supply is finite. Much is 'locked up' in rocks and is not available to organisms. Carbon is recycled so there is a continuous supply to plants in the form of carbon dioxide. Plants use carbon dioxide and transform it into sugars in photosynthesis.

STUDY FOCUS

Light energy is absorbed by plants and made available as chemical energy to animals. Eventually all the energy that entered a food chain passes to the environment as heat energy and cannot be used by plants. There is a continuous supply of energy from the sun and energy is **not** recycled from animals to plants.

We get most of our power from burning fossil fuels, such as oil, natural gas and coal. These compounds are **hydrocarbons**. They contain hydrogen, oxygen and carbon. These fuels were formed millions of years ago. Organisms were buried and did not decompose because there was not enough oxygen. They were fossilised. When we burn these fuels we are releasing energy that was captured by plants millions of years ago and is now being released. When we burn these fuels, the hydrocarbons in the fuels are oxidised to form carbon dioxide.

Before people discovered fossil fuels the main fuel was wood. This is still burnt in many parts of the world as a main fuel. As fossil fuels run out, many countries are turning to renewable forms of energy, such as wind energy and the energy in the wood of fast growing trees.

Figure 1.7.1 This power plant burns natural gas to provide Port of Spain with electricity

Respiration

You will read more about respiration in 3.4. Respiration is a chemical process. It occurs in all living cells to release energy from carbon compounds, such as carbohydrates, proteins and fats. Oxygen is required for the type of respiration that releases the most energy. This is the word equation for the aerobic respiration of glucose – one of the body's main fuels:

glucose + oxygen → carbon dioxide + water + energy released

Carbon dioxide is one of the waste products of respiration. As living organisms respire they replace the carbon dioxide that plants absorb. This helps to keep the carbon dioxide concentration in the atmosphere fairly constant and recycles carbon for plants to reuse.

The energy content of foods is determined by burning foods in oxygen. The heat energy released is measured and the energy content of foods is given in **kilojoules**, the unit for energy.

Decomposition

Decomposers are organisms that break down dead and decaying matter. They feed on the waste matter from plants and animals, such as dead leaves, urine and faeces. Many species of bacteria and fungi are decomposers. They grow on their food supply, making and releasing enzymes that digest their food. They absorb the products and use the sugars in respiration. Carbon dioxide is released into the surroundings. Decomposers need oxygen for aerobic respiration.

Figure 1.7.2 | These fungi are decomposing this old tree

In the **carbon cycle** carbon dioxide enters the atmosphere as a result of the following:

• Plants and animals use some of their food for respiration and release carbon dioxide.

• Decomposers use animal faeces and dead plants and animals for food and release carbon dioxide during respiration.

• Fossil fuels, such as oil, peat, coal, and natural gas, contain carbon. When these are burned, carbon dioxide is one of the gases released into the air.

These processes all release carbon dioxide into the air. This balances the uptake of carbon dioxide by photosynthesis. As a result the concentration of carbon dioxide in the atmosphere does not decrease with time.

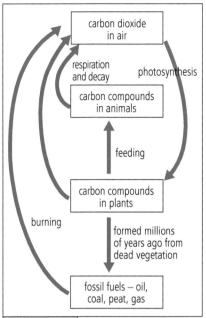

Figure 1.7.3 | The carbon cycle

LINK

If there is not enough oxygen present during combustion, carbon monoxide and methane are also produced. The effects of carbon monoxide are described in 3.5.

KEY POINTS

1 Carbon dioxide is a raw material for photosynthesis.

2 Wood and fossil fuels are burnt to provide us with heat and energy; carbon dioxide is produced unless there is not enough oxygen available, then carbon monoxide and methane are also produced.

3 Carbon dioxide is the end product of respiration; decomposers release carbon dioxide from carbohydrates during respiration.

4 Carbon is recycled. There is always a supply of carbon dioxide for plants.

SUMMARY QUESTIONS

1 a Define the following terms: *combustion*, *respiration* and *decomposition* and explain how these three processes are involved in recycling carbon.

   b Explain the term *fossil fuel*.

2 State three processes that add carbon dioxide to the atmosphere and one that removes it.

3 Describe the role of animals, such as cattle and goats, in the carbon cycle.

4 Why is there an 'energy crisis'?

5 'Energy flows, but carbon is recycled'. Explain this statement.

The nitrogen cycle

At the end of this topic you should be able to:

- state that plants absorb nitrogen in the form of nitrate ions and use them to make amino acids and then proteins

- understand that plants cannot use nitrogen gas (N_2) from the air as their source of nitrogen

- describe the roles of plants, herbivores and carnivores in recycling nitrogen

- describe the roles of microbes in recycling nitrogen and fixing nitrogen (N_2) from the air.

EXAM TIP

Be careful about writing 'plants absorb nitrogen' when you mean 'plants absorb nitrate ions'.
Also do not write that 'farmers add nitrogen to the soil'. They don't, they add fertilisers that provide nitrate ions.

The element nitrogen is part of many important compounds. Approximately 80% of the air is nitrogen gas (N_2), but it is inert. This means plants, animals and most microorganisms cannot use it. It has to be available in the form of compounds, such as amino acids and proteins, and as ions, such as nitrate and ammonium ions.

Here are forms of nitrogen important in biology:
- ammonia (NH_3) and ammonium ions (NH_4^+)
- urea
- amino acids and proteins (examples of proteins such as haemoglobin, amylase, catalase, antibodies, carrier proteins in membranes)
- nucleic acids (DNA and RNA).

Use the index to find out more about them.

Each of the following steps of the nitrogen cycle is shown in Figure 1.8.1:

- Plants absorb nitrogen in the form of nitrate ions (NO_3^-). These ions are transported to the leaves where they are used to make amino acids. Amino acids are made into proteins.

- Herbivores digest plant proteins into amino acids and then use them to make the proteins they require.

- Animals excrete **urea** in their urine. Their faeces contain protein and other nitrogenous compounds. These provide resources for decomposers (bacteria and fungi). The dead bodies of herbivores also provide food for decomposers.

- Decomposers break down animal wastes and the dead remains of plants and animals. This releases ammonium ions (NH_4^+) into the soil.

- Bacteria break down the urea in urine to ammonium ions. This process is called **ammonification**.

- **Nitrifying bacteria** in the soil change ammonium ions into nitrate ions. These bacteria gain their energy from this reaction.

- **Nitrogen-fixing bacteria** contribute to the recycling of nitrogen. They are found in the soil and convert nitrogen gas from the air into compounds of nitrogen that they use themselves. When they die and are decomposed, this fixed nitrogen is available to plants.

- Nitrogen-fixing bacteria are also found in the roots of **leguminous** plants such as peas, beans, alfalfa and clover and many tropical trees. The bacteria are inside swellings on the roots called root nodules. These bacteria change nitrogen gas into amino acids. The leguminous plants use these to make proteins. In return the leguminous plants provide a suitable environment for the bacteria (in the nodules – see Figure 1.8.2 opposite) and also provide all the sugars that they need. **Nitrogen fixation** requires a lot of energy.

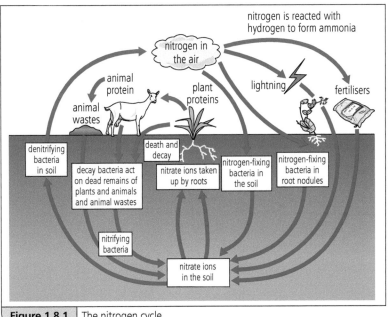

Figure 1.8.1 The nitrogen cycle

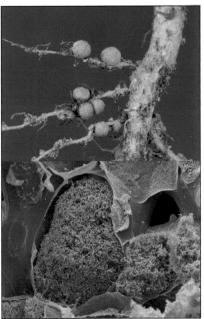

Figure 1.8.2 Top: root nodules on a peanut plant. Bottom: thousands of nitrogen-fixing bacteria live inside the cells of the root nodule

Denitrifying bacteria live in water-logged soil. They change nitrate ions back to nitrogen gas, which enters the atmosphere.

Lightning causes nitrogen and oxygen to react together at high temperatures. Nitrogen oxides are formed in the reactions. Rain washes these oxides into the soil where they form nitrate ions.

SUMMARY QUESTIONS

1 Explain why nitrogen is such an important element for living organisms.

2 Define the following terms: *nitrogen fixation*, *nitrification*, *denitrification*, *legume* and *root nodule*.

3 Describe the role of microbes in:
   a nitrification,
   b denitrification
   c nitrogen fixation.

4 Explain how nitrogen in the bodies of dead animals and plants is made available to plants in the form of nitrate ions.

KEY POINTS

1 Nitrogen is in the atmosphere as a gas (N_2) but is not available to most organisms as it is inert.

2 Some bacteria fix nitrogen (N_2) converting it to amino acids. Some nitrogen-fixing bacteria live inside root nodules of legumes.

3 Bacteria decompose protein and urea to ammonium ions. Nitrifying bacteria convert ammonium ions to nitrate ions.

4 Denitrifying bacteria convert nitrate ions to nitrogen gas (N_2).

5 Plants absorb nitrate ions and convert them to amino acids to make proteins. Herbivores obtain the amino acids they need by eating and digesting plant protein.

UNIT 1: Multiple-choice questions

1 All living things:

  a feed, grow and sleep

  b feed, respire and sweat

  c reproduce, move and respire

  d reproduce, walk and grow.

2 The list shows organisms in a food chain, but they are not in the correct order.

        bird; small fish; cat; seaweed.

  The correct sequence in the food chain is:

  a 1, 2, 4, 3

  b 2, 1, 4, 3

  c 3, 1, 2, 4

  d 4, 2, 1, 3.

3 A typical plant cell contains all of the following EXCEPT:

  a a cell membrane

  b a cell wall

  c a nucleus

  d small vacuoles.

4 What is the function of ribosomes?

  a Assemble proteins for organisms

  b Provide strength and structure for plants

  c Release energy for cells

  d Store genetic information for organisms

5 In active transport, energy is used:

  a to increase the rate of gaseous diffusion

  b to move ions against their concentration gradient

  c to move ions down their concentration gradient

  d to move respiratory gases from areas of high concentration to areas of low concentration.

Further practice questions and examples can be found on the accompanying CD.

UNIT 1: Short answer questions

1 a Figure 1 shows a diagram of a plant cell.

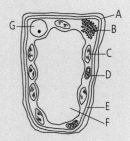

Figure 1

  i The table shows some functions of plant cell structures. Identify the part of the cell that carries out each function and complete the table. The first one has been done for you.

Function	Name of part of the cell	Letter on Figure 1
Maintains the fixed shape of plant cells	Cell wall	A
Stores water and ions		
Controls the movement of substances in and out of the cell		
Carries out aerobic respiration		
Controls all the cell's activities		
Contains chlorophyll		

                                              (5)

  ii State which of the structures shown in Figure 1 is **not** found in a fungal cell.

                                              (1)

b Plants can be destarched by keeping them in the dark for a period of time.

  i Describe how you would use a plant that had been destarched to show that light is necessary for photosynthesis.

    In your answer, list the apparatus you would use and describe the method that you would follow. *(6)*

  ii Explain how the results show that light is necessary for photosynthesis. *(3)*

Total 15 marks

2 a Explain what is meant by the term
      sensitivity.   (2)
   b Figure 2 shows a diagram of a nerve
      cell as it would be seen with an electron
      microscope.

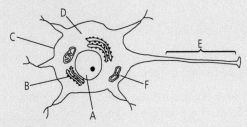

Figure 2

      i   Name the parts of the cell labelled **A**
          to **D**.   (4)
      ii State the functions of the structures
          labelled **E** and **F**.   (2)
      iii State the function of nerve cells.   (1)
   c State **three** ways in which a plant cell
      differs from the nerve cell shown in
      Figure 2.   (3)
   d Human cells remove sodium ions from the
      cytoplasm so that the concentration of
      these ions inside the cytoplasm is twelve
      times less than the concentration of
      sodium ions in the blood.

      Explain how the cells maintain this
      difference.   (3)

                              Total 15 marks

3 Epithelial cells form the lining of structures
   such as the trachea (windpipe), alveoli in the
   lungs, arteries, veins and the alimentary canal.
   a Explain how epithelial cells are specialised
      for the functions that they perform.   (4)
   b Specialised cells, such as epithelial cells
      and muscle cells, rely on other cells of the
      body for their survival.

      Explain how muscle cells rely on the
      activities of epithelial cells in the lungs and
      the alimentary canal for the substances
      that they require for respiration.   (3)

   c Explain what would happen to red
      blood cells, if they were placed into the
      following:
      i   distilled water
      ii a solution with a high concentration of
          salt.   (6)
   d State two ways in which a sperm cell is
      specialised for its function.   (2)

                              Total 15 marks

4 a Explain how the nutrition of bacteria and
      fungi differs from the nutrition of green
      plants.   (4)
   b The following passage describes some of
      the feeding relationships in an aquatic
      habitat.

      Sea grass provides food for sea urchins
      and turtles. Many organisms grow on
      the sea grass including photosynthetic
      algae which are grazed by parrotfish. Sea
      urchins are eaten by puffer fish. Groupers
      are predators of parrotfish. Humans catch
      and eat turtles, parrotfish and groupers.

      i   Draw a food chain showing the
          feeding relationships between four of
          the organisms given in the passage. (2)
      ii Identify the trophic levels of the four
          organisms you have given in the food
          chain.   (4)
   c The ecologist Paul Colinvaux wrote an
      essay with the title: 'Why big, fierce
      animals are rare'.

      He explains in the essay that this is due to
      the loss of energy in food chains.

      Explain why big, fierce animals are rare. (5)

                              Total 15 marks

Further short answer
questions can be found
on the CD.

2 Nutrition

2.1   Nutrients

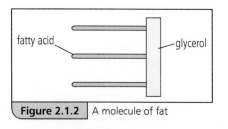

Figure 2.1.2   A molecule of fat

The human diet provides us with energy and the nutrients to be healthy. The energy is provided by the major nutrients, which are carbohydrates, fats and proteins. **Vitamins** and **minerals** are the minor nutrients. They do not provide energy and are needed in tiny quantities.

Carbohydrates

Examples of carbohydrates are sugars and starches. These contain the elements carbon (C), hydrogen (H) and oxygen (O).

Glucose is made during photosynthesis, used in respiration and transported in the blood. It is a simple sugar.

Two molecules of simple sugars (like glucose) are joined by chemical bonds to form a complex (or 'double') sugar. Complex sugars include **sucrose**, **maltose** and **lactose.** All the sugars are sweet and soluble and provide energy in a ready-to-use form.

Complex carbohydrates, such as starch, are made by joining many simple sugar molecules together by chemical bonds. Plants store starch in leaves, roots and seeds as an energy store. Starch is insoluble and does not taste sweet.

Proteins

Proteins are made up of carbon, hydrogen and oxygen, but they also contain nitrogen (N) and many have sulphur (S). Proteins are long chains made up of smaller molecules called **amino acids**. There are 20 different types of amino acid. Molecules of amino acids are made into chains (Figure 2.1.1). There are many different proteins. After formation they are either folded into different shapes (see 2.6 and 10.8) or become arranged into long fibres (see 5.1).

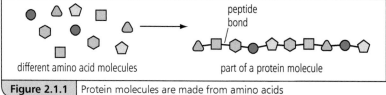

different amino acid molecules   part of a protein molecule

Figure 2.1.1   Protein molecules are made from amino acids

It is the sequence of the different amino acids in the chain that determines the type of protein that is formed.

Lipids

Lipids are made up of the elements carbon, hydrogen and oxygen. Each lipid molecule is made from one molecule of **glycerol** and three **fatty acids**. There are different types of fatty acids and these can form different lipids with different properties.

Vitamins and minerals

Vitamins and minerals are micronutrients because you need very small quantities each day. Vitamins are complex molecules that we cannot make from anything simpler. Minerals are elements that we need for many different functions as you can see in the table.

Micronutrient		Function(s) in the body	Good sources
Vitamins	A*	Helps receptors in the eye, known as rods, to detect light of low intensity (see 7.4)	Liver, milk, sweet potatoes, carrots
	B_1^+	Helps aerobic respiration in mitochondria	Cereals
	C^+	Helps tissue repair and resistance to disease	Oranges, lemons and other citrus fruits
	D*	Helps absorption of calcium in the gut and strengthening of bones and teeth	Fish oil, milk, butter (also made in the skin exposed to sunlight)
Minerals	Iron	Forms part of the haemoglobin in red blood cells that transports oxygen	Liver, meat, cocoa, eggs
	Calcium	Gives strength to bones and teeth; needed for nervous system and blood clotting	Milk, fish, green vegetables

STUDY FOCUS

*Vitamins A and D are fat soluble as are vitamins E and K. Vitamins B_1 and C are water soluble. There are many more vitamins and minerals that we require in our diet – only a few are given in the table.

SUMMARY QUESTIONS

1 Define the terms *nutrient*, *macronutrient*, *micronutrient*, *vitamin* and *mineral*.
2 Name two reducing sugars and one non-reducing sugar.
3 A food sample is thought to contain both glucose and sucrose. How would you prove this?
4 Explain how starch differs from glucose.
5 Name foods that are good sources of each of the following: starch, sucrose, protein and fat.

Testing for nutrients in foods

This table summarises the procedures and results for the tests that distinguish each of the different food nutrients from one another.

Nutrient	Reagent	Procedure	Positive result	Negative result
Starch	Iodine solution	Add a few drops to a sample of food	Blue-black	Yellow-orange
Reducing sugars (e.g. Glucose and fructose)	Benedict's solution	Heat in boiling water bath with a solution of the food	Colour change from blue to green, orange or red	No colour change – solution remains blue
Non-reducing sugars (e.g. Sucrose)	Hydrochloric acid (HCl), sodium hydroxide (NaOH), Benedict's solution	Boil sample with HCl; cool; neutralise with NaOH; test with Benedict's solution as above	Colour change from blue to green, orange or red	No colour change – solution remains blue
Protein	Biuret solution – a solution of sodium hydroxide (NaOH) and copper sulphate ($CuSO_4$)	Add a few drops of biuret solution to a solution of the sample	Colour change from blue to lilac/purple	No colour change – solution is blue
Lipids (fats and oils)	Piece of filter paper	Rub the sample on the filter paper and leave to dry	Greasy spot, the paper lets some light through	No greasy spot

LEARNING OUTCOMES

At the end of this topic you should be able to:

- explain the terms *balanced diet* and *deficiency disease*
- state the roles of water and fibre in the body
- state the causes, symptoms and treatment of anaemia, night blindness and rickets.

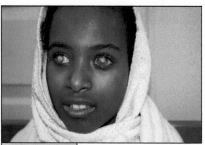

Figure 2.2.1 This child is blind because she did not have enough vitamin A in her diet

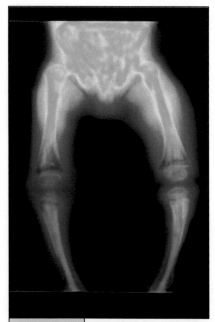

Figure 2.2.2 X-ray of the legs of a child with rickets

A **balanced diet** provides all the energy and nutrients that a person requires for their immediate needs. This includes:

- energy – macronutrients (carbohydrates, proteins and lipids) provide this energy
- **essential amino acids** – eight to nine types of amino acids that the body cannot make
- **essential fatty acids** – two fatty acids that the body cannot make
- vitamins and minerals, including calcium and iron (see 2.1)
- enough water to replace that which is lost each day
- fibre.

STUDY FOCUS

Organs, such as the liver, kidneys and brain, function to keep us alive. This is known as basal metabolism or the basal metabolic rate. Added to this, our muscles need energy so that they can contract when we are active. The more active you are the more energy you need above that required for your basal metabolism.

If a diet has too little or too much of one or more of the components it is *unbalanced*. If this continues for some time then **health** will suffer. **Deficiency diseases** are caused by the lack of micronutrients in the diet.

Deficiency diseases

- Without vitamin A in the diet the rods in the eye do not work properly resulting in **night blindness**. If the deficiency is serious then the front of the eye becomes cloudy and light cannot pass through easily.
- Without vitamin D bones become soft. Leg bones often bow outwards under the pressure of the body, indicating that a person has **rickets**. Children who do not go out in the sunshine, or who wear clothing that completely covers their body are most at risk of this deficiency disease.
- Without iron, the red blood cells contain less haemoglobin so the quantity of oxygen transported in the blood decreases. This is iron-deficiency **anaemia**. People who are anaemic have less energy and feel tired and lethargic because they have less oxygen available for aerobic respiration. They are also likely to grow and develop slowly. Girls and women are more at risk of iron deficiency anaemia because they lose blood in their monthly menstruation.
- A deficiency of calcium can lead to weak bones and teeth and slow blood clotting.

STUDY FOCUS

Deficiency diseases are treated by making sure people have a balanced diet and by giving dietary supplements, such as pills containing vitamins and minerals.

Water

Water makes up two-thirds of your body mass. You take in water when you drink or eat.

Water is needed in the body:

- as a solvent for all the water-soluble compounds inside cells and in body fluids, such as blood plasma, tissue fluid and lymph (see 4.4 and 4.6)
- as a reactant in chemical reactions, such as hydrolysis, which occurs during digestion (see 2.9)
- as a transport medium in the blood
- as a coolant when we sweat.

Our intake of water each day must equal our loss of water in urine, faeces, sweat and exhaled air otherwise we dehydrate. Without enough water in the body, the blood becomes too thick and sticky and the heart is forced to work harder to pump blood.

Diarrhoea is a **symptom** of many diseases. **Diarrhoeal diseases** are the main killers of young children, especially in poorer regions of the World. The intestines do not absorb water so that watery faeces are produced. These diseases can be prevented by drinking water from safe sources, boiling any water that is from an unsafe source and using hygiene in the preparation of food. This will reduce the presence of bacteria, which cause diarrhoea.

Fibre

Dietary fibre (or roughage) mainly consists of cellulose from plant cell walls. We do not have any enzymes to digest cellulose, so it does not provide us with any energy.

Fibre adds bulk to our food and helps the movement of food in the alimentary canal by peristalsis. The muscles of the gut wall need something to push against. Without fibre, food remains in the gut for longer, faeces are hard and difficult to pass because more water is absorbed from the large intestine and people have **constipation**. Fibre absorbs poisonous wastes from bacteria in our guts. High-fibre diets are thought to lower the concentration of **cholesterol** in the blood and reduce the risk of heart disease. Fibre is also linked to reducing the chances of developing bowel cancer.

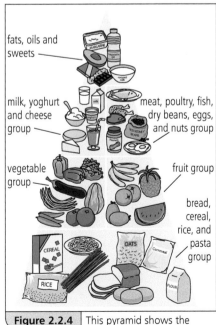

fats, oils and sweets

milk, yoghurt and cheese group

meat, poultry, fish, dry beans, eggs, and nuts group

vegetable group

fruit group

bread, cereal, rice, and pasta group

| **Figure 2.2.4** | This pyramid shows the relative quantities of different foods people should eat |

| **Figure 2.2.3** | High fibre foods include bran cereals, and the fruit and vegetables on this stall |

SUMMARY QUESTIONS

1. Define the following terms: *balanced diet*, *haemoglobin* and *dietary supplements*.

2. Why must each of the following be in a balanced diet: water, fibre, vitamin A, vitamin D, iron and calcium?

3. Explain how water is involved in the following processes in the body: digestion, transport, temperature control and excretion.

4. Make a table to show the causes, symptoms and treatment of the three deficiency diseases in this topic.

5. Explain why the quantity of iron recommended for women is higher than that for men.

6. Explain why diarrhoeal diseases are a major cause of death of young children.

2.3

Malnutrition

People who do not have a balanced diet may well suffer from some form of malnutrition. In the previous topic you read about deficiency diseases caused by a lack of specific micronutrients. There are also forms of **malnutrition** caused by insufficient macronutrients, or far too many.

Many people are malnourished. **Protein energy malnutrition** (PEM) occurs in children who do not receive enough energy in their diet and which is also deficient in protein. This results in children with the appearance of those in Figures 2.3.1 and 2.3.2. **Marasmus** is caused mainly by not receiving enough energy-providing foods. As a result growth is retarded and there is severe weight loss. **Kwashiorkor** is also the result of protein deficiency, which results in the swelling of body tissues and a swollen liver. Protein in the blood helps in absorbing water from the tissues.

| **Figure 2.3.1** | A child with marasmus |

| **Figure 2.3.2** | A child with kwashiorkor |

Children who are severely malnourished are often given a specially prepared food, such as Plumpynut. This is a peanut-based paste with sugar, vegetable fat and skimmed milk powder which is enriched with vitamins and minerals. Without this intervention children are not likely to make a full recovery.

Some people have psychological disorders, such as **anorexia** and **bulimia**, that affect their eating habits. People with anorexia eat so little that they do not obtain enough energy. Those with bulimia eat a large quantity of food (binge eating) and then deliberately reduce the chances of the food being digested and absorbed. They do this by:

- making themselves vomit
- taking laxatives so that food passes through the digestive system too quickly to be digested
- taking excessive exercise to reduce the quantity of food stored as fat.

Both conditions are more common among women than men and both tend to start in the early teenage years. Without treatment, these conditions can be fatal.

| **Figure 2.3.3** | This child is being fed with a ready-to-use therapeutic food |

Obesity

Consuming more food energy than required increases the quantity of body fat. There are two ways in which a person can be identified as obese:

- being 20% above the recommended weight for his or her height
- having a **body mass index (BMI)** greater than 30.

BMI is calculated using the following formula:

$$\text{BMI} = \frac{\text{body mass (in kg)}}{\text{height}^2 \text{ (in metres)}}$$

There is an obesity epidemic in many regions of the world including the Caribbean. The causes of this are:

- a change from traditional high-fibre diets to 'Western' diets rich in fatty foods and refined foods with a high sugar (especially sucrose) and low fibre content
- an increase in income with more money to spend on food
- a change from occupations that involved much physical activity to more sedentary occupations
- an increased use of cars and public transport rather than walking to work, school or the shops.

People who are overweight or obese are at high risk of developing serious health problems such as:

- high blood pressure
- coronary heart disease (see 4.5)
- diabetes (see 10.2)
- arthritis (damage to joints)
- many types of cancer, e.g. bowel and uterine cancers.

The different BMI categories are shown in the table.

Body mass index	Categories
Less than 18.5	Underweight
Between 18.5 and 24.9	Normal
Between 25 and 29.9	Overweight
Between 30 and 34.9	Obese (class 1)
Between 35 and 39.9	Obese (class 2)
Over 40	Seriously obese (class 3)

SUMMARY QUESTIONS

1 The table gives the body mass and height of four people.
  a Copy and complete the table.

Person	Body mass/kg	Height/m	BMI	Category
A	110	1.70		
B	50	1.75		
C	75	1.85		
D	125	1.73		

  b What advice would you give to each of these people?

2 a State what is meant by *protein energy malnutrition*.
  b Explain the differences between:
    i kwashiorkor and marasmus, and
    ii anorexia and bulimia.

3 Explain how obesity is a risk to one's health.

4 Suggest how governments could reduce the proportion of their populations who are obese.

Nutrition: Data analysis

Table 1

Age	Recommended energy intake per day/kJ	
	Males	**Females**
0–3 months	2280	2160
10–12 months	3850	3610
7–10 years	8240	7280
15–18 years	11510	8830
19–49 years	10600	8100
last 3 months of pregnancy		8900
breastfeeding		10900
60–64 years	9930	7990

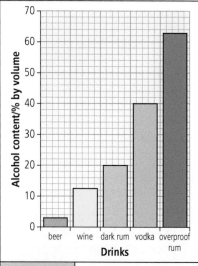

Figure 2.4.1	A bar chart showing the alcohol content of different drinks

Much of the information you will find about nutrition is in the form of tables and charts. You need to know how to construct these and how to use them by analysing and interpreting the information that they represent.

You should know how to put information into tables like those in this topic. Here are some simple rules to follow:

- Draw the table outlines in pencil and leave plenty of space above the table.
- Rule lines between the columns and rows.
- Rule lines around the whole table.
- Write brief, but informative headings for each column.
- Columns headed with quantities should have the appropriate units.
- When two or more columns are used to present data, the first column should be the independent variable; the second and subsequent columns should contain the dependent variables.

Table 1 shows recommended energy intakes from food for people who take little exercise.

You might be asked to analyse a table like this. Read the information systematically by looking at the column and row headings and then reading down each column and then across each row. Look for trends and patterns. Notice in Table 1 that the values for males are always higher than for females and that the values increase with age in children, but decrease in older people.

Information like this is presented as a bar chart (see Figure 2.4.1).

Always follow these instructions if you are going to draw a bar chart:

- Use at least half the grid provided and do not make the chart too small.
- Draw the chart in pencil.
- Use blocks of equal width which have gaps between them.
- The intervals between the blocks on the x-axis should be equidistant.
- The y-axis should be properly scaled with equidistant intervals.
- The y-axis should be labelled with units.
- Each block should be identified clearly.

Table 2 shows how the body mass of a woman changed over her lifetime.

This information can be presented as a line graph (see Figure 2.4.2). Always follow these instructions if you are going to draw a line graph:

- Use at least half the grid provided and do not make the graph too small.
- Draw the graph in pencil.

- The independent variable should be plotted on the *x*-axis – here it is age.
- The dependent variable should be plotted on the *y*-axis – here it is body mass.
- Use an appropriate scale for each axis; the *x*-axis should start at 0 (birth), the *y*-axis at 0 kg.
- Each axis should be scaled using multiples of 1, 2, 5 or 10 for each 20 mm square on the grid. This makes it easy for you to plot and extract data. Never use multiples of 3.
- Each axis should be labelled clearly with the quantity and unit, e.g. age (years) and body mass (kg).
- Plotted points must be clearly marked and easily distinguishable from the grid lines on the graph. Encircled dots (○) or saltire crosses (×) should be used, dots on their own should not. You can also use vertical crosses (+).

A South African teenager weighed the foods she ate each day. She calculated the mass of each of seven food groups as a percentage of the total mass of food eaten each day (Table 3).

Table 2

Age/years	Body mass/kg
Birth	3.5
1	9.5
2	12.0
3	13.6
5	17.3
10	33.0
15	52.0
17	36.2
20	58.9
25	60.3
30	72.4
40	64.7
50	73.2
60	75.3

Table 3

Food groups	Mass of each component/% of the daily diet
Cereals	53
Animal fats	3
Meat	10
Milk and milk products	5
Vegetables	15
Fruits	12
Sugars and sweeteners	2

This information can be presented as a pie chart (see Figure 2.4.3). Always follow these instructions if you are going to draw a pie chart:

- Draw a large circle leaving plenty of space for labelling and annotating.
- Calculate the size of each segment of the pie chart by calculating the angle to draw.
- Use a protractor to determine the angle for each segment.
- Draw straight lines between the segments.
- Label each segment clearly.
- Annotate the pie chart by giving the relevant figures. In Table 3 they are given as percentages.

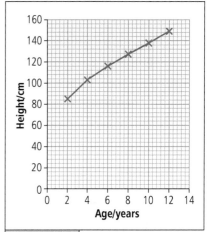

Figure 2.4.2 | A line graph to show the growth in height of a boy between the ages of 2 and 12 years

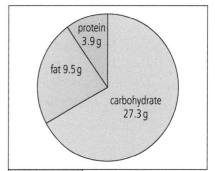

Figure 2.4.3 | A pie chart showing the macronutrients in 100 g of pumpkin pie. The rest of the pie is fibre, micronutrients and water

SUMMARY QUESTIONS

1 Draw bar charts for the information given in Table 1. Make one bar chart for males and another for females.

2 Use the data in Table 2 to draw a line graph to show how the woman's body mass changed during her lifetime.

3 Draw a pie chart to show the composition of the diet in Table 3.

We use teeth to bite into food and then to crush it into smaller pieces so making it easier to swallow.

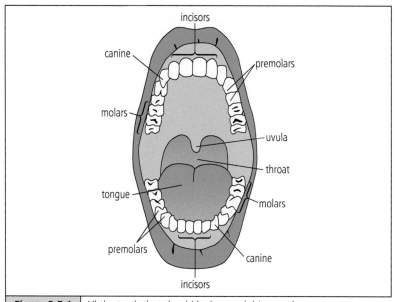

Figure 2.5.1 | All the teeth that should be in an adult's mouth

Adult humans have 8 incisors, 4 canines, 8 premolars, and 12 molars, making 32 teeth altogether, while children have 8 incisors, 4 canines, and 8 premolars, making 20 teeth altogether.

The four types of teeth have different shapes for performing different functions:

- **incisors** are chisel-shaped for biting and cutting
- **canines** are pointed for piercing and tearing
- **premolars** have uneven 'cusps' for grinding and chewing food
- **molars** are like premolars and are for chewing and grinding food.

Our first set of teeth, or **milk teeth**, are small and there are only eight molars as our jaws are too small for a full set. Between the ages of six and 12 these teeth gradually fall out, to be replaced by our **permanent teeth**.

Study the diagram of a section through a molar tooth (Figure 2.5.2).

- **Enamel** forms the hard, outer layer of the **crown** of the tooth, which is the part above the gum.
- Softer **dentine** is inside the enamel and is like bone in structure.
- **Cement** fixes the **root** of the tooth into a bony socket in the jaw. The root is the part that is below the gum.
- The space inside the tooth is the **pulp cavity**. It contains **nerves** and blood vessels.

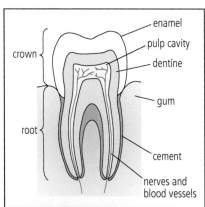

Figure 2.5.2 | Molar tooth (vertical section)

Tooth decay

Bacteria in the mouth cause tooth decay. The bacteria mix with saliva to form **plaque**, which is an invisible layer that sticks to teeth and gums.

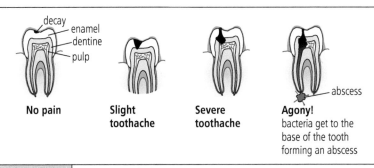

decay enamel dentine pulp **No pain**	**Slight toothache**	**Severe toothache**	abscess **Agony!** bacteria get to the base of the tooth forming an abscess

Figure 2.5.3 Stages in tooth decay

After a meal, food may be left between the teeth. Bacteria use any sugar and respire it anaerobically (without oxygen) producing acid as a waste product. Acid attacks the enamel starting the decay of the teeth. If the enamel is worn away the acid will attack the dentine underneath. Left untreated the damage may reach the pulp cavity and stimulate sensory nerve endings. The pain caused by this is toothache. The acid can also make gums red and swollen.

Periodontal disease occurs if the bacteria rot the fibres holding the teeth in place so that they fall out.

Guidelines for care of the teeth

- Avoid sugary food and drinks between meals.
- Clean teeth at least twice a day using a good toothbrush and toothpaste.
- Use dental floss to clear particles of food and plaque between the teeth.
- Use disclosing tablets to show areas of plaque.
- Replace your toothbrush when it wears out (every four to six months).
- Visit a dentist regularly. Dentists recommend that some people should visit as often as every three months if their teeth are at risk of decay. People not at risk may be recommended to visit once a year or even less frequently.

DID YOU KNOW?

Fluoride gives teeth a hard surface. It strengthens the enamel of the teeth. In some countries it is added to the drinking water. Some people oppose this since it denies them choice and they are concerned about the long-term effects of drinking fluoridated water.

STUDY FOCUS

Infants (babies in the first year of life) gain their milk teeth from the age of three months.

Figure 2.5.4 Dentists can tell if there is any damage to your teeth by examining X-rays

KEY POINTS

1 Incisors are for biting and cutting, canines for piercing and tearing and premolars and molars are for grinding and chewing.

2 Tooth decay is caused by bacteria in plaque, which produce acidic waste products. This attacks the enamel and dentine of the tooth.

3 Tooth decay can be avoided by following the guidelines given here.

SUMMARY QUESTIONS

1 a Name the four main types of teeth.
   b For each type, describe its shape and its function.

2 What are the differences between the milk teeth and the permanent teeth?

3 a Make a labelled diagram of a molar tooth showing some decay.
   b Describe the stages of tooth decay.
   c State three ways in which tooth decay can be prevented.

EXAM TIP

In mechanical digestion the particles of food become smaller – the food molecules are **not** broken down into smaller molecules.

LINK

See 2.9 for more about mechanical digestion in the stomach and in the small intestine.

STUDY FOCUS

A catalyst is any substance that speeds up a reaction and remains unchanged at the end of the reaction. Common catalysts are metals, such as nickel, and compounds, such as hydrochloric acid (see the non-reducing sugar test in 2.1) and manganese dioxide (see 2.8).

Digestion is the breakdown of large, insoluble food molecules into small, water-soluble food molecules so that they can be absorbed into the bloodstream. There are two forms of digestion:

- **Mechanical digestion** – food is broken down into smaller pieces. The teeth begin the process of mechanical breakdown.
- **Chemical digestion** – food molecules are broken down into smaller molecules so they can be absorbed. This is a slow process, so it needs to be speeded up by catalysts. The special catalysts are made of protein and are called **enzymes**.

Properties of enzymes

Most enzymes work inside cells, but those involved in chemical digestion work outside cells. Enzymes have the following properties:

- they are all proteins
- each enzyme catalyses one reaction
- only small numbers of enzyme molecules are needed to catalyse many reactions over a period of time
- they can be used again and again
- their activity is affected by temperature
- their activity is affected by pH.

Enzymes are made of protein molecules. They can be folded into many different shapes. Each enzyme molecule has a shape that makes it suitable for catalysing **one** reaction. This explains why there are many different enzymes. Only the substrate molecule with a shape that fits into the enzyme will take part in the reaction catalysed by this enzyme. This model of enzyme activity is known as the '**lock and key**'. The substrate (the 'key') must have a shape that fits exactly into the 'key hole' of the enzyme (the 'lock').

Enzymes are influenced by the conditions of their surroundings. If the conditions become too hot, too acid or too alkaline their shape changes and they stop acting as catalysts. At high temperatures and at extreme pH, the bonds holding the enzyme molecule together start to break down. This changes the shape of the **active site**, so the substrate no longer fits. We say that **denaturation** has occurred and the enzyme can no longer catalyse the reaction.

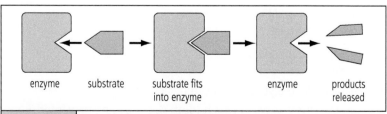

enzyme substrate   substrate fits   enzyme   products
                    into enzyme   released

Figure 2.6.1 Lock and key – a model of enzyme action

The figure below shows the enzymes that work in the gut.

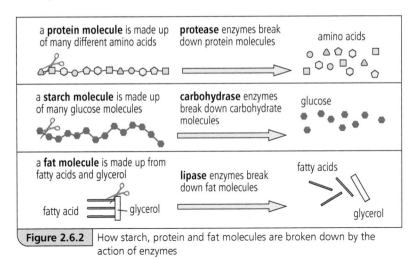

Figure 2.6.2 How starch, protein and fat molecules are broken down by the action of enzymes

EXAM TIP

Never say 'the enzyme is killed'. Enzymes are not organisms. They are protein molecules. The correct word to use is denatured.

EXAM TIP

Remember the shape of the substrate and the active site are **not** the same shape – they have different shapes that fit together – like a key fits into the key hole of a lock.

Enzymes in the digestive system

There are three types of enzyme involved in chemical digestion: carbohydrases that break down carbohydrates, proteases that break down proteins and lipases that break down lipids (fats).

Type of enzyme	Name of enzyme	Site of production	Site of action	Reaction catalysed by enzyme
Carbohydrase	Amylase	Salivary glands	Mouth	starch → maltose
		Pancreas	Small intestine	
	Sucrase	Wall of small intestine	Small intestine	sucrose → glucose + fructose
	Lactase	Wall of small intestine	Small intestine	lactose → glucose + galactose
	Maltase	Wall of small intestine	Small intestine	maltose → glucose
Protease	Pepsin	Stomach wall	Stomach	protein → **peptides**
	Trypsin	Pancreas	Small intestine	polypeptide → shorter peptides
	Peptidases	Wall of small intestine	Small intestine	peptides → amino acids
Lipase	Lipase	Pancreas	Small intestine	fats → fatty acids + glycerol

SUMMARY QUESTIONS

1 Define the following terms: *catalyst*, *enzyme*, *chemical digestion* and *denaturation*.

2 Make a table to summarise the digestion of starch, protein, fat and sucrose. Your table should have the following headings: food nutrient, enzyme, product(s) of digestion, site of digestion.

3 Make a model of an enzyme and its substrate to show how the two fit together. Modelling clay is a good substance to use for your model. Make a drawing of your model and use it to explain what happens when an enzyme is denatured.

KEY POINTS

1 Chemical digestion involves the breaking of chemical bonds to change large molecules to small molecules that can be absorbed into the blood.

2 Catalysts speed up a reaction and remain unchanged at the end. Enzymes are biological catalysts that are made of protein.

3 Enzymes are specific to certain reactions. Their activity is influenced by pH and temperature.

Investigating temperature and the activity of amylase

Amylase and temperature

Amylase catalyses the breakdown of starch to maltose. You will remember from 2.1 that iodine solution is used to detect the presence of starch. As the starch is broken down by amylase, there is less and less starch present in the reaction mixture. You can follow this by taking samples from the reaction mixture and testing with iodine solution as shown in Figure 2.7.1.

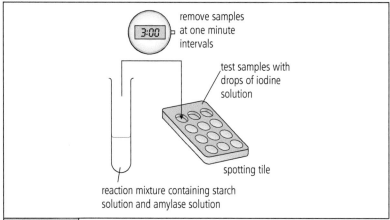

remove samples at one minute intervals

test samples with drops of iodine solution

spotting tile

reaction mixture containing starch solution and amylase solution

Figure 2.7.1 Samples taken from the reaction mixture in the test tube are added to drops of iodine solution each minute until there is no change in the colour

The table shows some results from a student's investigation in which seven reaction mixtures were kept at different temperatures.

Temperature/°C	Presence of blue-black colour when tested with iodine solution over 9 minutes									Time taken for starch to be digested/mins	Rate of reaction as 10/t
	1	2	3	4	5	6	7	8	9		
0	✓	✓	✓	✓	✓	✓	✓	✓	✓	–	0
10	✓	✓	✓	✓	✓	✓	✓	✓	✗	9	1.1
20	✓	✓	✓	✓	✓	✓	✗	✗	✗	7	1.4
30	✓	✓	✓	✓	✓	✗	✗	✗	✗	6	1.6
40	✓	✓	✓	✗	✗	✗	✗	✗	✗	4	2.5
50	✓	✓	✓	✓	✓	✓	✓	✗	✗	8	1.3
60	✓	✓	✓	✓	✓	✓	✓	✓	✓	–	0

Figure 2.7.2 shows the results.

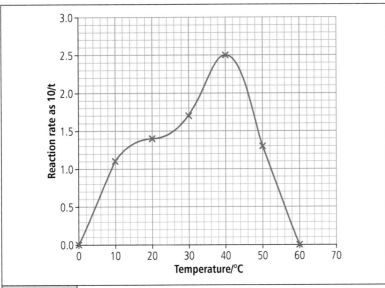

Figure 2.7.2 | The effect of temperature on the activity of amylase

EXAM TIP

When you look at the graph make sure you also look at the instructions about drawing graphs in 2.4. Make sure you know how to plot a graph like this.

Look at the graph and observe that the rate of reaction:

• is slow at low temperatures, e.g. at 10 °C
• increases as the temperature increases to 40°C
• reaches a maximum at 40 °C
• decreases at temperatures greater than 40 °C
• is zero at 60 °C.

The temperature at which the maximum rate of reaction occurs is called the **optimum temperature**. This is the best temperature for the enzyme. As the temperature increases towards the optimum, the molecules of substrate and enzyme move faster. They collide more often so there are more reactions occurring every second. At high temperatures the enzyme molecules are denatured and there is no reaction.

STUDY FOCUS

Here are some examples of optimum temperatures:

• fungal and plant enzymes – approximately 20 °C
• human enzymes – 37 °C (body temperature – see 6.3)
• enzymes produced by bacteria for use in industry – 90 °C.

SUMMARY QUESTIONS

1 Make a flow chart diagram to show how to investigate the effect of temperature on the activity of amylase.

2 a Sketch a graph to show the effect of increasing temperature on the rate of a reaction catalysed by a human enzyme, such as salivary amylase.

  b Describe, in words, what is shown by your graph.

  c Explain the effect of temperature on enzyme activity.

KEY POINTS

1 Increasing the temperature of an enzyme-controlled reaction increases the rate of reaction up to a maximum, which occurs at the optimum temperature.

2 At temperatures above the optimum the rate decreases until there is no reaction because the enzyme molecules are denatured.

2.8

Investigating pH and the activity of enzymes

Figure 2.8.1

The photograph in Figure 2.8.1 shows the results of an investigation into the effect of pepsin and acid on the breakdown of meat. The tubes were set up and left for several hours at 37 °C. There were no changes in the test tube of 'meat with acid' (on the left) and very little meat was broken down in the tube containing only pepsin. The meat has been entirely digested in the tube on the right with pepsin and acid.

Using different solutions of a milk protein is much quicker than using meat at different pH values. After adding the enzymes pepsin and trypsin, the time taken for the cloudiness of the milk protein to disappear can be recorded.

Proteases and pH

> **STUDY FOCUS**
>
> pH is a measure of the acidity or alkalinity of a solution. pH 1 is very acid, pH 14 is very alkaline and pH 7 is neutral (neither acid nor alkaline).

Tables 1 and 2 show results for such an investigation. Different acids and alkalis can be used to achieve the pH values indicated in the tables. It is possible to use special solutions that do not take part in the reaction but which maintain a constant pH throughout the time the reaction takes place. These solutions are called **buffer solutions**.

Table 1 The effect of pH on pepsin

pH	Cloudiness disappeared	Time taken for cloudiness to disappear/seconds	Rate of reaction as 1000/t
1	✓	30	33
3	✓	45	22
5	✓	87	11
7	✗	–	0
9	✗	–	0

Table 2 The effect of pH on trypsin

pH	Cloudiness disappeared	Time taken for cloudiness to disappear/seconds	Rate of reaction as 1000/t
1	✗	–	0
3	✗	–	0
5	✓	120	8.3
7	✓	100	10
9	✓	35	28

Figure 2.8.2 shows that:

- pepsin works best at pH 2.0 – that is its **optimum pH**
- the optimum pH for trypsin is pH 8.0
- up to pH 2.0 the rate of reaction increases for pepsin and then between pH 2.0 and pH 3.5 it decreases – there is no reaction above pH 3.5
- between pH 5.5 and pH 8.0 the rate of reaction increases for trypsin and then between pH 8.0 and pH 10.0 it decreases – there is no reaction below pH 5.5 and above pH 10.0.

Catalase is an enzyme found inside many cells. Its function is to catalyse the breakdown of hydrogen peroxide. This is a toxic substance that is produced by cells and which causes damage if allowed to accumulate. Hydrogen peroxide is used in haircare products as a bleaching agent. Catalase catalyses this reaction:

hydrogen peroxide → oxygen + water

Catalase is found in many plant and animal tissues. It is also found in bacteria and fungi.

This is the procedure you could follow to find out how quickly the reaction proceeds when the enzyme is at different values of pH.

LINK 🔗

Manganese dioxide catalyses the same reaction but it is not an enzyme. See 2.6 if you do not know why.

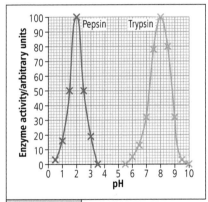

Figure 2.8.2 The effect of pH on the activity of pepsin and trypsin

1 Use a cork borer to remove several cores from a potato. Cut each core into 2 mm thick discs.

2 Put three discs into a solution with a pH of 7.0.

3 Put the same volume of hydrogen peroxide into three test tubes.

4 Put one potato disc into one of the test tubes at pH 7.0. It will sink towards the bottom of the test tube.

5 As soon as the disc starts to rise, time how long it takes to reach the surface.

6 The reaction between catalase and hydrogen peroxide produces oxygen which forms inside the potato and underneath the disc making the disc less dense so it floats. The faster the disc floats to the surface, the more oxygen is being produced. This indicates the speed of reaction of catalase.

Figure 2.8.3 Calalase in meat added to hydrogen peroxide gives a very vigorous reaction

7 Repeat steps 4 and 5 with two more discs so that there are three readings for pH 7.0.

8 Repeat the whole procedure with discs at a range of pH values.

The results are shown below:

pH	Time taken for discs to reach the surface/ seconds			
	First disc	Second disc	Third disc	Mean
4	36.03	37.13	38.59	28.94
5	15.77	12.93	14.35	12.01
6	12.06	10.05	11.03	9.79
7	9.13	10.13	9.63	8.97
8	9.67	10.29	9.98	9.49
9	10.81	12.69	11.87	11.09

STUDY FOCUS

Why take two repeat readings so that there are three results for each disc? Think about this and then answer question **3a**.

SUMMARY QUESTIONS

1 a Calculate the rate of the reaction of catalase at different values of pH as 1000/t.

 b Draw a line graph to show the effect of pH on the activity of catalase.

2 Use your graph to describe the effect of pH on the activity of catalase.

3 Explain:

 a why it is a good idea to have three results for each pH, and

 b the pattern that you have described in question **2**.

4 a Sketch a graph to show the effect of increasing pH on the rate of an enzyme-catalysed reaction where the optimum pH is 8.0 and there is no activity below pH 5.0 and none above pH 11.0.

 b Suggest why the enzyme in this example shows no activity below pH 5.0 and above pH 11.0.

The digestive system

At the end of this topic you should be able to:

- identify the main structures of the digestive system
- describe the functions of these structures.

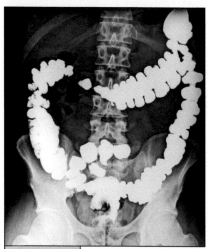

Figure 2.9.2 Fluoroscopy is a technique using X-rays to see the movement of the alimentary canal. Can you tell which part of the digestive system is shown in this X-ray?

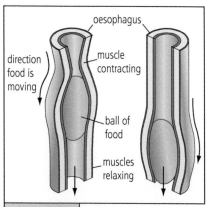

Figure 2.9.3 Peristalsis is a wave of contraction that moves food through the alimentary canal

The digestive system consists of all the organs, tissues and cells that ingest and digest food and then egest any undigested food. Starch, protein and fat are too large to be absorbed through the wall of the **alimentary canal** into the blood so they need to be broken down into smaller molecules by chemical digestion.

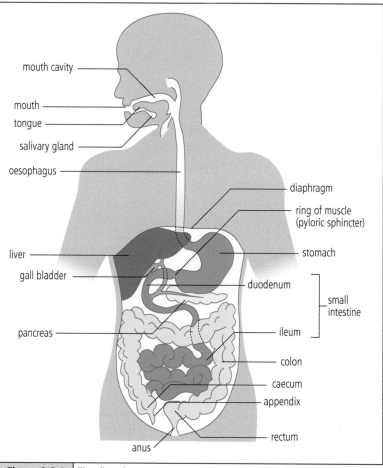

Figure 2.9.1 The digestive system

In **peristalsis** the circular muscles contract just behind the food and the longitudinal muscles relax thereby pushing the food along. In front of the bolus of food the circular muscles relax and the longitudinal muscles contract to allow the gut to widen. This 'wave' proceeds along the length of the alimentary tract from the oesophagus to the large intestine. In the small intestine food is 'shuttled' back and forth to increase its exposure to the villi, which absorb the products of digestion (see 2.10).

Table 1 The functions of the digestive system

Part of the digestive system	Functions
Mouth	• **Mastication** – mechanical digestion of food using the teeth and tongue • Secretion of saliva by salivary glands; salivary amylase begins the digestion of starch • Food formed into a bolus that can be swallowed
Oesophagus	• Transfers food by peristalsis from mouth to stomach
Stomach	• Wall of stomach secretes gastric juice containing hydrochloric acid and pepsin • Movements of muscular wall mixes food with gastric juice and breaks up large pieces of food into a creamy mixture called chyme • Pepsin begins the digestion of protein • No digestion of starch as amylase does not function in acid environment
Liver	• Secretes **bile** that contains bile salts to emulsify fats • Secretes sodium hydrogen carbonate to neutralise stomach acid
Gall bladder	• Stores bile and releases it into the small intestine through the bile duct
Pancreas	• Secretes pancreatic juice that contains amylase, trypsin and lipase • Secretes sodium hydrogen carbonate to neutralise stomach acid
Small intestine	• Secretes the enzymes sucrase, maltase, lactase and peptidase that complete the digestion of starch, protein and fat • Absorbs products of digestion into the bloodstream • Absorbs water, ions and vitamins into the bloodstream
Large intestine	• Absorbs the remaining water and ions • Stores faeces in the rectum
Anal canal	• Faeces pass out of the body

Fat is insoluble in water. This makes fat hard to digest because it forms spherical globules with a small surface area exposed to the water in the alimentary canal. When these globules reach the duodenum, bile salts break them up into smaller ones. This **emulsification** increases the surface area of the fat globules allowing lipase molecules easier access to the fat to break the bonds between the fatty acids and glycerol.

SUMMARY QUESTIONS

1 Distinguish between mechanical and chemical digestion, giving examples of each.

2 Make a large labelled diagram of the digestive system. Label all the main regions of the system. Alongside each label write out the main functions of each region.

3 Explain how peristalsis moves food along the alimentary canal.

4 Describe what happens to food in:
   a the stomach, and
   b the small intestine.

5 Describe the roles of the liver and the pancreas in the digestive system.

KEY POINTS

1 Peristalsis involves a wave of muscular contractions that squeeze the food bolus, carrying it down the oesophagus to the stomach.

2 In the stomach, food is churned up and mixed with gastric juice and hydrochloric acid. This starts the digestion of protein.

3 Bile emulsifies fats in the duodenum. The smaller fat globules have a larger surface area upon which lipase can act.

4 Enzymes produced by the pancreas and the small intestine complete the chemical digestion of starch, proteins and fat.

Absorption and assimilation

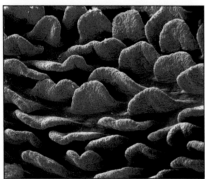

Figure 2.10.1 | Villi from the small intestine – leaf-like and full of blood capillaries

Absorption

Absorption is the movement of digested food molecules into the blood or the lymph. Simple sugars, amino acids, fatty acids and glycerol pass through the epithelial cells of the small intestine either by diffusion or by active transport.

The small intestine is very long (about 6 m in an adult) and is adapted for efficient absorption of food as it has:

- a very large surface area of about $9\,m^2$
- a thin lining of epithelial cells (only one cell thick) so that food molecules can move easily into the blood and lymph
- epithelial cells with **microvilli** (see Figure 1.2.3 in 1.2)
- cell membranes with many carrier proteins for active transport (see 1.4)

The large surface area of the small intestine fits into the small space within the abdomen because it has a folded inner lining with millions of tiny, finger-like or leaf-like projections called villi (the singular of villi is **villus**).

The digested food enters the capillaries and **lacteals** (lymph capillaries) in the villi. Absorbed food molecules are transported quickly to the liver by the **hepatic portal vein**. Fatty acids and glycerol are transported more slowly in the lymph. The villi have muscle inside them. When this contracts the lacteals are squeezed causing the lymph to move into lymphatic vessels. These vessels are thin walled like veins and they empty into blood vessels near the heart. As a result fat does not enter the bloodstream too quickly.

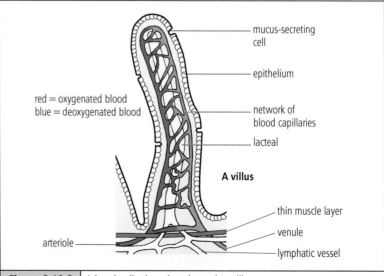

red = oxygenated blood
blue = deoxygenated blood

mucus-secreting cell

epithelium

network of blood capillaries

lacteal

A villus

thin muscle layer

venule

lymphatic vessel

arteriole

Figure 2.10.2 | A longitudinal section through a villus

When the food reaches the colon there is only fibre, dead cells and bacteria left. Most of the water has been absorbed in the small intestine and the rest is absorbed by the colon.

The solid waste or faeces are stored in the rectum. The indigestible food, in the form of faeces, passes out of the body through the anus. This is called **egestion**. Normally it takes between 24 and 48 hours for food to pass along the length of the digestive system.

Assimilation

The food molecules that have been absorbed are transported around the body and taken up by cells. **Assimilation** is the use of these molecules by the cells. As part of assimilation, the liver:

- takes up glucose molecules from the blood and stores them as **glycogen**. This helps to regulate the concentration of glucose in the blood (see 6.4)
- uses amino acids to make proteins, such as those involved with blood clotting
- breaks down surplus amino acids (see 6.1)
- converts fatty acids and glycerol into fat which is stored around the body, e.g. under the skin
- produces cholesterol from fats (see 4.5).

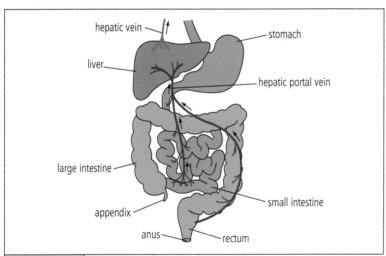

Figure 2.10.3 The hepatic portal vein carries blood from the stomach and intestines to the liver

SUMMARY QUESTIONS

1 Draw flow chart diagrams to show how starch, protein and fats are digested in the human alimentary canal.

2 Make a large labelled diagram of a villus. Annotate your diagram by writing notes about the functions of the parts that you have labelled.

3 Explain how the liver is involved in assimilating the products of digestion.

LINK

Undigested food is egested. Do not confuse this with excretion. See 1.1 and the glossary on the CD to remind yourself about the difference between them.

STUDY FOCUS

When you answer summary question **2**, use arrows to indicate the pathway taken by nutrients that are absorbed into the capillaries and into the lacteals. Annotate the arrows with the names of these nutrients: glucose, amino acids, fatty acids, glycerol, mineral salts, vitamins and water.

KEY POINTS

1 Absorption is the movement of digested food molecules through the wall of the intestine into the blood and lymph.

2 Assimilation is the use of food molecules by the cells of the body.

3 The small intestine is adapted for absorption by being very long and having a folded inner lining with millions of tiny villi.

4 The liver stores glucose as glycogen, makes proteins, breaks down surplus amino acids and converts fatty acids and glycerol back into fat for storage.

UNIT 2: Multiple-choice questions

1 Which vitamin when NOT present in the body or present in small quantities leads to rickets?

  a   A

  b B_1

  c   C

  d   D

2 Donna calculates her body mass index (BMI). She has a weight of 82 kg and her height is 1.5 m. What is her BMI?

  a   27.3

  b   36.4

  c   60.0

  d   270.0

3 Which of the following diseases related to nutritional deficiencies is associated with a lack of energy and protein in the diet?

  a   Anaemia

  b   Kwashiorkor

  c   Night blindness

  d   Scurvy

4 All of the following affect the activity of enzymes EXCEPT:

  a   type of substrate

  b   pH of the surroundings

  c   temperature

  d   type of product.

5 What is the muscular activity that moves food through the intestines?

  a   Assimilation

  b   Mastication

  c   Peristalsis

  d   Secretion

Further practice questions and examples can be found on the accompanying CD.

UNIT 2: Short answer questions

1 Catalase is an enzyme that catalyses the decomposition of hydrogen peroxide:

$$H_2O_2 \rightarrow O_2 + 2H_2O$$

Some students investigated the effect of temperature on the activity of this enzyme. Figure 1 shows the apparatus that they used. They measured the volume of oxygen that collected in two minutes.

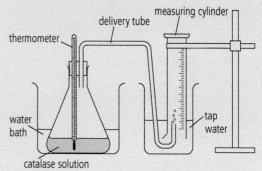

Figure 1

  a   Explain how the students would set up and use this apparatus to find the volume of oxygen produced at 30 °C.   *(4)*

  b   The table shows the results collected by the students.

Temperature/°C	Mean volume of oxygen collected/cm³
0	0
10	5
20	11
30	21
40	25
50	13
60	4
70	0

    i   Draw a graph to show the data collected by the students.   *(4)*

    ii   Use the graph to describe the effect of increasing temperature on the activity of catalase.   *(3)*

    iii   Explain the effect of temperature on the activity of catalase.   *(4)*

Total 15 marks

2 a Figure 2 is a diagram of the human alimentary canal.

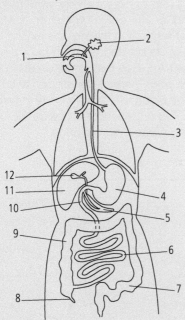

Figure 2

Copy and complete the table to show the part of the alimentary canal that is identified by each function. Write one number for each function. You may use each letter from Figure 2 once, more than once or not at all. One has been completed for you.

Function	Part of the alimentary canal
Peristalsis	3
Starch is digested	
Protein digestion	
Water is reabsorbed	
Partially digested food is mixed with bile	

(4)

b Dialysis (Visking) tubing can be used as a model of the lining of the alimentary canal.

In an investigation, two pieces of dialysis tubing were set up as shown in Figure 3 and left for 20 minutes. Samples were then taken from inside the bags and from the water surrounding the bags. The samples were tested with iodine solution and Benedict's solution and the results are shown in the table below.

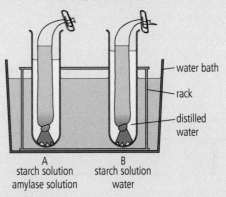

Figure 3

Tube	Sampling site	Results with iodine solution	Results with Benedict's solution
A	Inside bag	Negative	Positive
	Outside bag	Negative	Positive
B	Inside bag	Positive	Negative
	Outside bag	Negative	Negative

i Explain what has happened to give the results inside and outside the bag in tube A. (5)

ii Explain the results for tube B. (3)

iii State and explain what would happen if the starch solution in tube A was made with a solution having a very low pH. (3)

Total 15 marks

Further short answer questions can be found on the CD.

3 The respiratory system

3.1 Breathing

LEARNING OUTCOMES

At the end of this topic you should be able to:

• explain the importance of breathing for humans

• name and identify on diagrams the parts of the respiratory system: larynx, trachea, bronchi, bronchioles and alveoli

• relate the structures of the respiratory tract to their functions

• explain how to measure vital capacity.

STUDY FOCUS

Look carefully at the word equation for respiration in 1.1. Oxygen is required for aerobic respiration and carbon dioxide is the waste product.

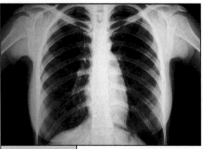

Figure 3.1.2 An X-ray of a pair of healthy lungs. Compare with the X-ray in 3.5

One of the characteristics of life is respiration. This is the chemical process that occurs in all living cells to release energy from food molecules, such as glucose and fat. **Aerobic respiration** is when oxygen is involved. This type of respiration releases the most energy. It produces carbon dioxide as a waste substance, which must be removed otherwise it becomes toxic. **Gas exchange** occurs in the lungs and involves the movement of molecules of oxygen and carbon dioxide between the air and the blood. **Breathing** is the movement of air in to and out of the lungs. This refreshes the air inside the lungs, providing oxygen and removing waste carbon dioxide.

The respiratory system

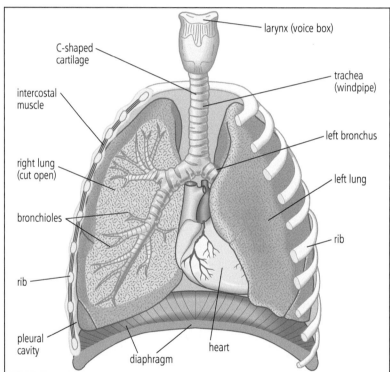

Figure 3.1.1 The respiratory system

The lungs are spongy organs situated within the **thorax** (chest). They are protected by the ribcage and the backbone. The **diaphragm** is a sheet of muscle and fibrous tissue separating the thorax from the abdomen. When the muscle contracts the diaphragm moves downwards and when it relaxes it is pushed upwards.

The pleural cavity is filled with fluid and lies between two pleural membranes. This fluid is a lubricant which reduces friction between the ribs and the lungs which move when we breathe in and out.

The **intercostal muscles** contract to move the ribs during breathing, especially when we take deep breaths.

Air enters the mouth or nose and passes through the throat to the **larynx**, which contains the vocal cords. Air then enters the **trachea**, and passes through the neck and into the thorax. The trachea branches into the two **bronchi**, which enter each lung. The bronchi continue to branch to form many small **bronchioles**, which end in tiny air sacs, each of which is called an **alveolus**. Around each alveolus are many blood capillaries for efficient gas exchange.

The tubes through which air moves to reach the alveoli are often called the airways.

You cannot breathe and swallow at the same time. When you swallow the **epiglottis** covers the opening to the larynx to stop any food from going into the trachea. C-shaped rings of cartilage keep the trachea open. The 'arms' of each C are joined by muscle at the back of the trachea. The cartilage prevents the trachea from collapsing when you breathe in and the air pressure decreases.

Vital capacity

Take the deepest breath that you can. Now breathe out as much air as you can from your lungs. The volume of air that you have breathed out after taking a deep breath is known as the **vital capacity**. The apparatus shown below can be used to measure your vital capacity.

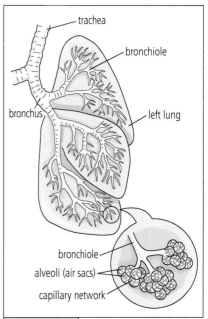

Figure 3.1.3 | The structure of the left lung

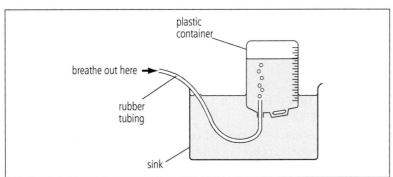

Figure 3.1.4 | Vital capacity can be measured by using a large plastic container and some tubing in a sink or large bowl

LINK

For a graph showing vital capacity see Figure 2 on page 59.

SUMMARY QUESTIONS

1 Define the following: *breathing*, *respiration* and *vital capacity*.

2 Describe the pathway taken by air as it moves from the atmosphere into the respiratory system. You could draw this as a flow chart diagram.

3 Make a table to show the functions of all the structures of the respiratory system labelled in Figures 3.1.1 and 3.1.3.

4 Explain how you would use the apparatus shown in Figure 3.1.4 to measure someone's vital capacity.

5 Make a diagram of the respiratory system. Add labels and annotate with the functions of the different structures. You will find some of the functions in 3.2 and 3.3.

KEY POINTS

1 Breathing is the movement of air in and out of the lungs.

2 Inspired air enters the nose or mouth, passes through the throat and then the larynx, which contains the vocal cords.

3 The air passes through the trachea, bronchi and bronchioles to the alveoli, where gas exchange occurs.

4 Vital capacity is the maximum volume of air forcibly breathed out after taking as deep a breath as possible.

3.2 Factors affecting breathing

LEARNING OUTCOMES

At the end of this topic you should be able to:

- describe what happens during breathing in and out
- state the factors that influence breathing
- outline how these factors affect the rate and depth of breathing.

STUDY FOCUS

You are a good model for breathing in and out. Put your hand on your abdomen while breathing in and out a few times. The outward movement of your abdomen is due to the downward movement of the diaphragm. Now put your hands on your ribcage and breathe deeply. You can feel the effect of the external intercostal muscles raising the ribs, as you breathe in.

When you breathe it feels as if the lungs are expanding to push your ribs outwards. This is not so. Your lungs work on the same principle as an accordion or concertina.

Breathing in (inspiration)

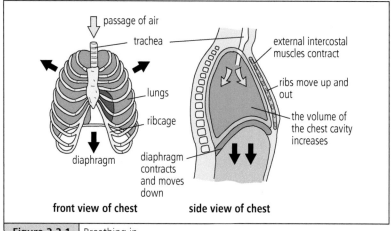

Figure 3.2.1 Breathing in

- The muscles of the diaphragm contract and flatten the central part of the diaphragm, which is made of tough fibrous tissue. These muscles are strong and connect to the backbone, the lower ribs and the **sternum**.
- The external intercostal muscles **contract** and the internal intercostal muscles **relax**. This moves the ribs and sternum (breast bone) upwards and outwards.
- These movements **increase** the volume inside the thorax, which **decreases** the air pressure inside the lungs.
- The air pressure inside the lungs is less than atmospheric pressure, so air moves in through your nose or mouth **into** the lungs and they inflate.

STUDY FOCUS

Use a model like the one in Figure 3.2.2. The rubber sheet represents the diaphragm.

Pull the rubber sheet down and then push it up.

Do this a few times and watch what happens to the balloons.

This model shows how movement of the diaphragm changes the volume and pressure in the thorax (represented by the bell jar). As the diaphragm contracts and moves downwards, the balloons inflate as a result of an increase in volume and decrease in pressure in the space around the balloons.

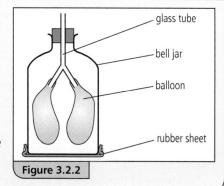

Figure 3.2.2

Breathing out (expiration)

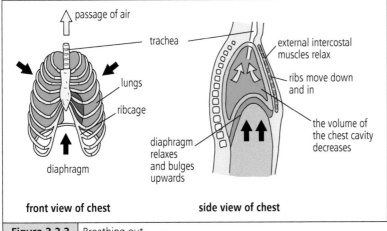

passage of air

trachea

external intercostal muscles relax

ribs move down and in

lungs

ribcage

the volume of the chest cavity decreases

diaphragm

diaphragm relaxes and bulges upwards

front view of chest   **side view of chest**

Figure 3.2.3 | Breathing out

- The diaphragm muscles **relax** and the pressure exerted by the abdomen pushes the central fibrous tissue upwards.
- The internal intercostal muscles **contract** and the external intercostal muscles **relax** to move the ribs downwards and inwards.
- These movements **decrease** the volume inside the thorax, which **increases** the air pressure inside the lungs.
- The **elastic tissue** around the alveoli recoils and this helps to force air **out** of the lungs.

During quiet or shallow breathing the diaphragm alone may be moving. Both the diaphragm and the ribcage move when taking deep breaths, for example during exercise.

Factors that affect breathing

The rate and depth of your breathing are influenced by many factors.

The following factors **increase** the rate and depth of breathing: exercise, anxiety, excitement, moving to high altitude (e.g. visiting cities such as Mexico City, Quito and La Paz), increase in weight, smoking, sitting in a stuffy space with no fresh air, and taking stimulant drugs, such as **amphetamines**.

The following factors **decrease** the rate and depth of breathing: recovering from exercise, sleep, returning to low altitude, moving from a stuffy place into fresh air, and taking depressant drugs, such as **barbiturates**. People with **asthma** and **bronchitis** often have bronchi partially blocked by **mucus**, so they have difficulty breathing and usually take shallow breaths.

The main internal factor that influences breathing is the carbon dioxide concentration in the blood. The brain detects how this changes and then determines how often and how deeply you breathe to keep the carbon dioxide concentration constant in the body. This is an example of homeostasis. See 6.1 for more information on homeostasis.

See 6.1 for more information on homeostasis.

KEY POINTS

1. When breathing in, the diaphragm contracts and moves down and the external intercostal muscles contract to raise the ribcage. This increases the volume of the chest and decreases the air pressure in the lungs. Atmospheric pressure forces air into the lungs.

2. When breathing out, the diaphragm relaxes and is pushed up and the ribcage falls. These movements decrease the volume of the chest and increase the air pressure in the lungs. Air pressure in the lungs forces air out.

3. Many factors affect the rate of breathing. Examples are exercise, drugs, anxiety, smoking, altitude and weight.

SUMMARY QUESTIONS

1. Make a table to show what happens to the diaphragm, intercostal muscles, volume of the lungs and air pressure inside the lungs during breathing in and breathing out.

2. a State which part of the model (see Figure 3.2.2) represents each of the following: lungs, trachea, bronchi, ribs.

   b Explain how the model shows what happens when you breathe in and out.

   c Make criticisms of the model.

3. Most of the time we do not think about our breathing. There are times when we voluntarily control the rate and depth of our breathing. List some examples of this.

Gaseous exchange and resuscitation

LINK

See 1.4 to remind yourself about diffusion and concentration gradients. A steep gradient is one where the concentrations on either side of the surface are very different.

LINK

See 1.3 to remind yourself about squamous epithelial cells.

EXAM TIP

Beware! You can say that alveoli and capillaries have **walls made of cells**, but not **cell walls** – remember plant cells have cell walls, but animal cells do not.

Gaseous exchange surfaces

We breathe in and out to refresh the air that is in the alveoli (i.e. where gaseous exchange occurs). Gaseous exchange is the diffusion of oxygen from alveolar air into the blood and the diffusion of carbon dioxide from the blood into the air. Our gaseous exchange surface shares features in common with other gaseous exchange surfaces of other creatures, such as the gills of fish, the breathing tubes of insects and the internal surfaces of leaves. All gaseous exchange surfaces are in contact with their surroundings, even if they are enclosed deep inside the body. They all have the following features that adapt them for efficient exchange of oxygen and carbon dioxide:

• a large surface area for diffusion of gases

• a moist surface so that gases can dissolve before diffusion

• thin walls so that gases do not have to diffuse very far.

Steep concentration gradients for oxygen and for carbon dioxide are maintained between alveolar air and the blood because of:

• a good blood supply, bringing carbon dioxide for efficient removal and for absorption of lots of oxygen

• breathing that constantly supplies fresh oxygen-rich air and removes waste carbon dioxide.

Gas exchange at the alveolus

When inspired (breathed-in) air reaches the alveoli it contains a lot of oxygen. Oxygen dissolves in the watery lining of each alveolus and then diffuses through the walls of the alveolus and the capillary and into the blood. There is a very short diffusion distance because the cells are simple squamous cells.

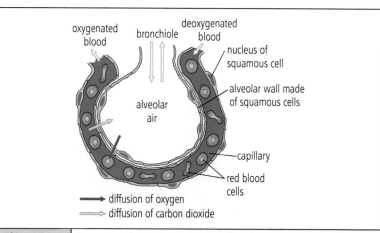

Figure 3.3.1 Gaseous exchange in an alveolus. The alveolus and the capillary are each lined by one layer of squamous cells

Each alveolus has many capillaries around it. Oxygen molecules from the alveolus diffuse into the red blood cells and combine with **haemoglobin**. The blood cells transport oxygen to the body tissues (see 4.1 and 4.4).

Carbon dioxide is carried from respiring tissues to the alveoli in the blood. Carbon dioxide molecules diffuse in the opposite direction, through the capillary wall, across the alveolar wall and into the space inside the alveolus. From here they are breathed out.

The elastic tissue around each alveolus stretches when you breathe in. When you breathe out it recoils to help remove air from your lungs.

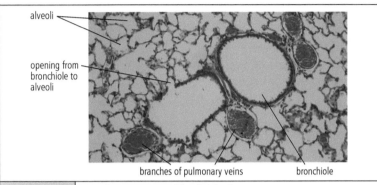

alveoli

opening from bronchiole to alveoli

branches of pulmonary veins   bronchiole

Figure 3.3.2 | Lung tissue as seen with a light microscope

Rescue breathing

When a person has an accident and stops breathing, they should be placed on their back and rescue breathing (which used to be called mouth-to-mouth resuscitation) should be carried out. **Rescue breathing** puts oxygen into the lungs in an attempt to keep the person alive.

Step 1 – Pinch the nostrils shut and tilt the head back and push the lower jaw forward. This opens the airways.

Step 2 – Take a deep breath and open your mouth and seal your lips against the person's mouth. Breathe out firmly but gently into the person's mouth. This puts air into the person's lungs.

Step 3 – Lift your mouth away and turn your head to look at the person's chest. If you have been successful you will see that the chest has risen and is now falling as air is leaving the lungs.

Step 4 – Repeat steps 2 and 3 at a steady rate. Breathing should start again.

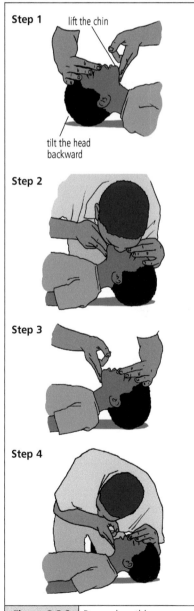

Step 1   lift the chin

tilt the head backward

Step 2

Step 3

Step 4

Figure 3.3.3 | Rescue breathing

Aerobic and anaerobic respiration

EXAM TIP

Cells also respire fats and proteins to provide energy, but you only have to know about the respiration of glucose, which is a carbohydrate. You should know that 1 g of fat releases far more energy than 1 g of carbohydrate.

DID YOU KNOW?

ADP has two phosphates whereas ATP has three. Adding the phosphate to ADP is driven by energy released from glucose. When ATP transfers energy to other compounds or to parts of the cell that do things, such as active transport, it loses the phosphate to become ADP.

Respiration takes place in **all** living cells **all of the time**. It provides a constant supply of energy for cells. They need this energy to stay alive and to carry out processes such as active transport, protein synthesis and cell division. Glucose and fat are the fuels used to provide energy in the cells. During respiration, the energy is released very gradually in a series of small, enzyme-controlled reactions.

Aerobic respiration

In **aerobic respiration** oxygen is used in the breakdown of glucose as shown by the word equation:

glucose + oxygen → carbon dioxide + water + energy released

The reactions of respiration use the energy in glucose to convert the substance **adenosine diphosphate** (ADP) into **adenosine triphosphate** (ATP). No energy transfer reaction is 100% efficient, so some of the energy from glucose is also released as heat.

ATP is good at transferring energy from respiration to the energy-consuming processes in cells. ATP diffuses easily through the cell and it breaks down readily so energy is transferred. When this happens it becomes ADP. The ADP molecules return to the mitochondria to be changed back to ATP using energy from the breakdown of glucose.

The **mitochondrion** is where aerobic respiration occurs. Cells that need a lot of energy have many mitochondria.

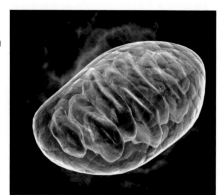

Figure 3.4.1 A computer-generated image of a mitochondrion. It is in these cell structures that most of the ATP is made. Each is 0.002 mm long

Anaerobic respiration

In **anaerobic respiration** energy is released from glucose without using oxygen. This is because mitochondria do not function if oxygen is not available. The word equation for anaerobic respiration shows that **lactic acid** is produced:

glucose → lactic acid + energy released

Some bacteria produce lactic acid when they respire without oxygen. Our muscles respire anaerobically during fast bursts of exercise, such as sprinting and weightlifting.

When yeasts respire anaerobically they make alcohol and carbon dioxide as shown in this word equation:

glucose → alcohol + carbon dioxide + energy released

Far less energy is released from each molecule of glucose in anaerobic respiration compared to aerobic respiration. This is because glucose is not completely broken down and a lot of energy remains in lactic acid and alcohol in the form of chemical bond energy.

Uses of anaerobic respiration

Yoghurt is made when bacteria respire lactose (milk sugar) to produce lactic acid. This is the substance that causes milk to taste sour.

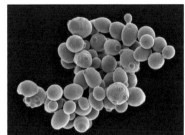

When yeast is kept in a sugar solution with little access to air, it respires anaerobically to release energy for growth and produces alcohol and carbon dioxide as waste products. This is why yeast is used to make alcoholic drinks, such as wine and beers.

| Figure 3.4.2 | Some yeast cells growing by producing 'buds' that will break off to give new yeast cells |

| Figure 3.4.3 | Copper fermentation tanks in a brewery |

Wine is made by adding special strains of yeast to sugar-rich juices extracted from grapes and other fruits.

Beer is made from barley which is germinated so that starch is converted to maltose. The germinating grain is boiled in water to extract the maltose. The mixture is fermented with special strains of yeasts that break down maltose to glucose and produce alcohol when they respire.

Carbon dioxide produced by yeasts in wine making and brewing escapes from the fermenters into the air.

In bread making, dough is prepared from flour, water, sugar and special strains of yeast. The dough is kept warm. Carbon dioxide produced by yeast through aerobic and anaerobic respiration cannot escape, so the dough fills with gas bubbles and so it rises. While the dough is baking, the alcohol produced by yeast, through any anaerobic respiration, evaporates into the air.

| Figure 3.4.4 | The baker is kneading dough to mix in some air. The dough will rise because yeast will respire aerobically and anaerobically releasing carbon dioxide |

SUMMARY QUESTIONS

1 Describe the importance of ADP and ATP in cells.

2 Yeast cells have a cell wall, cell membrane, cytoplasm, mitochondria and a nucleus. Make a diagram of a yeast cell and show the exchanges that occur with a sugar solution during fermentation to produce wine.

3 Explain the roles of yeast in the production of wine, beer and bread.

4 Explain how bacteria are involved in the production of yoghurt.

5 Make a table to compare aerobic and anaerobic respiration.

KEY POINTS

1 ATP is the energy currency of cells. ATP is used to transfer energy between respiration and energy-consuming processes.

2 Glucose is respired in cells to release energy that is used to convert ADP to ATP.

3 In aerobic respiration this occurs with oxygen with the maximum release of energy. Less energy is released in anaerobic oxygen when oxygen is not used.

4 Muscle tissue and some bacteria respire anaerobically to produce lactic acid; yeast respires anaerobically to produce alcohol and carbon dioxide.

Smoking

Addicted to smoking

If you smoke or know someone who smokes, you will know that it is very hard to give up the habit. Smokers have a craving that is only prevented by having another smoke. That craving is partly psychological but it is also physical. The body relies on the drug in tobacco smoke in order to function properly because its molecules interact with synapses in our nervous system. That drug is **nicotine** and it is one of the most addictive substances known.

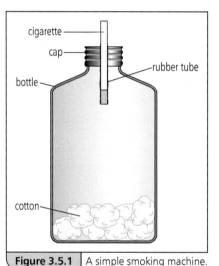

Figure 3.5.1 A simple smoking machine. Scientists have used more sophisticated machines to mimic our smoking behaviour to analyse the contents of tobacco smoke

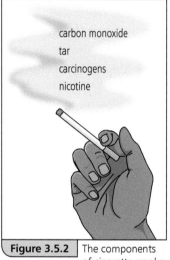

Figure 3.5.2 The components of cigarette smoke

Damage to the lungs

Tar is the black sticky material that collects in the lungs as smoke cools. It does not pass into the bloodstream. Tar irritates the lining of the airways stimulating the epithelial cells to produce more **mucus**. This tends to accumulate, narrowing the airways. Smokers have to cough to make this material move to the back of the throat.

Tar causes the cilia on the cells that line the air passages to stop beating. Mucus and the dust, dirt and bacteria that stick to it, are not removed from the lungs. The mucus accumulates and bacteria multiply. White blood cells congregate where this happens – particularly in the bronchi. The bronchi become blocked with **phlegm** (a mixture of mucus, bacteria and white blood cells), which people attempt to cough up. This condition is known as **chronic bronchitis**. People with chronic bronchitis find it difficult to breathe as the bronchi are partly blocked.

Particles, bacteria and tar reach the alveoli. White blood cells digest a pathway through the lining of the alveoli to reach the bacteria. Eventually this weakens the walls of the alveoli so much that they break down and burst, reducing the surface area for gas exchange. This condition, known as **emphysema**, leaves people gasping for breath. They cannot absorb enough oxygen or remove carbon dioxide efficiently. Many long-term smokers have both these conditions.

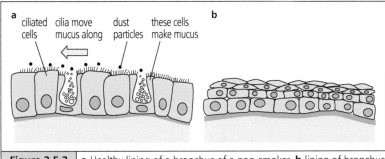

Figure 3.5.3 **a** Healthy lining of a bronchus of a non-smoker, **b** lining of bronchus of a long-term smoker: the ciliated cells are replaced by squamous cells

Lung cancer

About 90% of the cases of lung cancer occur in people who smoke or who have smoked. The **carcinogens** in the tar cause lung cancer. These substances promote changes, known as **mutations**, to occur in the DNA of cells lining the airways. These mutations cause the cells to grow and divide out of control. This growth is very slow and it may take 20 years before there are any symptoms. The cells form a **tumour**. If this is not discovered it may grow to occupy a large area of the lung pushing against airways and blood vessels to block them. Worse still, a part of the tumour may break off and spread into other organs. If a tumour is discovered before it has spread then it may be removed by surgery. If the tumour has spread then the cancer is much more difficult to treat.

Effects on transport of oxygen

Carbon monoxide combines permanently with haemoglobin in red blood cells reducing the volume of oxygen that the blood can carry. There may be as much as a 10% decrease in the oxygen transported. This is particularly dangerous for pregnant women (see 8.5).

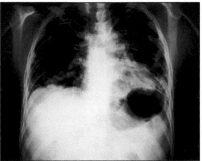

Figure 3.5.4 Lung cancer is often diagnosed using X-rays. Compare this with the X-ray of healthy lungs in 3.1

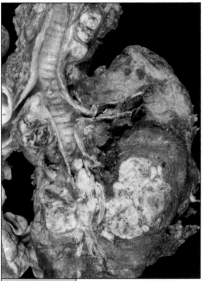

Figure 3.5.5 This cancer has spread through the lung, blocking blood vessels and airways

KEY POINTS

1 Nicotine is the addictive substance in tobacco smoke.

2 Tar damages the lining of the airways, stimulating excess production of mucus and destroying ciliated cells.

3 Carcinogens in smoke cause lung cancer.

4 Carbon monoxide combines with haemoglobin in red blood cells to reduce the blood's oxygen-carrying capacity.

SUMMARY QUESTIONS

1 State the components of tobacco smoke.

2 Smoking-related diseases are often classified as self-inflicted diseases. Discuss whether this is true.

3 Research the wider health risks of smoking and make a presentation to warn young children against smoking.

4 Explain why smokers find it hard to give up their habit.

Vital statistics – measuring breathing

SUMMARY QUESTIONS

1 a Complete the tally chart in Table 2 to analyse the data in Table 1, and plot a histogram.

  b Calculate the mean and determine the median and mode for the data in Table 1.

  c Suggest reasons for the variation in vital capacities.

2 Describe how the results after exercise differ from the results before exercise as shown in Table 3. Explain the differences.

3 a Draw a line graph of the data in Table 4.

  b Describe and explain the changes in oxygen consumption.

4 Suggest why sprinters can rely on anaerobic respiration, whereas long-distance runners cannot.

LINK

There is a histogram in 9.3 that you can look at. Also you can check your answer to question 1 by looking on the CD.

Vital capacities

The vital capacity (see 3.1) is the maximum volume of air that can be exhaled after breathing in fully. Vital capacity varies between different people. A sample of people picked at random had their vital capacities measured. The results are shown below.

Table 1 Vital capacities of 30 people in dm^3

3.5	4.6	6.2	5.9	3.9	5.8	5.6	5.9	6.0	4.6
3.8	3.9	4.1	3.9	5.4	5.3	5.9	3.9	4.3	4.4
4.9	4.3	4.6	3.2	6.3	5.7	5.6	3.8	4.7	4.8

The variation in the vital capacities of these people can be presented as a histogram. Here are the steps to convert this raw data into a histogram:

1 Group the figures. Ideally, you need about seven groups or classes. The difference between the lowest and highest figures in Table 1 is the range. Divide this range into classes, e.g. 3.0 to 3.4, 3.5 to 3.9, etc. until 6.0 to 6.4. There is no overlap between the classes. Create a tally chart for each chart.

Table 2

Classes	Tally	Totals
3.0–3.4	/	1
3.5–3.9	## //	7

2 Draw a histogram. Follow these rules when drawing a histogram:

• Use at least half the grid provided and do not make the histogram too small.

• Draw the histogram in pencil.

• The classes will be on the x-axis. In this case all the classes are the same size so they should be given the same distance on the x-axis. There should be no gaps between the classes

• The blocks should be drawn carefully. The area of each block is proportional to the size of the class. It is usual to have similar-sized classes so the widths of the blocks are all the same.

• The blocks should be labelled, so the first is labelled '3.0 to 3.4'.

• The y-axis represents the number or frequency and should be properly scaled with equidistant intervals.

• The axes should be labelled and any units given, e.g. dm^3.

Finding averages

When you have collected data for vital capacity, you can find out an average. There are three ways that you can do this:

- **Arithmetic mean** – add all the numbers and divide by the total number of readings. In this example, add all the vital capacities and divide by the total number of people in the sample which is 30.
- **Median** – find the middle number by arranging the data in numerical order and choosing the middle figure.
- **Mode** – arrange the data in a tally table and find the most common number. In a histogram the mode is the most common class.

The effect of exercise on breathing

Some students used a spirometer to investigate the effect of exercise on breathing.

Table 3 Aspects of breathing before and after exercise

Aspect of breathing	Before exercise	Immediately after 20 minutes of running
Rate of breathing/breaths/min^{-1}	12	20
Average volume of air taken in with each breath/dm^3	0.5	3.5
Ventilation rate/dm^3 min^{-1}	6.0	70
Percentage of oxygen	17.2	15.3
Percentage of carbon dioxide	3.6	5.5

In an investigation in an exercise laboratory, an athlete ran on a treadmill (similar to that shown in Figure 3.6.2) for 13 minutes. The scientists recorded the uptake of oxygen by his body before, during and after exercise. The results are shown in Table 4.

These results show that oxygen consumption does not return to resting levels immediately after exercise finishes. Oxygen is required to repay an **oxygen debt**. During hard, strenuous exercise not enough oxygen may reach the muscles for aerobic respiration to supply all the energy needed. Muscle tissue respires anaerobically so that there is enough energy released. Some glucose is broken down to lactic acid. The extra oxygen absorbed after exercise is used to respire the lactic acid.

Figure 3.6.1 | This apparatus measures vital capacity

Figure 3.6.2 | An athlete on a treadmill

Table 4 Change in oxygen absorption before, during and after exercise

Time/min	Oxygen consumption/ dm^3 min^{-1}
0	0.25
1	0.25
5	0.25
7	1.10
9	2.20
15	2.40
18	2.40
20	1.40
22	0.70
30	0.25
35	0.25

Figure 3.6.3 | Jamaican sprinter, Shelly-Ann Fraser Pryce

Figure 3.6.4 | Tirunesh Dibaba, Ethiopian long-distance runner

LINK

Before you answer these questions read through 2.4 to remind yourself about how to draw bar charts and line graphs.

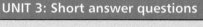

UNIT 3: Multiple-choice questions

1 Vital capacity is the volume of air:
  a breathed in during normal breathing
  b forced out after breathing in as much as possible
  c taken in during a deep breath after normal breathing
  d that cannot be expelled from the lungs.

2 During aerobic respiration:
  a carbohydrates are converted to carbon dioxide and water
  b carbohydrates are converted to lactic acid
  c muscle converts carbohydrates to fat
  d muscle converts excess carbohydrates to more muscle.

3 During inspiration (breathing in):
  a the diaphragm curves upward
  b the muscles of the diaphragm contract
  c the pressure in the lungs first increases and then decreases
  d the volume of the lungs decreases.

4 Which of the following is NOT a feature of the human gas exchange surface?
  a A large surface area
  b A poor supply of deoxygenated blood
  c A short diffusion distance for oxygen and carbon dioxide
  d A very large number of alveoli

5 Anaerobic respiration occurs in humans. Which of the following does NOT occur?
  a The production of lactic acid in muscle
  b The production of ATP
  c The use of carbon dioxide instead of oxygen
  d The breakdown of glucose

> Further practice questions and examples can be found on the accompanying CD.

UNIT 3: Short answer questions

1 a Write out and complete the word equation for aerobic respiration.

    ____ + oxygen → ____ + ____ + ____ (4)

A student set up the apparatus shown in the diagram to find the rate of respiration of crickets.

The student took several readings from the apparatus. After each reading the clip was opened for several minutes before being sealed again.

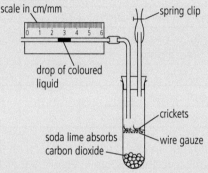

Figure 1

  b The coloured drop moves from left to right along the scale as the crickets respire in the apparatus. Explain why this is so. (3)
  c Explain why the clip is opened before taking the readings. (2)
  d State one factor that should be kept constant during the investigation. (1)
  e The table shows some results that the student obtained.

Time/seconds	Distance travelled by coloured drop/mm
0	0
30	5
60	10
90	15
120	20
150	25
180	27

i   Draw a graph to show these results. *(4)*

ii Suggest why the distance travelled by the coloured drop decreased in the last 30 seconds. *(1)*

Total 15 marks

2 The diaphragm, ribcage and intercostal muscles are involved in breathing movements.

a   Describe how these three structures are responsible for moving air into the lungs. *(4)*

b   i   Explain how air is moved out of the lungs during quiet breathing when at rest. *(4)*

   ii Explain how breathing out during recovery from strenuous exercise differs from breathing out when at rest. *(2)*

c   A student used a spirometer to measure her vital capacity. The trace is shown in Figure 2.

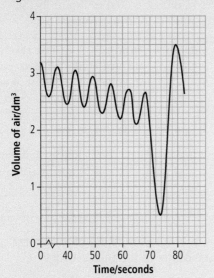

Figure 2

i   Define the term *vital capacity*. *(2)*

ii State the student's vital capacity. *(1)*

d   State two factors that INCREASE the rate of breathing. *(2)*

Total 15 marks

3 A long-term study into the link between smoking and lung cancer collected information on a large number of smokers and non-smokers. The researchers recorded the age at which people started to smoke and how many cigarettes they smoked each day. The causes of death were recorded and the percentage of deaths caused by lung cancer in each group is shown in the table below. 11% of those who never smoked died of lung cancer.

Age at which started smoking/ years	Percentage of deaths caused by lung cancer in each group	
	Number of cigarettes smoked per day	
	10–20	21–39
Before 15	26	40
15–19	24	33
20–24	19	23
25 and over	13	17

a   State the group:

   i   most at risk of dying from lung cancer *(1)*

   ii least at risk of dying from lung cancer. *(1)*

b   Explain how the results of this study help to show a link between smoking and lung cancer. *(4)*

c   Explain how lung cancer develops. *(4)*

d   Describe two lung diseases, OTHER THAN LUNG CANCER, that are caused by smoking. *(5)*

Total 15 marks

Further short answer questions can be found on the CD.

4.1   Transport systems

At the end of this topic you should be able to:

• define the term *transport system*

• explain why humans need a transport system

• list what is transported around the human body.

The students calculated the surface area and the volume of the cubes. The smallest cube has a ratio of surface area to volume of 6 : 1, whereas the largest cube has a ratio of 1 : 1. The results show that we cannot use our body surface for gas exchange. Very small organisms, such as bacteria, and very thin organisms, such as tapeworms, have a large body surface compared with their volume (or body mass) and use their body surface for gas exchange.

In question **2a** you should plot the time taken as the vertical axis, but what to choose as the horizontal axis? You could plot the length of each side of the cubes (column 1) or the ratio given in column 4 (in which case plot 1, 1.2, 1.5, 2, 3 and 6). Remember to scale the axis correctly (see 2.4).

Oxygen in the lungs and **glucose** in the intestine are absorbed into your blood. Your blood transports these substances to all the living cells of the body so that they can respire, grow and repair themselves.

The cells, tissues and organs of the circulatory system together make up a system that carries substances around the body. The circulatory system is our main transport system. The other system is the **lymphatic system** (see 4.6).

Without a transport system we would have to rely on **diffusion** for the movement of substances through the body. Just think about getting oxygen from your lungs to your big toe.

Problems with diffusion

This practical demonstration will help you to understand the difficulty of relying on diffusion alone. **Agar**, a special jelly, is mixed with an alkali and a pH indicator. The jelly is cut into cubes of different sizes and placed into dilute hydrochloric acid. The colour of the pH indicator changes as the acid diffuses into the blocks. Eventually, the whole block changes colour. The time this takes is a measurement of how long the acid takes to diffuse to the centre of the block. The table shows some students' results for this investigation.

Cube of side/mm	Surface area/mm^2	Volume/mm^3	Ratio of surface area to volume	Time taken for block to change colour in acid/s
1	6	1	6 : 1	8
2	24	8	3 : 1	26
3	54	27	2 : 1	43
4	96	64	1.5 : 1	65
5	150	125	1.2 : 1	112
6	216	216	1 : 1	160

The time taken for acid to diffuse to the centre of the largest cube is 20 times slower than to the centre of the smallest cube.

Movement of substances by diffusion is not an efficient way of getting oxygen and glucose to cells far removed from the places where they are absorbed into the body.

The ratios of surface area to volume given in the table **decrease** as the cubes **increase** in size. This is because the volume of the cubes increases much more each time than the increase in the surface area. Your bodies are much bigger than these cubes, so your own surface area to volume (or body mass) ratio will be even smaller. With such a **small** surface area to volume ratio we cannot rely on diffusion from the body surface to cells deep in the body. The distances are too great and there is not enough surface area to absorb enough oxygen.

Another reason we do not absorb oxygen through our body surface is that we have skin. Look at 6.3 to find out why we do not use the skin for gas exchange.

Substances transported by the circulatory system

The circulatory system carries substances from place to place within the body. For example, glucose enters the blood that flows through the small intestine when you are absorbing a meal. Much of this glucose leaves the blood to enter liver cells to be stored as glycogen. The rest travels around the body in the blood entering other cells that use glucose for respiration. Between meals liver cells break down glycogen to release glucose for cells to use.

SUMMARY QUESTIONS

1 The table shows information about three spherical organisms.

Feature	Spherical organism		
	A	B	C
Radius/mm	1	2	3
Surface area/mm^2	12.57	50.27	113.10
Volume/mm^3	4.19	33.51	113.10

  a State which organism has the highest surface area:volume ratio.

  b Explain why B and C may need a transport system, whereas A may not.

2 a Plot a line graph of the results in the table opposite.

  b Use the graph you have drawn to explain why humans need a transport system.

3 Make a large drawing of the human body showing the location of the major organs. Label all the organs and then annotate your drawing with details of the exchanges that occur between the blood and the cells in the organs. You may want to add more information from Units 1 to 8.

4 Make a table to show what is transported in the circulatory system, where each substance enters the blood and where it leaves the blood.

  Here is a list of substances that you will find in this book:

  water; *ions*; *glucose*; *amino acids*; *proteins*; *fats*; *cholesterol*; *respiratory gases* (*oxygen* and *carbon dioxide*); *urea*; *lactic acid*.

  Use the index to find them as you construct your table.

  The blood also transports heat and you can include this as well, even though it is not a substance.

  You can also write in the topics in this book (4.1, 4.6, etc.) or the pages where you find the information.

STUDY FOCUS

Glucose is not the only substance transported in the blood; there are many more. Make a list of as many substances that are transported by the blood as you can. Think about where each substance enters the blood and where it leaves it. Your answer to summary question 3 should help you to do this. Now try making the table as required by summary question 4.

KEY POINTS

1 Transport systems move substances around the bodies of organisms.

2 The human body needs a transport system because distances are too great for this to occur by diffusion alone.

3 Nutrients, water, oxygen, carbon dioxide, hormones, antibodies, urea and heat are transported around the human body.

The heart

At the end of this topic you should be able to:

- describe the structure of the heart including the four chambers, valves and the major blood vessels
- explain how the heart functions to move blood to the lungs and to the rest of the body
- describe what happens during one heartbeat.

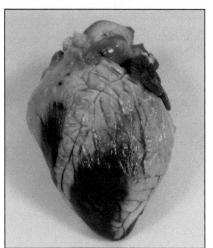

Figure 4.2.2 The heart viewed from the front of the body

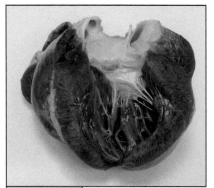

Figure 4.2.3 The inside of the left side of the heart

The human heart consists almost entirely of **cardiac muscle** tissue. This is specialised muscle that can contract about 70 times a minute for up to a hundred years or more without tiring.

We need a heart to pump blood around the body. The heart contracts and 'squeezes' the blood, applying a pressure to it. The blood can then flow through the vessels and overcome the pressure exerted on our bodies by the atmosphere. The heart is a 'double pump'. The right side of the heart pumps blood to the lungs and the left side pumps blood to the rest of the body.

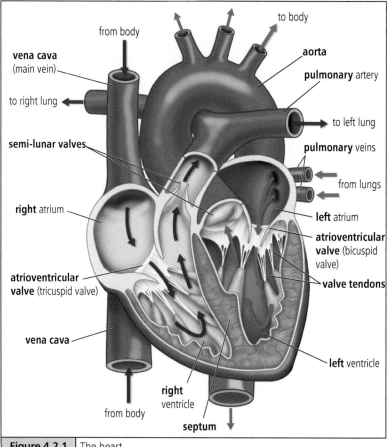

Figure 4.2.1 The heart

The septum separates the two halves of the heart. This prevents the mixing of deoxygenated and oxygenated blood. On each side of the heart there are two chambers. The upper chamber is the **atrium**. Blood empties into the atria from **veins**. When each atrium contracts it pumps blood into a **ventricle**. The ventricles have much more muscular walls than the atria as they have to pump the blood at higher pressure over a great distance.

Between each atrium and ventricle is an **atrioventricular valve** which is the white area in Figure 4.2.3. These **valves** prevent the blood flowing back into the right and left atrium when the right and left ventricles contract. At the base of the **pulmonary artery** and the **aorta** there are **semi-lunar valves**. In Figure 4.2.3 the semi-lunar valves at the base of the aorta are the pink structures just above the atrioventricular valve. These prevent blood flowing back into the ventricles when they relax.

The left ventricle has a more muscular wall than the right ventricle. This is because it has to pump blood a further distance – around the entire body. It has to overcome much more resistance to flow around the body than the blood that flows through the lungs, because the lungs have a spongy texture and are a short distance from the heart.

Heart action

The heart does not need to be 'told' to contract by the brain. In the wall of the right atrium are some specialised cardiac muscle cells that act as the heart's **pacemaker**. These cells send out pulses of electricity that instruct the atria and then the ventricles to contract.

The heart pumps blood when its muscles contract. When the muscle contracts the chamber gets smaller and squeezes the blood out. After each chamber contracts it relaxes so it fills up with blood again.

Systole is when the heart muscles contract. **Diastole** is when the heart muscles relax. During systole, the atria contract to force blood into the ventricles. The valves between the atria and ventricles open due to the higher pressure of blood in the atria pushing against them. The atria relax and then the ventricles contract to force blood out into the arteries. The higher pressure in the ventricles closes the atrioventricular valves to prevent blood flowing back into the atria. The increase in pressure also causes the semi-lunar valves at the base of the arteries to open. This allows blood to flow from the right ventricle to the lungs in the pulmonary arteries and from the left ventricle to the rest of the body in the aorta (main artery).

The chambers fill with blood during diastole. Deoxygenated blood returns to the right atrium in the **vena cava** (main vein). Oxygenated blood returns to the left atrium in the **pulmonary veins**.

LINK

There is more about artificial pacemakers in 4.5.

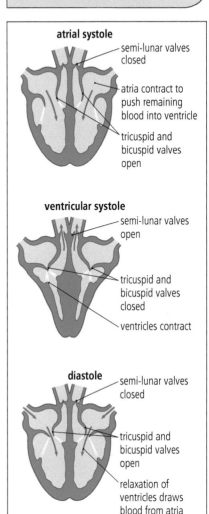

Figure 4.2.4 The changes that occur in the heart during one heartbeat

SUMMARY QUESTIONS

1 Draw a flow chart diagram to show the flow of blood through the four chambers of the heart and the major blood vessels of the body.

2 Explain why we need a heart.

3 Explain the difference between diastole and systole.

4 The heart is sometimes described as a 'double pump'. Explain what this means.

5 Explain how one-way flow of blood through the heart is achieved.

KEY POINTS

1 The heart consists of two muscular pumps divided by a septum.

2 Each side has two chambers: an atrium and a ventricle.

3 Ventricles contract to force blood into arteries. Valves make sure that blood flows in one direction through the heart.

Double circulation

At the end of this topic you should be able to:

- define the term *double circulatory system*
- describe the circulation in humans
- state the functions of arteries, capillaries and veins
- explain how the structure of arteries, capillaries and veins is related to their functions.

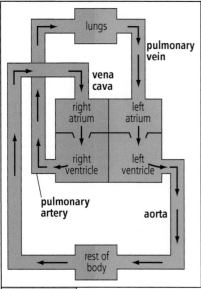

Figure 4.3.1 Double circulatory system

Squamous cells are very thin. They line the alveoli as well as capillaries. They are thin so that the diffusion distance from one side to the other is very short. As you have seen in 4.1, diffusion becomes less efficient the further the distance.

In 4.2 you saw the major blood vessels that are attached to the heart. Blood travels away from the heart in the arteries and towards the heart in veins. We have a **double circulatory system** in which blood flows through the heart **twice** during one complete circulation of the body. To prove this, follow the blood around the diagram in Figure 4.3.1 from the lungs, around the system and back to where you started. The two circulations are:

- **pulmonary circulation** – deoxygenated blood flows from the heart, through the pulmonary arteries to the lungs and back to the heart in the pulmonary veins as oxygenated blood
- **systemic circulation** – oxygenated blood flows from the heart, through the aorta and other arteries to all the other organs of the body and then back to the heart through the venae cavae as deoxygenated blood.

The circulation is also described as a closed circulation because the blood remains inside blood vessels during its journey throughout the body.

Not all animals have blood vessels. Animals such as crabs and insects have an open circulation with blood in large spaces in the body, not in blood vessels.

Blood vessels

The walls of arteries and veins are made of three different tissues:

- **squamous cells** that form a smooth lining
- muscle tissue
- fibrous tissue that contains **elastic tissue** and **collagen** fibres.

The walls of capillaries do not have muscle or fibrous tissue. They are only composed of the squamous cells.

Blood is red. Oxygenated blood is bright red and deoxygenated blood is dark red. On diagrams of the blood system it is a convention to use blue to represent deoxygenated blood. It doesn't mean that deoxygenated blood is **actually** blue. It isn't.

The following table summarises the structure and function of blood vessels.

Blood vessel	Relationship between structure and function
Artery	• Blood flows away from the heart at high pressure • Elastic tissue in the walls stretches and recoils to maintain the blood pressure • Blood is delivered to the organs at a pressure slightly less than it left the heart • Walls have thick layers of muscle and fibrous tissue to withstand high blood pressures
Vein	• Blood flows towards the heart at low pressure • Vessels expand to take increasing volumes of blood, e.g. during exercise • As blood pressure is low, backflow of blood is prevented by semi-lunar valves at intervals along veins • Walls have thin layers of muscle and fibrous tissue as they do not have to withstand high blood pressures
Capillary	• Blood flows between smaller arteries (arterioles) and smaller veins (venules) at low pressure • Oxygen and carbon dioxide diffuse through the walls • Water and solutes, such as glucose and amino acids, pass across the walls into tissue fluid surrounding the cells • Walls are thin so there is a short diffusion distance between the blood and the tissue fluid

KEY POINTS

1 In a double circulation, blood travels through the heart twice in one complete circuit of the body.
2 Blood flows from the heart to the lungs and back in the pulmonary circulation and from the heart to the rest of the body and back in the systemic circulation.
3 Blood flows away from the heart in arteries, towards the heart in veins and through tissues in capillaries.
4 Arteries have thick walls to withstand high pressure and veins have thin walls as blood pressure is low. Capillaries are exchange vessels and have very thin walls.

SUMMARY QUESTIONS

1 a Define the term *double circulatory system*.
  b Explain what is meant by a closed circulatory system.
2 Find a diagram of the circulatory system showing the blood vessels and the following organs: heart, lungs, liver, kidney, brain and muscles in the legs and in the arms. Label all the blood vessels and the direction of flow of the blood. Use the diagram to explain the advantages of a double circulatory system.
3 Explain how the circulatory system ensures that blood flows in one direction.
4 Explain how the structures of arteries, veins and capillaries are related to the functions of these blood vessels.

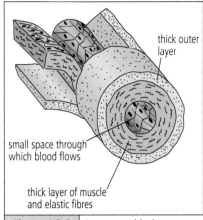

thick outer layer

small space through which blood flows

thick layer of muscle and elastic fibres

Figure 4.3.2 An artery with the outer layers cut away

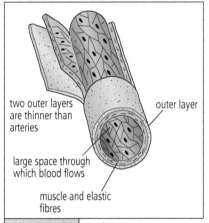

two outer layers are thinner than arteries

outer layer

large space through which blood flows

muscle and elastic fibres

Figure 4.3.3 A vein

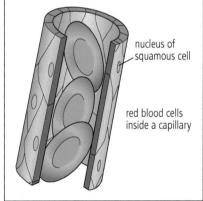

nucleus of squamous cell

red blood cells inside a capillary

Figure 4.3.4 A capillary magnified ×1000 to show the detail of the cells that make up the wall. Part is cut away to show the red blood cells inside

4.4

Blood

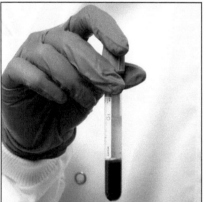

Figure 4.4.1 This sample of blood has been spun at high speed in a centrifuge

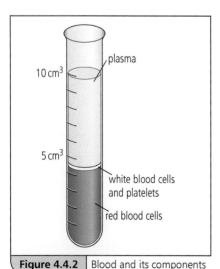

10 cm³ — plasma

5 cm³

white blood cells and platelets

red blood cells

Figure 4.4.2 Blood and its components

Blood is the fluid that is pumped around the cardiovascular system by the heart. As blood flows through capillaries in the organs, substances are exchanged with the surrounding tissues. We have seen that in the lungs there is gaseous exchange with the air in the alveoli. In respiring tissues there is exchange with the cells that need to gain oxygen and to lose waste carbon dioxide.

Blood is a tissue that consists of cells and of cell fragments suspended in a liquid called **plasma**.

This table shows the features of the blood cells you can see in Figures 4.4.3 and 4.4.4.

Type of blood cell	Features	Relationship between structure and function
Red blood cell	• Small cell • Shape: biconcave disc • No nucleus, mitochondria or endoplasmic reticulum • Cytoplasm is full of **haemoglobin**	• Can change shape and fit easily through capillaries • More space to fill with haemoglobin to transport oxygen and carbon dioxide
Phagocyte	• Large cell • Lobed nucleus • Cytoplasm with mitochondria and endoplasmic reticulum • Many small vacuoles containing enzymes	• Lobed nucleus helps cells leave blood through small gaps in the capillary walls • Vacuoles contain enzymes to digest bacteria
Lymphocyte	• Small cell • Small quantity of cytoplasm with few mitochondria and little endoplasmic reticulum	• When activated during an infection more endoplasmic reticulum is made to produce antibodies (B lymphocytes) that are made of protein (see 10.8)

LINK

Platelets are small pieces of cells. There is more information about them in 4.5.

There is more information about phagocytes and lymphocytes in 10.8.

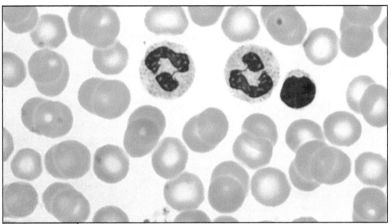

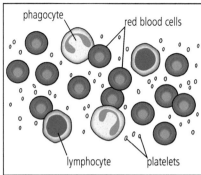

Figure 4.4.4 A drawing made from a photograph similar to the one in Figure 4.4.3

Figure 4.4.3 In this photograph you can see red blood cells, two phagocytes and a lymphocyte. Compare with Figure 4.4.4 to identify them

Plasma is the liquid part of the blood. It is composed mostly of water, which is a solvent for:

• nutrients, e.g. glucose, amino acids, vitamins B and C and minerals, such as calcium

• carbon dioxide, urea and other wastes

• blood clotting proteins

• antibodies and other proteins for defence against invading pathogens.

In addition, the plasma transports heat around the body.

Plasma is a source of many compounds that are used in treatment. Antibodies from blood donors are collected and used for **passive immunity** (see 10.8). **Serum** is plasma with the clotting proteins, such as fibrinogen, removed. If plasma is exposed to air it clots. Serum does not clot. Serum is prepared from blood samples that are taken for diagnostic tests. An example is the test for iron to see if someone has iron-deficiency anaemia.

KEY POINTS

1 Blood is composed of red blood cells, **white blood cells** (phagocytes and lymphocytes) and platelets suspended in liquid plasma.

2 Red blood cells are filled with haemoglobin for transporting oxygen, phagocytes containing enzymes for digesting bacteria, and lymphocytes containing endoplasmic reticulum for producing **antibody** molecules.

3 Serum is produced by removing the clotting agents from plasma.

SUMMARY QUESTIONS

1 a List the components of blood.
  b What percentage of the total volume of blood does each component occupy?

2 Blood consists of cells and fragments of cells suspended in plasma.
  a Make a labelled drawing of each type of cell.
  b State the function of each cell.
  c What are the fragments of cells called and what is their function?

3 Explain how each of the cell types you have drawn in question 2 is adapted to its function.

4 What is *serum* and what is it used for?

Heart attacks

At the end of this topic you should be able to:

- state what is meant by blood clotting, when and where it occurs and why it is important
- state the sequence of events that occurs during blood clotting
- explain the causes and effects of heart attacks.

Figure 4.5.1 Red blood cells trapped in a mesh of fibrin

LINK

Where a wound happens in the skin, the stem cells at the base of the epidermis divide by mitosis to form new skin cells to repair the damage. See 6.3 and 9.1 for information about stem cells in the skin and mitosis.

You cannot afford to lose too much blood. It is a precious fluid. The blood system has a way of sealing any breakages in the blood vessels to limit blood loss. Whenever blood is exposed to air or there is a break in a blood vessel, blood starts to clot. It is important that this does not happen too easily; otherwise the flow of blood through the circulation would be blocked too frequently. Instead, there is a complex system to ensure that clotting only occurs when and where necessary.

Platelets are small fragments of cells. When a blood vessel is damaged it releases substances that interact with calcium ions in the plasma to activate **prothrombin**. This changes into the active enzyme **thrombin**, which catalyses the conversion of the soluble protein **fibrinogen** into the insoluble protein **fibrin**. Fibrin forms a mesh of fibres to trap platelets and blood cells. The mesh of fibres and cells dries to form a scab.

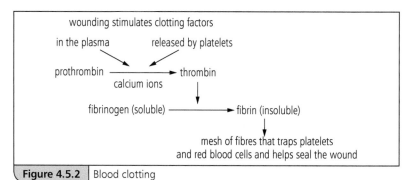

Figure 4.5.2 Blood clotting

Blood clotting seals wounds to restrict the loss of blood and to prevent the entry of pathogens through open wounds.

Heart disease

Healthy arteries have a smooth lining which allows blood to flow easily. The plasma contains small particles that transport a fatty substance called cholesterol, which is needed by all the cells in the body for making cell membranes. If the walls of arteries are damaged in any way these particles enter the lining and deposit cholesterol. With time this fatty deposit – known as plaque – builds up. It blocks the opening (or lumen) through which the blood flows and roughens the lining. This makes it more likely that blood will clot and form a blood clot or **thrombus** within the artery.

The build-up of fatty tissue in artery walls is **atherosclerosis**. When this happens in coronary arteries it leads to coronary heart disease (CHD). The supply of blood to cardiac muscle is reduced and some tissues will not receive enough oxygen and nutrients, such as glucose. This may mean that the tissue has to respire without oxygen and may even die. This happens when a person has a heart attack.

One of the first signs of heart disease is an increase in blood pressure as the heart works harder to pump blood around the circulation. High blood pressure is know as **hypertension** (see 10.2).

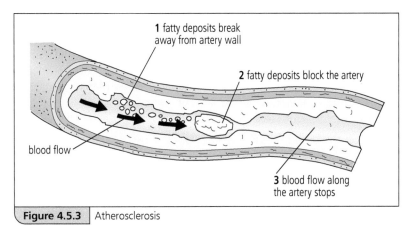

1 fatty deposits break away from artery wall

2 fatty deposits block the artery

3 blood flow along the artery stops

blood flow

| **Figure 4.5.3** | Atherosclerosis |

Certain factors increase the risk of developing heart disease. These factors fall into two groups:

Factors you cannot do anything about	Factors you can do something about
• Inheritance – some genes increase the chances of developing CHD as they control the metabolism of cholesterol • Age – the risk increases as people get older • Sex – men are more at risk of CHD than women	• Eating a diet rich in animal fat • Being overweight or obese • High blood pressure • Smoking • Taking little or no exercise • A stressful way of life

Artificial pacemakers

Some people have poorly functioning pacemakers. This can be treated by inserting an artificial pacemaker into their chest. The pacemaker sends electrical impulses to the heart causing it to contract in just the same way as it would have done from the natural pacemaker. It is also possible to get pacemakers to respond to the different demands of the body.

SUMMARY QUESTIONS

1 Explain why blood clotting is important.

2 Platelets, calcium ions, thrombin and fibrinogen are involved in blood clotting. Explain how.

3 Explain the terms *coronary heart disease* and *atherosclerosis*.

4 List the risk factors for heart disease.

5 Suggest how people can reduce their risk of developing heart disease.

STUDY FOCUS

Coronary arteries branch from the aorta and carry oxygenated blood to cardiac muscle. They are the heart muscle's own blood supply. They follow the lines you can see on the surface of the heart in Figure 4.2.2 and you should look for them if you dissect a heart.

LINK

The natural pacemaker is in the muscle tissue of the right atrium. Study Figure 4.2.1 to remind yourself where that is.

KEY POINTS

1 Platelets respond to blood loss by releasing clotting factors which interact with calcium ions to activate the enzyme thrombin.

2 Thrombin converts soluble fibrinogen to insoluble fibrin that forms a mesh over a wound preventing further blood loss.

3 Atherosclerosis is the gradual build-up of fatty tissue in the walls of arteries. Factors that promote this are poor diet, smoking, obesity and lack of exercise.

4 Heart attacks are caused by blockages in coronary arteries supplying blood to heart muscle.

4.6

Lymph

All of our cells are surrounded by tissue fluid. This is formed when the liquid part of blood leaks out of the blood vessels into the spaces surrounding our cells. The liquid comes from blood plasma as blood flows through capillaries. Tissue fluid provides a constant environment for our cells.

Although the blood pressure in capillaries is lower than in arteries, it still forces water and other small molecules through tiny gaps in the walls into the spaces around the cells. Red blood cells remain in the blood, but white blood cells can squeeze through the gaps, to help remove any pathogens.

Tissue fluid helps substances, such as glucose and oxygen, pass from tissue fluid into cells. Carbon dioxide and other wastes, such as urea and lactic acid, pass out of cells into the tissue fluid.

Blood pressure decreases along the length of capillaries. When it has decreased sufficiently the water moves from the tissue fluid back into the blood. This reabsorption occurs by osmosis as there is high concentration of solutes in the blood. However, not all of the fluid is reabsorbed and that is why tissues need a 'drainage' system. As you can see in Figure 4.6.1 there are blind-ending **lymph capillaries** for the absorption of this excess fluid.

STUDY FOCUS

Fluid flows constantly from the plasma to form tissue fluid and then about 90% of it is reabsorbed into the plasma, with the rest draining into the **lymphatic system**.

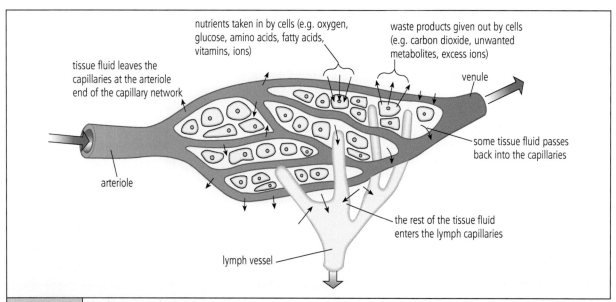

nutrients taken in by cells (e.g. oxygen, glucose, amino acids, fatty acids, vitamins, ions)

waste products given out by cells (e.g. carbon dioxide, unwanted metabolites, excess ions)

tissue fluid leaves the capillaries at the arteriole end of the capillary network

venule

arteriole

some tissue fluid passes back into the capillaries

the rest of the tissue fluid enters the lymph capillaries

lymph vessel

Figure 4.6.1 The formation of tissue fluid and lymph

Look carefully at Figure 4.6.1. Before blood flows into capillaries it passes through arterioles. These control the blood flow into capillaries as you will see in 6.3. Blood flows from capillaries into venules which are wider than capillaries, but not as wide as veins.

Our lymphatic system is not so obvious as the blood circulatory system, but you can feel the **lymph nodes** beneath your lower jaw. Adenoids and tonsils are similar to lymph nodes. These glands are all connected together by **lymph vessels**.

Tiny valves allow tissue fluid to flow in one direction only. The walls of the capillaries have clefts which allow the fluid to enter the lymph capillaries but do not let the lymph pass out. The capillaries join up to form lymph vessels. These are thin-walled vessels in which the lymph flows in one direction because of semi-lunar valves.

There is no pump in the lymphatic system so the flow of **lymph** is slow. Surrounding muscles contract and squeeze the vessels to make it flow.

The smaller lymph vessels join into two large lymph vessels. These empty into the subclavian veins under the collar bones. Here the lymph mixes with the blood before joining the vena cava just before it enters the heart.

Sometimes the drainage of tissue fluid into lymph vessels becomes blocked. Tissue fluid builds up leading to swelling. This is known as oedema (pronounced 'eedema'). Oedema in the lungs is very dangerous.

Lymph nodes are filled with lymphocytes. During an infection their numbers increase and they make antibodies. The antibodies leave the lymph nodes, travel in the lymph and enter the blood to be carried around the body. Some lymphocytes circulate around the body in the blood patrolling for invasions of pathogens all the time. The lymphatic system is an important part of the body's defence system (see 10.8).

1 When tissue fluid enters the lymph capillaries it is termed lymph.

2 Lymph consists of plasma and white blood cells, but has no red blood cells or large plasma proteins.

3 The lymphatic system has a separate circulation which returns lymph to the blood.

4 Lymphocytes in lymph nodes multiply during an infection and produce antibodies.

Figure 2.10.2 shows that each villus in the small intestine has a blind-ending lacteal - a thin walled vessel that absorbs fat from the gut. Lacteals are part of the lymphatic system too.

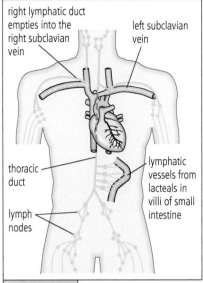

right lymphatic duct empties into the right subclavian vein

left subclavian vein

thoracic duct

lymph nodes

lymphatic vessels from lacteals in villi of small intestine

Figure 4.6.2 | The lymphatic system

1 a What is tissue fluid and what are its functions?

   b What is lymph and what are its functions?

2 Explain in as much detail as you can why the flow of lymph is so slow and how the circulation is maintained.

3 What are lymph nodes, where are they found and what is their main function?

4 Describe **in detail** the pathway taken by a molecule of water that is absorbed in the stomach and that travels via the blood to tissue fluid in the muscle tissue in the leg. It is then returned to the blood via the lymphatic system.

Unit 4   Practice exam questions

1 Which part of the heart prevents the backflow of blood from the left ventricle into the left atrium?
  a Aorta
  b Atrioventricular valve
  c Pulmonary vein
  d Semi-lunar valve

2 The progressive build-up of yellowish fatty deposits within the walls of arteries is called:
  a arthritis
  b atherosclerosis
  c plaque
  d thrombus.

3 Blood clotting involves the following events:
  i fibrinogen is converted into fibrin; **ii** red blood cells and platelets become trapped in a mesh of fibrin; **iii** platelets come into contact with damaged tissue; **iv** a mesh of fibres is formed.
  Which is the correct sequence in which these events occur?
  a i, ii, iii, iv
  b ii, iii, iv, i
  c iii, i, iv, ii
  d iii, iv, i, ii

4 A blood clot can cause a heart attack when the clot enters:
  a an atrium of the heart
  b a ventricle of the heart
  c the aorta
  d a coronary artery.

5 Which of the following statements best describes lymph?
  a Lymph is the fluid that drains into blind-ending tubes from the tissues in the body.
  b Lymph is the liquid part of blood that squeezes out of the blood vessels.
  c Lymph is the fluid that fills the spaces between the cells of the body.
  d Lymph is the plasma from the blood without any fibrinogen.

> Further practice questions and examples can be found on the accompanying CD.

1 Two students did a stepping exercise to compare their athletic fitness. They each used a heart monitor to record their heart rate. The table shows their heart rates at the end of each minute. They exercised for three minutes.

Time/minutes	Heart rate/beats per minute	
	Student A	Student B
0	60	70
1	60	70
2	116	140
3	118	168
4	120	170
5	63	100
6	60	78
7	60	77

  a Draw a graph to show the changes in heart rate for the two students.   (5)
  b **i** Describe the changes in heart rate for Student A.   (3)
      ii Describe how the changes in Student B's heart rate differ from those of Student A.   (3)
  c Suggest why the heart rate did not decrease to the value at rest immediately after the students stopped exercising.   (4)

  Total 15 marks

2 a A person has an irregular heartbeat and is prescribed an artificial pacemaker.
    Explain how such a pacemaker functions to control the heart.   (2)

  The table shows data about deaths from heart disease in the member countries of the Caribbean Epidemiology Centre (CAREC).

Year	Number of deaths from heart disease	Total number of deaths	Percentage of deaths caused by heart disease
1985	6504	38 526	16.88
1990	6629	37 855	17.51
1995	7206	43 219	16.67
2000	6764	43 036	

b Calculate the percentage of deaths in CAREC countries that were caused by heart disease in 2000. Show your working. (2)

c Explain how you could assess the importance of heart disease as a cause of death in different countries in the different member states of CAREC. (3)

d i Explain what causes a heart attack to occur. (5)

ii Suggest the steps that governments of member countries of CAREC could take to reduce the number of deaths from heart disease. (3)

Total 15 marks

3 a Copy and complete the table to compare arteries with veins and capillaries.

Feature	Arteries	Veins	Capillaries
squamous cells		form the lining	form the wall
muscle tissue	thick layer	some	
elastic tissue		some	none
relative thickness of wall		thin	very thin
direction of blood flow		organs to heart	arteries to veins

(5)

b Explain how the structure of a capillary helps it to carry out its function. (2)

c i When the heart contracts it increases the pressure of the blood. Explain why it is necessary for blood to have a pressure. (3)

ii Explain how the structure of the heart ensures that blood flows in one direction. (5)

Total 15 marks

4 The blood is a suspension of cells and cell fragments in plasma.

a Describe the structure and functions of red blood cells, phagocytes and lymphocytes. (8)

b i Explain the importance of blood clotting. (3)

ii Describe how blood clotting takes place. (4)

Total 15 marks

5 a Explain why humans need a transport system. (4)

b i Describe how lymph is formed. (3)

ii Describe the functions of lymphatic vessels and lymph nodes. (4)

c i State the difference between plasma and serum. (1)

ii Explain how serum is used by the medical profession. (3)

Total 15 marks

Further short answer questions can be found on the CD.

5 The skeletal system

5.1 The human skeleton

The skeletal system is composed of bones that are joined together at **joints**.

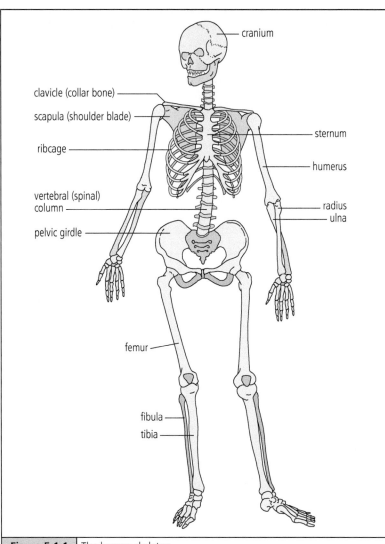

Figure 5.1.1   The human skeleton

The skeleton is composed of two main tissues – **bone** and **cartilage**. Both tissues consist of cells within an extensive matrix of **collagen** fibres and other material that the cells produce. Table 1 summarises the differences between bone and cartilage.

Cartilage is found in places where flexibility is required, such as the external ears, end of the nose and supporting the trachea and bronchi. The ends of bones and the discs between the vertebrae are made of cartilage. Cartilage is smooth and protects bones so they do not wear away by rubbing against each other.

Table 1

Bone	Cartilage
Matrix consists of tough collagen fibres hardened by calcium salts	Material between the cells is softer and is much more flexible
Many blood vessels in bone tissue providing cells with oxygen, nutrients, such as glucose, amino acids, calcium and phosphate, and hormones, such as vitamin D	No blood vessels

The functions of the skeleton are shown in Table 2.

Table 2

Function	Comments
Movement	• Bones are a firm structure for muscle attachment by **tendons** • The skeleton has systems of levers to move the whole body from place to place or move parts of the body relative to one another
Protection	• The cranium protects the brain, the eyes and ears • The ribcage protects the lungs and heart • The **vertebral column** protects the spinal cord • The **pelvis** protects the uterus
Support	• The bones provide a framework for all the other systems of the body – digestive, excretory, nervous, endocrine, muscular, for example. • The backbone provides support for the limbs and the head • The jawbones support the teeth
Breathing	• The ribcage is moved up and down by the intercostal muscles to increase and decrease the volume of the thorax (see 3.2)
Production of red blood cells	• Red **bone marrow** in the interior of the short bones and at the ends of long bones have **stem cells** that divide by mitosis to produce red blood cells to replace those that are removed from the circulation

A **Rounded head** fits into the shoulder blade to form a ball and socket joint allowing movement in three planes.

B The ends of the humerus are made of spongy bone, which is light and strong and withstands stresses in all directions. Spongy bone consists of struts of bone separated by softer bone marrow.

C Growth of the bone occurs here.

D Red bone marrow in the ends of the bone produces red blood cells.

E Yellow bone marrow is a store of fat.

F The long shaft is hollow which reduces the chances of a break occurring across the bone.

G The outer part of the shaft is made of compact bone which is very strong.

H Rounded ends form hinge joint with radius and ulna.

J The surface of the shaft provides sites of attachment for the triceps and other muscles, but not the biceps which are attached to the scapula.

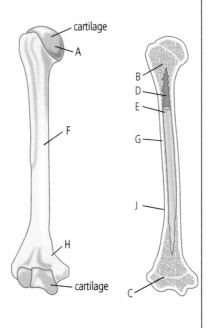

Figure 5.1.2 The humerus bone and how it is adapted for its functions

Joints

At the end of this topic you should be able to:

- explain why it is important for humans to be able to move
- distinguish between ligaments and tendons
- define the term *joint* and describe the structure of a named joint
- identify hinge joints, fixed joints and ball and socket joints
- describe the lever action of the arm.

Movement is crucially important to humans. We are **bipedal** – we walk upright. This enables us to have our front limbs free to manipulate objects. We have opposable thumbs, which have allowed us to make and use tools. Movement involves the skeleton, skeletal muscles and joints between the bones.

The place where two bones meet is a joint. There are two types of joint:

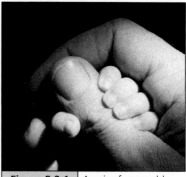

Figure 5.2.1 A pair of opposable thumbs belonging to a father and daughter!

1 Fixed joint where there is no movement, e.g. between the bones of the cranium.

2 Moveable (or synovial) joint where there is movement:

 a hinge joint in which movement occurs in one plane, e.g. at the elbow and the knee

 b ball and socket joint where movement occurs in all three planes, e.g. at the shoulder and the hip.

You can learn a lot by dissecting a pig's trotter. Remove the skin and then separate the tendons that are attached to the bones. Manipulate the tendons and bones to see the movement across the hinge joints. Cut through the ligaments around the joints and open up the hinge joints to find cartilage and the synovial fluid – the oily lubricant.

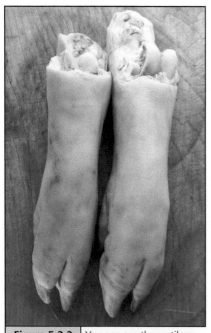

Figure 5.2.2 You can see the cartilage at the end of the bones of these pig's trotters

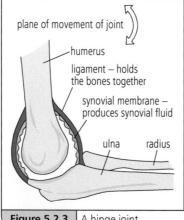

plane of movement of joint

humerus

ligament – holds the bones together

synovial membrane – produces synovial fluid

ulna   radius

Figure 5.2.3 A hinge joint

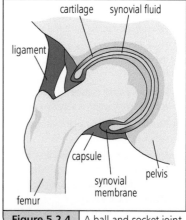

cartilage   synovial fluid

ligament

capsule

pelvis

synovial membrane

femur

Figure 5.2.4 A ball and socket joint

Muscle is attached to bones by tendons. These are full of tough collagen fibres that run deep into the muscle and the bone providing firm anchorage at either end. When muscles contract and shorten they pull on the tendons, which do not stretch so all the force is transmitted to the bone causing it to move.

Ligaments attach bones together. Most of these are also made mostly of collagen and are tough, but they have some elastic tissue which means that they can stretch a little. Ligaments provide support to the joints and form capsules around the joints. Some ligaments, such as those at the back of the neck, have elastic tissue so they do stretch. This helps with the support of your head.

Cartilage covers the ends of bones at moveable joints. It is softer than bone and smooth so it glides over the ends protecting the bone from wear and tear.

Synovial fluid is secreted by the synovial membrane surrounding the joint. This fluid is an oily liquid that lubricates the joint.

Lever action

Levers are ways of achieving the movement of a load with most efficiency. Wherever there is a moveable joint in the body there is a lever action. Joints act as fulcrums. These are the points about which a lever pivots. Muscles provide the effort to move levers. For each lever there is a load which is supported by the lever or is moved by it.

Levers in the body support the weight of the body. The arm acts as a lever which can move. The muscle provides the effort, the joint is the fulcrum and what is held in the hand is the load. The arrangement of the muscle minimises the effort needed to move the load. In the arm, a very small movement of the biceps produces a much larger movement of the hand. For example, a movement of 25 mm of the biceps results in a movement of 457 mm of the hand at the end of the lever.

The lever action in the diagram applies if the hand is holding something still or is moving upwards.

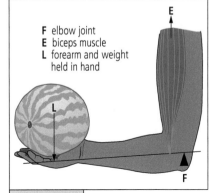

F elbow joint
E biceps muscle
L forearm and weight held in hand

Figure 5.2.5 Lever action of the arm

Movement

At the end of this topic you should be able to:

- describe movement at a hinge joint
- identify the antagonistic muscles that move the elbow
- explain the role of the antagonistic muscles in the movement of the lower arm
- list the factors that affect the skeletal system adversely.

STUDY FOCUS

We have three types of muscle tissue: skeletal muscle, cardiac muscle and the visceral muscle tissue that is in the digestive system and other muscular tube-like organs. Skeletal muscle moves your body, cardiac muscle pumps blood and visceral muscle in your gut moves food along by peristalsis.

LINK

You need to know about movement of the forearm when studying the withdrawal reflex. See 7.3.

Muscles only contract. To move about or to move part of your body, muscles contract and shorten, pulling on a bone. To get a bone to move back another muscle is needed. For example, there are two muscles that move the forearm and they form an **antagonistic** pair. They are the **biceps** and **triceps** muscles.

The biceps and triceps muscles are attached to the skeleton and are known as **skeletal muscles**. At either end of a muscle are the tendons. The origin of a muscle is where the tendon (or tendons) holds the muscle stationary. At the end that moves during muscle contraction is the insertion. You can see the origin and insertion of each of the antagonistic muscles in the arm in Figure 5.3.1.

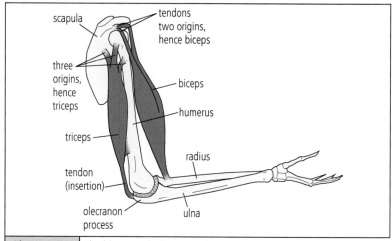

Figure 5.3.1 The biceps and triceps are the antagonistic pair of muscles that move the lower arm (forearm)

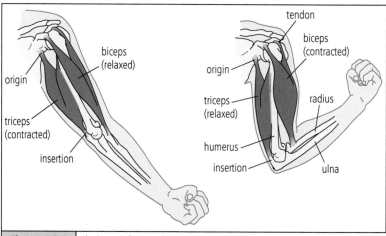

Figure 5.3.2 Flexion and extension

Contraction and shortening of the **biceps muscle** raises the forearm. This is called flexion and the biceps is the **flexor** muscle. The antagonist muscle, the triceps, relaxes and is pulled to become longer.

Contraction and shortening of the **triceps muscle** lowers the forearm. This is called extension and the arm is now extended; the triceps is the **extensor** muscle. The antagonist muscle, the biceps, relaxes and is pulled to become longer.

Muscle tissue is always slightly contracted. This maintains the position of the body and stops us flopping to the ground. This state of slight contraction is **muscle tone**. Muscle needs to be kept in good condition if it is to provide good support to the body.

Factors that affect the skeletal system

Our **diet** provides protein to make the collagen fibres, calcium and phosphate to harden the bones, and vitamin D to stimulate uptake of calcium and its deposition in bones. A lack of calcium and vitamin D in our diet can lead to **osteoporosis** in later life (see question **3** on page 81).

> **LINK**
>
> See 2.2 for more about the deficiency of vitamin D in children.

Exercise puts strains on the bones which respond by laying down extra mineral matter to increase bone density. This helps lower the risk of the bone disease osteoporosis. In response to exercise, joints produce more synovial fluid which maintains them in a supple state.

Obesity – the extra weight puts a lot of strain on the body, particularly at the joints. Obesity increases the likelihood that **arthritis** will develop.

Posture is the relative position of different parts of the body when sitting, standing or moving. Good posture involves balancing the body's weight about the centre of gravity in the lower spine. This is maintained by muscle tone. Sitting hunched over a desk is an example of bad posture, which can lead to a deformed spinal column.

Footwear – people who wear badly fitting footwear can get **bunions**. These are swollen joints at the base of the big toe, which can lead to deformed feet.

High-heeled shoes are very bad for the skeleton. The feet point nearly downwards so pressure increases on the front of the feet. To balance, the lower body leans forward and the upper body leans back. This is bad posture and may cause deformity in the spinal column.

Figure 5.3.3 These heels may be very fashionable but what long-term damage are they doing?

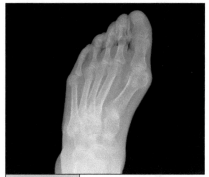

Figure 5.3.4 A bunion revealed by X-ray

> **KEY POINTS**
>
> **1** Flexion is bending the arm. The opposite action is extension.
>
> **2** Movement at joints is by antagonistic pairs of muscles, e.g. biceps and triceps, which are the flexor and extensor muscles.
>
> **3** Deficiencies of vitamin D and calcium, lack of exercise, repetitive exercise, bad posture and ill-fitting footwear all affect the skeleton adversely.

> **SUMMARY QUESTIONS**
>
> 1 Explain the term antagonistic muscles.
>
> 2 Explain how the forearm is raised and lowered.
>
> 3 Describe and explain the effects of the following on the skeletal system: deficiency of vitamin D, poor posture, lack of exercise and poor footwear.

UNIT 5: Multiple-choice questions

1 Which of the following is NOT a function of the skeleton?

   a To produce blood cells

   b To produce vitamin D

   c To protect delicate internal organs

   d To provide support for the body

2 Lack of vitamin D in children results in:

   a osteoporosis

   b night blindness

   c anaemia

   d rickets.

3 The opposing actions of the biceps and triceps muscles are examples of which of the following?

   a Peristalsis

   b Homeostatic control

   c Antagonistic action

   d Flexion

4 Which of the following is NOT an example of locomotion in humans?

   a Chewing

   b Running

   c Jumping

   d Swimming

5 Bunions are caused by:

   a bad posture when sitting at a desk

   b standing for long periods of time

   c walking in bare feet

   d wearing badly fitting shoes.

> Further practice questions and examples can be found on the accompanying CD.

UNIT 5: Short answer questions

1 a i Make a diagram to show the major bones of the shoulder, the upper arm and the forearm. *(3)*

   ii Label the following on your diagram: ball and socket joint, hinge joint, humerus, radius, scapula and ulna. *(3)*

   iii Draw on your diagram the biceps and triceps muscles. Label the two muscles and also their sites of origin and insertion. *(3)*

  b Explain why the movement of the forearm requires a pair of antagonistic muscles and not just one muscle. *(4)*

  c Distinguish between tendons and ligaments. *(2)*

Total 15 marks

2 a Describe how the ribcage is involved in breathing. *(6)*

  b Make a drawing of a long bone to show how it is adapted for its functions in support, movement and the production of red blood cells. *(6)*

  c State where cartilage is found in the body and explain why it is present in those places rather than bone. *(3)*

Total 15 marks

3 a The skeletal tissues are bone and cartilage. Explain how the structure of bone differs from the structure of cartilage. *(3)*

One of the functions of the skeleton is as a store of calcium and phosphate. Throughout life some cells in bone tissue constantly break down the hard matrix to release calcium into the blood. Other cells absorb calcium from the blood and use it to make more of the matrix material.

b Calcium and phosphate are important minerals in the body. State one function of each of these minerals **other than as components of bone**. *(2)*

Two hormones control the movement of calcium between blood and bone cells as shown in Figure 1.

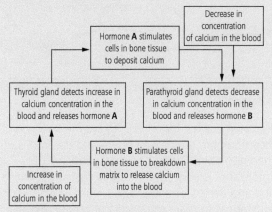

Figure 1 The balance between bone matrix formation and breakdown

Osteoporosis is a disease of the skeleton. There is a reduction in bone density as the mechanism shown in Figure 1 becomes unbalanced. The people most at risk of osteoporosis are post-menopausal women as they no longer produce oestrogen. The most common feature of the disorder is a hunched appearance of the back.

c Using the information in Figure 1, suggest:

i TWO ways in which the reduction in bone density may occur *(2)*

ii how oestrogen may prevent osteoporosis occurring. *(2)*

d Explain the role of vitamin D in bone health. *(3)*

MRI scans of the body, such as those in Figures 2 and 3, are used to examine the health of the skeleton.

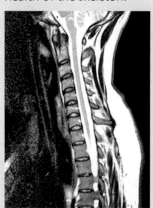

Figure 2 An MRI scan of a healthy spine

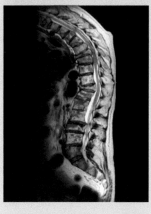

Figure 3 An MRI scan of the spine of someone with osteoporosis. The front of the body is to the left

e Describe how the appearance of the spine in the MRI scan of the person with osteoporosis differs from the scan of a healthy spine. *(2)*

f Discuss the advantages of early diagnosis of osteoporosis using MRI scanning. *(4)*

g Describe how poor footwear may affect the skeletal system adversely. *(2)*

Total 20 marks

6.1   Excretion

STUDY FOCUS

You have seen how one substance, hydrogen peroxide, is produced by cells and is immediately broken down to harmless substances by the enzyme catalase (see 2.8).

LINK

See 1.4 to remind yourself why cells swell and possibly even explode if there is too much water in the body.

Metabolism is the term used to describe all the chemical and physical changes that occur in the body. Some of the chemical processes produce substances that are of no use to the body and may even be toxic if allowed to accumulate.

Amino acids are absorbed from the gut during digestion and can be used to make proteins but they cannot be stored. Any amino acids that we do not use are broken down in the liver to form ammonia and simpler compounds that can be respired. Ammonia is toxic and is immediately converted by the liver into urea.

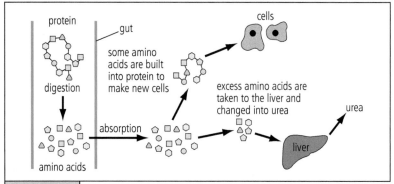

Figure 6.1.1   This shows what happens to amino acids absorbed from the small intestine

The liver breaks down old red blood cells to release haemoglobin. Molecules of haemoglobin are broken down and the iron is recycled to make new haemoglobin. The rest of the haem part of haemoglobin molecules is converted into bile pigments, which are excreted in urine and faeces. The liver also breaks down hormones into inactive substances that are removed from the body.

DID YOU KNOW?

Hormones are removed from the body in the urine. This is the basis of tests for pregnancy, fertility and drug-taking in sport.

The body also has too much of some substances. Water is absorbed into the blood from food and drink. It is also produced as a waste product of aerobic respiration. If water builds up in the body, cells could start to swell and even explode! The body can also have too many salts, especially potassium, sodium and chloride. These are controlled and then any excess removed.

Excretory organs

The organs involved in excretion are shown in Figure 6.1.2.

- **Lungs** – excrete carbon dioxide, which is lost from the blood by diffusion across the walls of the alveoli (see 3.3).
- **Kidneys** – filter the blood to produce urine, which is water with dissolved waste substances, such as urea and salts and water in excess of requirements (see 6.2).
- **Liver** – produces bile pigments and spent hormones.
- **Skin** – some urea and salts are lost when we sweat.

Homeostasis

Many chemical reactions occur inside the body during metabolism. Enzymes control these reactions and they work best when conditions in the body, such as temperature, pH and concentration of water, are kept suitable and constant.

Any slight change in the conditions in the body can slow down or stop enzymes from working. **Homeostasis** is the maintenance of constant internal conditions in the body, so that enzymes control metabolism efficiently.

Keeping conditions near constant requires several important components:

- receptors
- coordination systems
- control centre
- effectors.

Conditions in the body are monitored all the time to check whether changes in the body are effective at keeping conditions constant. This is the concept of **feedback**. This involves controlling a system, monitoring the effects of change continually and making adjustments.

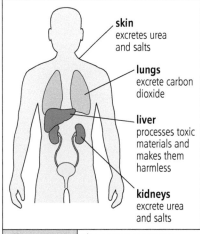

Figure 6.1.2 | The excretory organs

skin
excretes urea and salts

lungs
excrete carbon dioxide

liver
processes toxic materials and makes them harmless

kidneys
excrete urea and salts

LINK

See 2.7 and 2.8 to see how temperature and pH influence enzyme activity.

KEY POINTS

1 Metabolism is all the chemical and physical changes that occur in the body. Excretion is the removal from the body of the waste products of metabolism, toxic substances and substances in excess, such as water and ions.

2 The main metabolic wastes are urea and carbon dioxide.

3 The kidneys, lungs and skin are excretory organs.

4 Homeostasis is the maintenance of constant conditions in the body.

5 Feedback is the control of a system by monitoring the effects of change continually.

SUMMARY QUESTIONS

1 Define the terms *excretion*, *homeostasis* and *metabolism*.

2 Make a table to show the main metabolic waste substances, where they are produced and where they are excreted.

3 Explain why excretion and homeostasis are important.

4 State some internal conditions of the body that must be kept constant.

5 Suggest why you cannot rely on the skin as an excretory organ all the time.

6.2

The kidney

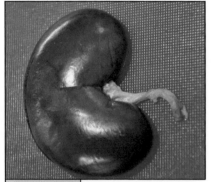

Figure 6.2.1 A kidney with part of the ureter attached

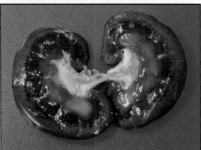

Figure 6.2.2 A kidney cut open vertically to show the cortex (brown outer area), medulla (reddish inner area) and pelvis (white area connected to the ureter that takes urine to the bladder)

The internal structure of the kidneys

The photographs (Figures 6.2.1 and 6.2.2) show the external and internal structures of the kidney.

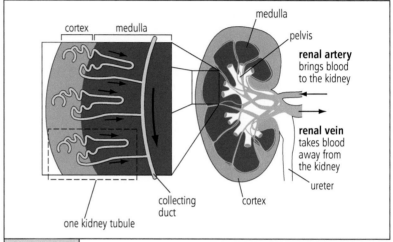

Figure 6.2.3 A vertical section of the kidney with a detailed view of three nephrons on the left

There are thousands of tiny tubes called **nephrons** inside each kidney. Nephrons are only visible with a microscope. Nephrons filter the blood, remove waste chemicals, reabsorb useful substances and determine how much water is excreted. The filtering is carried out in the **cortex**. The waste chemicals and excess water are removed from the body in **urine**.

Structure of a nephron

Blood flows into a kidney in a renal artery, which branches many times to form arterioles. Each arteriole supplies blood to a **glomerulus** which is a group of capillaries that fits inside a cup-like structure called **Bowman's capsule**. Blood flows out of the capillaries in the glomerulus into another arteriole. Blood then flows into capillaries around the rest of the nephron and into the renal vein.

The nephron passes through the cortex and **medulla**. The first coiled part of the nephron is the proximal convoluted tubule. This is followed by the loop of Henle, which dips down into the medulla. After leaving the loop of Henle the filtrate flows through the second coiled tube or distal convoluted tubule to drain into a **collecting duct**, which goes through the medulla and empties into the **pelvis** of the kidney. Urine collects in the pelvis and flows into the **ureter**.

Filtration and reabsorption

The kidneys are close to the heart so the blood pressure in the renal artery is high. You can see (in Figure 6.2.4) that the blood vessel entering the glomerulus is wider than the one leaving it. This causes pressure to increase inside the glomerulus so that blood is filtered. Small molecules, including water, leave the blood plasma through the walls of the capillaries so that less blood leaves the glomerulus than enters it.

The lining of the capillaries is like a net with tiny holes in it. Blood cells and large molecules, like blood proteins, are too big to pass through the capillary lining and so stay in the blood. Small molecules, like urea, glucose, amino acids, salts and water, pass through the holes in this net and are filtered into Bowman's capsule. The fluid that collects in Bowman's capsule is called filtrate.

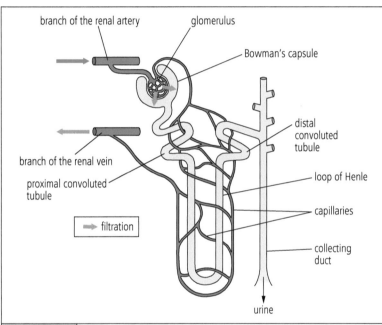

Figure 6.2.4 | A nephron

All the glucose, some salts and much of the water are needed by the body. The cells that line the first part of the nephron reabsorb these substances from the filtrate (see Figure 6.2.4). The substances move through the cells and enter the blood in the capillaries around the nephron. This process of **selective reabsorption** reduces the volume of the filtrate and prevents the loss of useful substances. Urea and excess salts dissolved in water pass on into the loop of Henle. As this fluid flows on through the nephron some more water may be **reabsorbed** if the body is low in water. The fluid that enters the collecting ducts is **urine**. The blood, with a lower concentration of waste chemicals, leaves the kidney in the renal vein.

Some people have kidney failure. If nothing is done about it they will die quickly. **Renal dialysis** is used to treat these people. Their blood flows through a dialysis machine that removes most of the excretory waste without unbalancing the salt, glucose and water content of the plasma.

Homeostasis – the skin and temperature control

At the end of this topic you should be able to:

- identify the structures in the skin
- explain how the structures in the skin carry out their functions
- distinguish between heat and temperature
- describe how body temperature is regulated.

The actions taken by effectors in the body to maintain the body temperature within narrow limits are called corrective actions. This is because their effect is to correct the rise or fall of body temperature.

The hypothalamus is the body's thermostat. It regulates other aspects of homeostasis. See 7.1 to see its location in the brain.

The skin and its functions

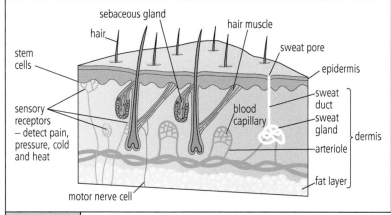

Figure 6.3.1 | The skin

The skin is the largest organ in the body. It has important roles in the interactions between the body and the surroundings. The functions of the structures labelled on Figure 6.3.1 are:

- Epidermis – this is made of layers of squamous cells filled with the tough **fibrous protein**, **keratin**; these cells provide mechanical protection against injury and are gradually rubbed away.
- Layer of stem cells (**Malpighian layer**) – these cells divide by mitosis to replace cells lost from the surface of the epidermis.
- Hair – provides some insulation on the head.
- **Sweat glands** – secrete sweat, which travels up sweat ducts to sweat pores; sweat evaporates to lose heat.
- Blood capillaries – apart from usual functions, these also lose heat.
- Arterioles - control the flow of blood to capillaries.
- **Sebaceous gland** – secretes **sebum**, which is a mild **antiseptic**.
- Sensory receptors and sensory cells – detect changes in temperature, pressure and pain.
- Motor nerve cells – instruct the hair muscles to contract and raise the hairs.
- Fat – store of energy and also a thermal insulator.

Temperature control

Heat is thermal energy and is dependent on the mass of material present. Temperature is a measure of the average kinetic energy of particles in a material, however much there is present. Mice, elephants and humans have a body temperature of about 37 °C; but there is far more heat in an elephant than there is in a mouse or a human.

Even if the weather is very hot or very cold your body temperature stays at 37 °C all the time – unless you have a fever.

Sensors in the skin detect changes in air temperature. Receptors in the spinal cord and hypothalamus detect changes in the temperature of the blood.

If the temperature of the blood flowing through the hypothalamus in the brain is **warmer than 37 °C** it sends nerve impulses to the skin to promote heat loss. The hypothalamus sends nerve impulses to the skin to stimulate:

- **vasodilation** – arterioles widen so more blood flows through the capillaries and loses heat to the surroundings by **convection** and **radiation**
- the sweat glands to produce sweat by filtration from the blood plasma – the heat of the body causes the sweat to evaporate so having a cooling effect.

When we feel cold and our blood temperature **decreases below 37 °C**, the hypothalamus sends nerve impulses to the skin to reduce heat loss by stimulating:

- **vasoconstriction** – arterioles contract so reducing blood flow through the capillaries
- the sweat glands to stop producing sweat.

If the blood temperature continues to fall then the hypothalamus stimulates heat production in the liver and sends impulses to skeletal muscles to contract to release heat by shivering. Blood flowing through the liver and muscles is warmed and it then distributes heat to the rest of the body.

Temperature sensors in the skin are particularly useful in the cold as they give an early warning about possible loss of heat to the surroundings before the blood temperature falls.

The effects of the adjustments made by the body in response to changes in temperature are monitored continually by the hypothalamus to detect whether they have had the desired result.

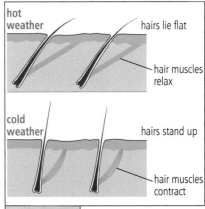

Figure 6.3.2 Hairs can be raised or lowered to help reduce or increase heat loss

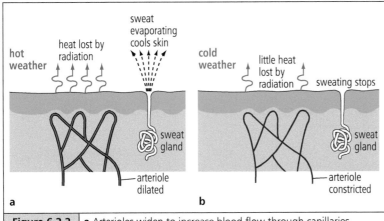

Figure 6.3.3 **a** Arterioles widen to increase blood flow through capillaries thereby increasing heat loss; **b** they constrict to reduce flow thereby conserving heat

SUMMARY QUESTIONS

1 List the structures that are in the skin.

2 Identify the structures that are involved in:
   a excretion
   b sensitivity (irritability)
   c temperature regulation
   d protection.

3 Explain how the skin helps to reduce heat and conserve heat.

Homeostasis – control of the blood

Temperature regulation

The control of body temperature described in 6.3 is one example of **negative feedback**. The same control system is used to regulate the temperature of an oven by ensuring that the actual temperature stays close to the pre-set temperature. In our body, if the temperature increases above or below the normal 37 °C then the hypothalamus responds by stimulating effectors to take actions to bring it back to normal. Negative feedback is used in the control of blood glucose concentration, the water content of the blood, blood pH and the oxygen and carbon dioxide concentrations of the blood.

Carbon dioxide concentration

The carbon dioxide concentration of the blood is detected by sensory cells in the medulla oblongata in the brain, in the aorta and in the carotid arteries that carry blood to the head. If the concentration increases, the medulla sends impulses to increase the rate and depth of breathing. More carbon dioxide is breathed out and the concentration returns to normal.

LINK

The medulla oblongata controls breathing and the activity of the heart. See 7.1 to see its location at the base of the brain.

ADH and water regulation

The quantity of water in the body affects the concentration of the blood plasma. If it decreases to below normal then this is detected by sensory cells in the hypothalamus. These cells stimulate the release of antidiuretic hormone (**ADH**) from the pituitary gland. ADH instructs the cells of the collecting ducts to become permeable to water which is absorbed by osmosis from the urine. If the level of water rises, then no ADH is secreted and the excess water passes out of the body in the urine.

Glucose control

Cells absorb glucose and respire it to release energy. Therefore they need a constant supply from the blood.

The blood glucose concentration can increase by a factor of 20 following a meal that is high in carbohydrates. However, the concentration does not remain that high – it would be dangerous if it did. Cells in the pancreas detect the high glucose concentration in the blood and respond by secreting the hormone **insulin** into the blood. Insulin stimulates liver cells and muscle cells to use glucose in respiration and convert it into the storage compound glycogen.

As a result, insulin has the effect of increasing the uptake of glucose by liver cells and by muscle cells so the concentration of glucose in the blood decreases and returns to normal.

During a race or some other type of exercise, muscles absorb lots of glucose from the blood to provide energy. The blood glucose concentration decreases as a result, but it does not keep decreasing. Other cells in the pancreas detect this decrease and secrete the hormone **glucagon** into the blood. Glucagon stimulates liver cells to break down glycogen to glucose, which diffuses out of the cells and into the blood. The blood glucose concentration increases so returning to normal.

EXAM TIP

Insulin and glucagon are hormones. They are chemical messengers, not enzymes. You should always state that insulin and glucagon stimulate the changes to glucose. Do not state that 'insulin converts glucose to glycogen'. The conversion is done by enzymes inside cells, such as those in the liver and muscles.

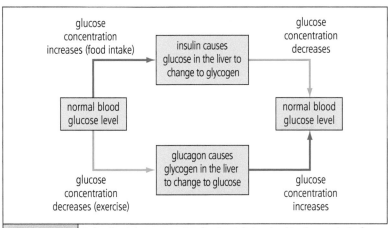

Figure 6.4.1 A feedback loop: negative feedback is involved in the control of blood glucose

This is an example of negative feedback because the pancreas releases insulin to stimulate a decrease in blood glucose concentration if it is too high and releases glucagon to stimulate an increase in blood glucose concentration if it is too low. The pancreas continually monitors the glucose in the blood so is aware of the effects of the hormones it releases.

SUMMARY QUESTIONS

1 Draw a flow chart diagram to summarise the feedback control of water in the blood.

2 Define the term *negative feedback*.

3 Explain why the water and carbon dioxide content of the blood needs to be controlled.

4 Draw a feedback loop to show how carbon dioxide is controlled.

5 Explain why feeding stations provide marathon runners with water and glucose drinks.

KEY POINTS

1 Homeostasis is the maintenance of constant internal conditions, such as body temperature.

2 Homeostasis involves negative feedback to maintain constant conditions of glucose, water, carbon dioxide and oxygen in the blood and also its pH.

3 The pancreas controls the concentration of glucose in the blood by secreting the hormones insulin and glucagon which stimulate the liver.

UNIT 6: Multiple-choice questions

1 When the body temperature rises, the internal diameter of arterioles near the surface of the skin widens. This is referred to as:

   a evaporation

   b insulation

   c vasoconstriction

   d vasodilation.

2 Which of the following detects changes in blood temperature and therefore aids the control of body temperature?

   a Hypothalamus

   b Medulla oblongata

   c Pituitary gland

   d Temperature receptors in the skin

3 Which of the following components of blood plasma is NOT filtered from the glomerulus to the Bowman's capsule in the kidney?

   a Glucose

   b Protein

   d Urea

   e Water

4 ADH causes an increase in:

   a the permeability of the collecting ducts to water

   b the rate of filtration in the glomeruli

   c the reabsorption of salts by the nephron

   d the supply of blood to the kidneys in the renal arteries.

5 Which of the following is an excretory product made by the liver from the contents of dead red blood cells?

   a Cholesterol

   b Bile pigments

   c Iron

   d Urea

Further practice questions and examples can be found on the accompanying CD.

UNIT 6: Short answer questions

1 Two people took a glucose tolerance test. They fasted for 12 hours and then drank identical solutions of glucose. Blood samples were taken from both people at intervals for 270 minutes. The results are shown in the table below.

Time/min	Blood glucose concentration/ $g\,dm^3$	
	Person A	Person B
0	0.85	1.10
30	0.85	0.95
60	0.90	0.85
90	1.05	1.40
120	1.60	2.10
150	1.35	2.40
180	0.85	2.30
210	0.85	2.00
240	0.80	1.85
270	0.85	1.60

   a Draw a graph of the results for the two people. *(5)*

   b Compare the results of the glucose tolerance test for the two people. *(4)*

   c Suggest why Person B's results are greater than the normal upper limit for blood glucose concentration. *(3)*

   d Explain why Person A's blood glucose concentration does not go beyond $0.85\,g\,dm^{-3}$. *(3)*

Total 15 marks

2 Figure 1 is a drawing made from a vertical section of the kidney.

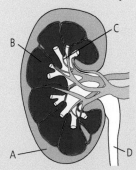

Figure 1 A vertical section of a kidney

a   Name A, B, C, and D.   (4)

The table below shows the composition of blood plasma in the renal artery, filtrate in the Bowman's capsule and urine.

Substance	Concentration/g dm³		
	Blood plasma in renal artery	Filtrate in Bowman's capsule	Urine
Urea	0.2	0.2	20.0
Glucose	0.9	0.9	0.0
Amino acids	0.05	0.05	0.0
Salts	8.0	8.0	16.5
Protein	82	0	0

b   Explain why:

   i   there is no protein in the filtrate   (1)

   ii   the concentration of urea is the same in the plasma as the filtrate but is much higher in the urine   (3)

   iii glucose and amino acids are in the filtrate but not in the urine   (3)

   iv   salts are present in the urine.   (2)

c   The volume of blood filtered by the kidneys is 1.18 dm⁻³ min⁻¹. Calculate the total volume of blood filtered in 24 hours. Show your working.   (2)

Total 15 marks

3 a   Make a diagram of the skin to show the following structures:

   epidermis; dermis; blood vessels; fat tissue; a sweat gland, duct and pore.   (6)

b   Explain how the structures you have drawn are involved in maintaining the temperature of the body.   (6)

c   The control of body temperature is an example of negative feedback.

   Describe how negative feedback is involved in the control of body temperature.   (3)

Total 15 marks

4 a   Make a drawing of a kidney nephron. Label the following on your drawing: glomerulus, Bowman's capsule and collecting duct.   (8)

b   i   Explain how blood is filtered in the kidney.   (4)

   ii   Explain why less than 1% of the filtrate produced each day becomes urine.   (3)

Total 15 marks

5 a   Define the term *homeostasis*.   (1)

b   Discuss the importance of homeostasis for the efficient functioning of the body.   (8)

c   Draw a diagram to show how negative feedback is involved in the control of the concentration of glucose in the blood.   (6)

Total 15 marks

6 a   i   Define the term *excretion*.   (3)

   ii   Explain why excretion is important for humans.   (4)

b   The concentration of the blood is kept within very narrow limits. If the concentration decreases, red blood cells tend to swell and if the concentration increases they shrink.

   Explain how the body regulates the concentration of the blood.   (8)

Total 15 marks

The nervous system

At the end of this topic you should be able to:

- state that the nervous system is one of the coordination systems
- state that the nervous system is divided into the central nervous system and the peripheral nervous system
- describe the main parts of the two systems
- state the functions of four regions of the brain and the pituitary gland.

We respond to changes in our surroundings and inside our bodies. Each change is a **stimulus**. You respond very quickly indeed to certain stimuli and much slower to others. We have two organ systems that coordinate our responses to different stimuli:

- the nervous system
- the **endocrine** (hormonal) system (see 7.6).

The nervous system communicates between **receptors** that give information about the external and the internal environment, the parts that make decisions and the **effector** organs that carry out the responses.

The diagrams (Figures 7.1.1 and 7.1.2) show the structure of the nervous system. The **central nervous system (CNS)** consists of the brain and the **spinal cord**; the **peripheral nervous system (PNS)** consists of all the **nerves** from the CNS that spread throughout the body.

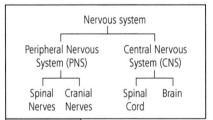

Figure 7.1.1 | The organisation of the nervous system

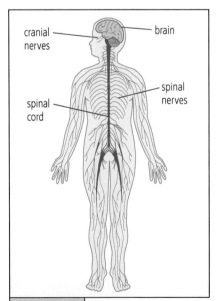

Figure 7.1.2 | The human nervous system

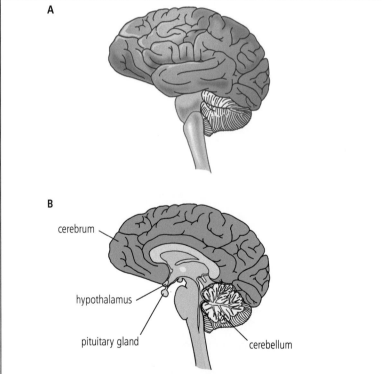

Figure 7.1.3 | The brain showing the location of the four areas listed in the table and the pituitary gland

Each **cranial** and **spinal nerve** contains the long extensions, known as **axons**, of many nerve cells. Individual nerve cells are known as **neurones**.

The brain

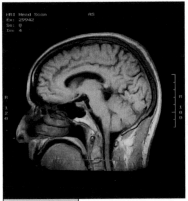

MRI Head Scan   AS
Ex: 29942
Se: 0
Im: 4
R 1 2 0
R 1 0 0

Figure 7.1.4 A vertical section of the brain as seen in an MRI scanner

EXAM TIP

Do not confuse the spinal cord with the spinal column. See 5.1 to be sure of the difference.

The cerebrum, cerebellum, hypothalamus and medulla oblongata are four of the main areas of the brain. The table below shows the functions of each of these areas.

Part of the brain	Functions
Cerebrum consisting of the left and right cerebral hemispheres	• Conscious thought • Coordination of voluntary actions • Memory, learning and reasoning • Understanding language and control of speech • Interpretation of sensory information from sense organs
Hypothalamus	Controls: • body temperature (body's thermostat) • water and salt content of the blood, by secreting ADH • reproduction by stimulating the release of hormones from the pituitary gland • sleep • feelings of thirst and hunger
Pituitary gland	• Releases ADH • Secretes hormones to control growth, metabolism and the activity of the testes and ovaries
Cerebellum	• Receives information from balance receptors in the ear and from stretch receptors in muscles and tendons • Coordination of balance, posture and movement
Medulla oblongata	Controls many **involuntary actions**, such as: • rate and depth of breathing • **heart rate** and blood pressure • peristalsis

SUMMARY QUESTIONS

1 Explain the terms: *central nervous system* and *peripheral nervous system*, *cranial nerves* and *spinal nerves*.

2 Distinguish between the spinal column and the spinal cord.

3 Make a simple drawing of the nervous system and use colour coding to distinguish between the CNS and the PNS.

4 Make a large drawing of the brain; label the parts in the table and annotate with their functions.

5 A girl was in a car accident. Afterwards she had memory loss, found it difficult to speak and her sense of balance was impaired.

   a Which areas of her brain may have been affected to have caused these effects?

   b Explain your answer.

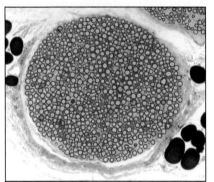

Figure 7.2.1 The many small circles are cross sections of neurones

EXAM TIP

Nerve cells transmit electrical impulses, not 'signals' or 'messages'. Never write these words in an examination answer about the nervous system.

LINK

The nervous system and the endocrine system work together to control our responses to danger. See 7.6 for the hormonal side of this control.

Nerves

Nerves are surrounded by tough fibrous tissue. The photograph in Figure 7.2.1 is part of a section through a spinal nerve.

Some nerves take information from sensory cells within a sense organ to the CNS. The **optic nerve** from the eye to the brain is an example (see 7.4). Some nerves only carry information from the CNS to effectors. Several **cranial nerves** are like this such as those that control movement of the eyeball and the tongue. Most nerves, including all the spinal nerves, are **mixed nerves** carrying information from sensory cells to the CNS and information from the CNS to effectors.

Neurones

Nerve cells (neurones) are highly specialised cells that show the properties of irritability and conductivity. Irritability means that the nerve cells respond to being stimulated. Conductivity means that they transmit electrical impulses. One part of the cell is specialised to be stimulated by receptor cells or other neurones and the other part is specialised to send impulses to other neurones or to effectors. Often these impulses travel long distances along neurones. There are three types of neurone:

Sensory neurones conduct electrical impulses from sensory cells, such as receptor cells in the eye, to other neurones in the CNS.

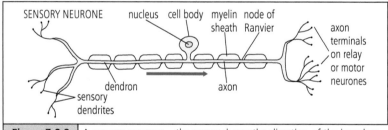

Figure 7.2.2 A sensory neurone – the arrow shows the direction of the impulses

Motor neurones conduct electrical impulses from the central nervous system to effectors. These effectors are muscles and glands, such as the medulla of the adrenal gland.

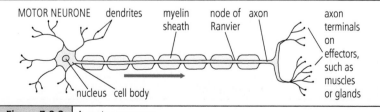

Figure 7.2.3 A motor neurone

Relay neurones are only found in the CNS. They transmit information between sensory and motor neurones. Other types of neurone in the CNS integrate and store information and make decisions.

Motor and sensory neurones have the same basic structure:

- **cell body** with endoplasmic reticulum, ribosomes and a nucleus – *this is where proteins are made for the cell*

- **dendrites** which are thin extensions all over the cell body – *these receive impulses from many other neurones; these impulses are integrated by the cell body that determines whether it sends impulses or not*

- **axon** which is a thin extension of the cell body that terminates a long distance away – *this conducts impulses over a long distance, e.g. from the base of the spinal cord to the foot*

- **synaptic bulb**, also called the axon terminal – *a swelling at the end of the axon where the impulse is transmitted to the next neurone or to an effector*

- **myelin sheath** which is a protective covering made by many cells along the length of the axon – *myelin acts as an insulator so that the impulse travels very fast.*

Synapses

At the end of every axon there is a swelling and then a gap. This gap is crossed by the release of a chemical transmitter substance to stimulate the next neurone or effector. A synapse is the gap and the parts of the cells on either side. **Synapses** are found between neurones and between motor neurones and effectors.

Synapses allow impulses to travel in one direction only. They also allow many neurones to influence the activity of another and for each neurone to receive information from many other neurones. This means that they are useful for the integration of information.

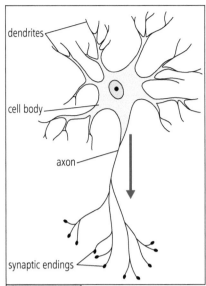

| **Figure 7.2.4** | A relay neurone |

SUMMARY QUESTIONS

1 Define the terms *neurone*, *nerve*, *motor neurone*, *sensory neurone* and *synapse*.

2 Describe the roles of neurones and synapses.

3 a Make large labelled drawings of a motor neurone and a sensory neurone.
  b Annotate your drawings with the functions of the different parts you have labelled.
  c Explain the function of chemical transmitter substances.

4 a Myelin is **not** part of motor or sensory neurones. Explain why.
  b Many nerves in the CNS are not myelinated, but those that pass along the length of the spinal cord and into the brain are myelinated. Suggest why.

KEY POINTS

1 Neurones each have a cell body with a nucleus, mitochondria and endoplasmic reticulum. The cytoplasmic extensions of neurones are dendrons, small dendrites and axons.

2 Nerves are bundles of axons surrounded by fibrous tissue.

3 Synapses are gaps between neurones and between motor neurones and effectors. Chemical transmitter substances transmit impulses across these gaps.

Reflex actions

At the end of this topic you should be able to:

- explain the difference between voluntary and involuntary actions
- define the term *reflex action*
- explain the advantages of reflex actions
- identify the components of a reflex arc
- describe spinal and cranial reflexes.

EXAM TIP

Remember to identify the stimulus and the response in anything you write about reflexes.

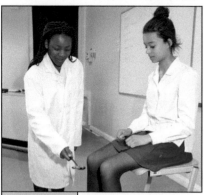

Figure 7.3.1 The knee jerk reflex – you can try this for yourself

STUDY FOCUS

Some physics is useful here: the neurones that control simple reflex actions are in series – one after the other.

Voluntary and involuntary actions

We make two types of action. Some happen automatically without us having to think about them. These are **involuntary actions**. Swallowing, blinking, breathing and the beating of the heart are examples of actions that are unconscious, but we can choose to control occasionally. Movement of food in the gut and urine from the kidneys by peristalsis are other involuntary actions that we cannot control by thinking about them. Motor neurones of the **autonomic nervous system** control these involuntary actions. **Voluntary actions** are those we choose to make and the decisions to make them occur in our brains. Impulses are sent via neurones of the **voluntary nervous system** in cranial or spinal nerves to the muscles required to make the actions.

STUDY FOCUS

Read about peristalsis in the alimentary canal again (2.9). Peristalsis also occurs in the tube that moves urine from the kidney to the bladder. Find the name of the tube if you cannot remember. Now answer question 2.

When a person sits on a sharp object, such as a thumb tack, without realising, there is a very quick, automatic response that the person does not need to think about.

This is an example of a simple **reflex**, which is an involuntary action.

The stimulus is the thumb tack touching the skin and the receptors are pain sensors. The effectors are the muscles in the legs that cause the person to get up quickly.

The sequence of events is:

stimulus → receptor → coordinator → effector → response

In **cranial reflexes**, the neurones pass through **cranial nerves**; in **spinal reflexes** they pass through **spinal nerves**.

Reflexes are protective. Withdrawing from the tack protects the skin from further damage. The pupil reflex (see opposite) protects the retina from the damaging effect of bright light, which could destroy the receptor cells.

Knee jerk reflex

Medical staff use this spinal reflex to check the nervous system. A tap on the knee stretches a tendon. Stretch receptors in the tendon send impulses along a sensory neurone to the spinal cord. There is no relay neurone so the sensory neurone stimulates a motor neurone that conducts impulses to a muscle in the upper leg. The effector muscle contracts to move the lower leg (see Figure 7.3.2).

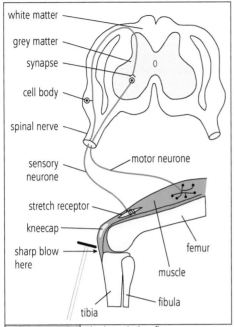

Figure 7.3.2 | The knee jerk reflex – an example of a spinal reflex

Labels: white matter, grey matter, synapse, cell body, spinal nerve, sensory neurone, stretch receptor, kneecap, sharp blow here, motor neurone, femur, muscle, fibula, tibia

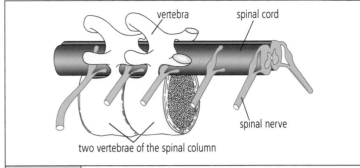

Figure 7.3.3 | Here you can see where the cross section in Figure 7.3.2 is taken

Labels: vertebra, spinal cord, spinal nerve, two vertebrae of the spinal column

Pupil reflex

Move from a well lit place into a dark place. It takes a while before you can see. When you go from a dark place and enter somewhere very bright, for a moment you are almost blinded by the light until your eyes adjust. These eye adjustments are a reflex that occurs through your brain using neurones in two cranial nerves. There are two types of muscle in each **iris**. The circular muscles contract to **decrease** the diameter of the pupil; the radial muscles contract to **increase** its diameter.

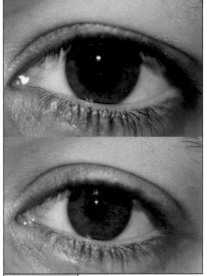

Figure 7.3.4 | Changes in the diameter of the pupil are controlled by the iris in this cranial reflex

7.4 The eye

The eye is one of our sense organs. It contains receptor cells in the **retina** and has a number of extra structures. These are involved in moving the eye, focusing and in protection. Receptor cells respond to light by stimulating sensory neurones to conduct impulses to the brain via the **optic nerve**. The brain interprets all the impulses that it receives to form an image of what we are looking at.

The table below shows all our major sense organs. Remember that we have receptor cells in other places, such as tendons and muscles.

Sense organ	Sense	Stimulus
Eye	Sight	Light
Ear	Hearing	Sound, sensory cells for gravity in the inner ear
Tongue	Taste	Chemicals in food
Nose	Smell	Chemicals in the air
Skin, e.g. lips and fingertips	Touch	Temperature, pressure/touch, pain

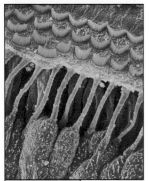

Figure 7.4.1 Sensory hair cells from the cochlear in the ear

STUDY FOCUS

The ear drum and three bones convert sound waves into movement of a fluid. This causes the 'hairs' that you can see in the photo to bend. The lower part of the cell stimulates a sensory neurone to transmit impulses to the hearing centre in the cerebrum.

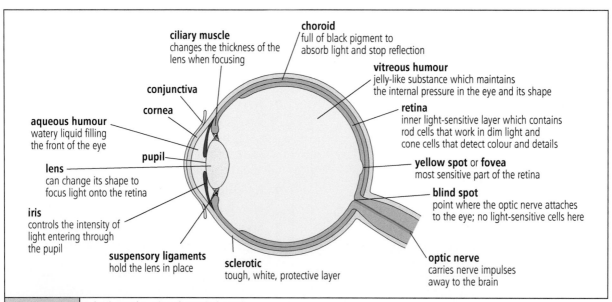

ciliary muscle
changes the thickness of the lens when focusing

choroid
full of black pigment to absorb light and stop reflection

vitreous humour
jelly-like substance which maintains the internal pressure in the eye and its shape

conjunctiva

cornea

aqueous humour
watery liquid filling the front of the eye

pupil

lens
can change its shape to focus light onto the retina

iris
controls the intensity of light entering through the pupil

suspensory ligaments
hold the lens in place

sclerotic
tough, white, protective layer

retina
inner light-sensitive layer which contains rod cells that work in dim light and cone cells that detect colour and details

yellow spot or **fovea**
most sensitive part of the retina

blind spot
point where the optic nerve attaches to the eye; no light-sensitive cells here

optic nerve
carries nerve impulses away to the brain

Figure 7.4.2 A horizontal section through the eye

Image formation

When light enters the eye it is focused onto the retina. Most of the focusing occurs as the light passes through the **cornea**. This is because it was travelling through the air and now enters a denser medium. If we relied on the cornea alone for our focusing we would see a very blurred image of the world around us. The **lens** provides the fine focusing so that we see sharp images. Figure 7.4.4 shows how this focusing by the cornea and the lens is achieved. Each medium has a refractive index and when light passes from one medium to another it is refracted or 'bent'.

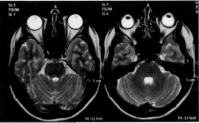

Figure 7.4.3 This MRI scan shows a horizontal section through the head at the level of the eyes. You can see the optic nerves between the eyes and the brain

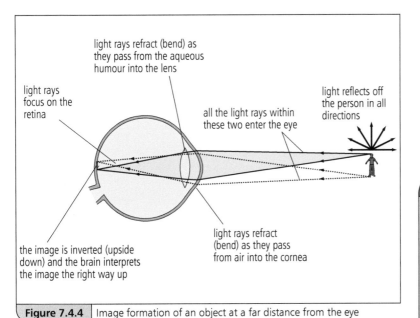

Figure 7.4.4 Image formation of an object at a far distance from the eye

LINK

Common problems with image formation are long and short sight. See 7.5 for more about these.

SUMMARY QUESTIONS

1 Use the information in Figure 7.4.2 to make a table showing the functions of the parts of the eye.

2 Make a large drawing of the human body and indicate the position of the CNS and all the sensory organs of the body. Annotate the structures you have labelled with their functions.

3 There are many internal receptor cells. Use the index of this book to find out what stimuli are detected by receptors in the following regions: hypothalamus, spinal cord, tendons, pancreas and the aorta and arteries to the brain.

KEY POINTS

1 Sensory cells are specialised cells that detect certain stimuli. Some of these are concentrated into sense organs. The retina in the eye and the cochlea in the ear are full of sensory cells.

2 The ear, eye, nose, tongue and skin are the sense organs, but there are many sensory cells throughout the body, e.g. in tendons and muscles.

3 The eye is a complex sense organ that focuses light on the sensitive retina. It changes the focal length of the lens and controls how much light enters the eye.

4 Light is refracted (bent) as it passes through the cornea and the lens. The lens is adjusted to form sharp images of far and distant objects.

Accommodation and eye defects

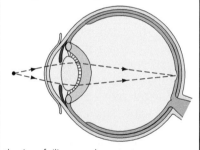

looking at a near object

the ring of ciliary muscle contracts and the lens becomes rounder

Figure 7.5.2 Focusing on an object close to the eye

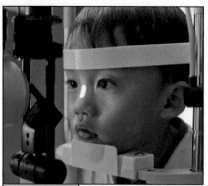

Figure 7.5.3 Opticians carry out tests to check for eye defects. This is important for children to make sure they are corrected from a young age

Accommodation

The changes that occur in the eye when we focus on far and near objects are known as **accommodation**. As light enters the eye it is refracted or bent to form a clear image on the retina that is in focus. Most of the **refraction** (about 60%) occurs as light enters the cornea. The lens is responsible for the rest which ensures that the image is in sharp focus. Elastic tissue surrounding the lens can be stretched and can recoil. The shape of the lens is controlled by the **ciliary muscles** and suspensory ligaments (see Figure 7.4.2).

If you are looking at a distant object the ciliary muscles **relax**. The pressure of the fluids inside the eye pulls the suspensory ligaments tightly (or taut) so the lens is pulled into a thin shape as the lens does not need to do too much focusing.

If you are looking at a near object the lens needs to become fatter so that more refraction occurs. The ciliary muscles **contract** to counteract the pressure of the fluids inside the eye. This reduces the stretch of the suspensory ligaments so they become slack, letting the elastic tissue around the lens recoil.

Accommodation is another simple reflex. This too is protective – if your surroundings are out of focus you are likely to come to some harm.

Eye defects

Long sight is caused by having an eyeball that is too short or a lens that is not convex enough. Objects close to the eye are out of focus because the light rays are not focused as they reach the retina. Convex or **converging lenses** in spectacles or contact lenses are used to correct long sight.

Short sight is caused by having a long eyeball or a lens that is too convex. Distant objects are blurred because the light rays are focused in front of the retina. Concave or **diverging lenses** are used to correct short sight.

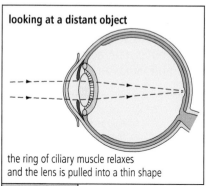

looking at a distant object

the ring of ciliary muscle relaxes and the lens is pulled into a thin shape

Figure 7.5.1 Focusing on an object far away from the eye

STUDY FOCUS

Converging lenses are *thicker in the middle* than they are at the edges so they are convex in shape. Diverging lenses are *thicker at the edges* than they are in the middle so they are concave in shape (remember that they 'cave in').

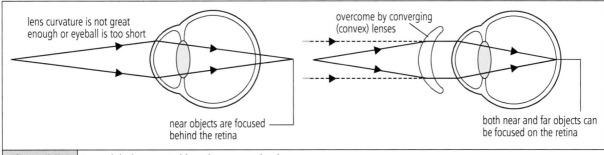

Figure 7.5.4 Long sight is corrected by using converging lenses

lens curvature is not great enough or eyeball is too short

near objects are focused behind the retina

overcome by converging (convex) lenses

both near and far objects can be focused on the retina

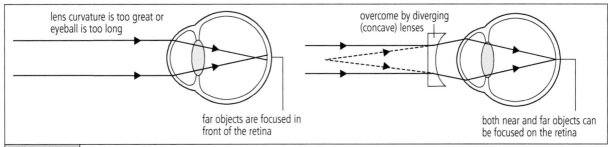

Figure 7.5.5 Short sight is corrected by using diverging lenses

lens curvature is too great or eyeball is too long

far objects are focused in front of the retina

overcome by diverging (concave) lenses

both near and far objects can be focused on the retina

Astigmatism is a problem with the cornea. It is uneven and does not focus all the light entering the eye in the same way. Vision is blurred and people with astigmatism may also be short-sighted or long-sighted as well.

Glaucoma is the result of increased pressure in the eyeball. The pressure increases because of poor drainage of the fluids in the eye. The fluids in the eyeball press on the blood vessels that supply the optic nerve obstructing the flow of blood. Neurones in the nerve start dying – first those that supply the periphery of the retina and later those from the fovea. People are often unaware of the changes as glaucoma develops slowly with a slow deterioration in their peripheral vision. Some children are born with it and their eyes are often cloudy and watery.

Cataracts are often a problem associated with age. The lens becomes cloudy, making it difficult for people to see. Left untreated, people will go blind. It is an easy condition to treat by replacing the cloudy lens with an artificial lens. Some children are born with cataracts in one or both eyes. They may also need replacement lenses.

LINK

There is more about glaucoma and cataracts in question 3 on page 105. Vitamin A deficiency is a cause of night blindness and also of total blindness in children (see 2.2).

SUMMARY QUESTIONS

1 a Explain what happens to the following when the eye focuses on a distant object:
   i the ciliary muscles
   ii the suspensory ligaments
   iii the lens.

 b Explain what happens to each of these structures when the eye focuses on a nearby object.

2 Define the terms *accommodation, astigmatism, glaucoma, cataract, long sight* and *short sight*.

3 Explain how opticians correct short and long sight.

4 Find out more about different eye defects and write a health leaflet to explain the conditions, their diagnosis and treatment.

KEY POINTS

1 Accommodation is the focusing of the lens to form a sharp image on the retina. For distant objects the suspensory ligaments are taut and the lens is narrow. For far-away objects the suspensory ligaments are slack and the lens is fatter.

2 Defects with eyesight can be caused by misshapen eyeballs (long sight and short sight), unevenness of the cornea, poor drainage of fluid (glaucoma) and cloudiness of the lens (cataracts).

Hormones

At the end of this topic you should be able to:

- define the terms *hormone* and *endocrine system*
- name the organs that secrete the major hormones
- explain the roles of thyroxine, growth hormone and adrenaline
- state the differences between endocrine and nervous control of body functions.

LINK

You can see the position of the pituitary gland in Figures 7.1.3 and 7.1.4.

Endocrine organ	Hormone(s) secreted
Pituitary gland	• FSH • LH • Growth hormone, • Thyroid stimulating hormone • ADH
Pancreas	• Insulin • Glucagon
Adrenal gland	• Adrenaline
Testis	• **Testosterone**
Ovaries	• **Oestrogen** • **Progesterone**

The endocrine system

Hormones are chemicals that are secreted by specialised cells in endocrine organs. Hormones travel in the blood to stimulate other cells, tissues and organs. Figure 7.6.1 shows where the major endocrine organs are located. They do not have ducts like sweat glands. Instead, the hormones leave the cells and go straight into the blood in the capillaries. The most important endocrine organ is the pituitary gland, which is located beneath the brain. It is important because it releases many hormones, including some that control the activities of other endocrine organs such as the **thyroid gland**, ovaries and testes.

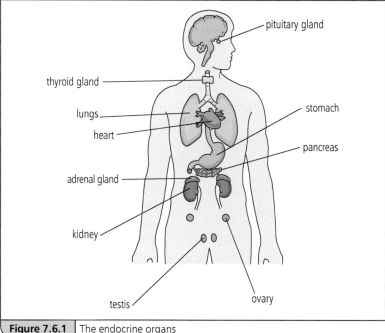

Figure 7.6.1 The endocrine organs

Adrenaline

Adrenaline is a hormone released by the adrenal glands that are located just above the kidneys.

Adrenaline is released during times of excitement, fear or stress. It is often called the 'flight or fight' hormone as it helps prepare the body for action. It stimulates:

- liver cells to convert glycogen to glucose – the glucose diffuses into the blood to give muscles enough energy for the contractions needed for sudden action
- the heart rate to increase – more blood goes to the muscles delivering glucose and oxygen

- dilation (widening) of the airways – more air reaches the alveoli in the lungs for more gas exchange
- dilation of arterioles in the brain and muscles – more glucose and oxygen are delivered to these organs
- constriction of arterioles in the gut and other organs allows blood to be diverted to the muscles.

The pituitary gland

The pituitary gland secretes:

- anti-diuretic hormone (ADH) that controls the kidney (see 6.1 and 6.4)
- **follicle stimulating hormone** (FSH) and **luteinising hormone** (LH) that control the ovaries and the testes (see 8.2 and 8.3) – these hormones stimulate the development of gametes and the secretion of the **sex hormones** – oestrogen, progesterone and testosterone
- a hormone that stimulates the thyroid gland to release **thyroxine**, which controls metabolism, growth and development
- **growth hormone** that stimulates protein synthesis throughout the body and growth of muscles.

The endocrine system and the nervous system

The endocrine system and the nervous system both control and coordinate the activities of the body. The table below compares the ways in which they work:

Nervous system	Endocrine system
Made up of nerve cells or neurones	Glands containing secretory cells
Information passes as electrical impulses along neurones	Hormones (chemicals)
Along neurones	In the blood
The effects are rapid and short-lived e.g. muscle contracts for a short time	The effects are usually slow and longer lasting (some are rapid, e.g. response to adrenaline)
Affects particular organs	Affects the whole of the body
Often involves reflexes	Controls growth, development, metabolism and reproduction

LINK

See 6.3 for another example of dilation and constriction of the arterioles to control the flow of blood through capillaries.

LINK

The pituitary gland is located just below the hypothalamus in the brain. The two work very closely together to control many aspects of our physiology, such as controlling the water content of the blood, core body temperature and the activity of the reproductive organs.

KEY POINTS

1 Hormones are chemical messages that travel around the body in the blood. The endocrine system consists of organs that secrete hormones directly into the blood.

2 The main endocrine organs are shown in Figure 7.6.1.

3 Thyroxine and growth hormone control aspects of metabolism, growth and development.

4 Adrenaline works alongside the nervous system to control our responses to danger.

5 The endocrine system is slower than the nervous system and the effects are usually long-term rather than short-term.

SUMMARY QUESTIONS

1 Use the index to find information for a table showing the hormones mentioned in this topic, their sites of production and their functions.

2 Distinguish between the endocrine and the nervous systems.

3 Explain the advantages of having two coordination systems.

UNIT 7: Multiple-choice questions

1 The largest part of the brain is the:
   a cerebellum
   b cerebrum
   c hypothalamus
   d medulla oblongata.

2 In the nervous system:
   a motor neurones conduct impulses to muscle fibres
   b relay neurones conduct impulses from motor neurones to sensory neurones
   c sensory neurones conduct impulses to muscle fibres
   d sensory neurones conduct impulses towards receptors.

3 In the eye:
   a images are formed on the iris
   b rods are involved with night vision
   c the lens is biconcave
   d the retina covers the lens at the front of the eye.

4 Which of the following statements is NOT correct?
   a Short-sightedness is corrected by the use of a concave (diverging) lens.
   b Short-sightedness occurs when the eyeball is too long.
   c Short-sightedness occurs when the iris is too large.
   d Short-sightedness occurs when the lens is too curved.

5 Which of the following statements about hormones is correct?
   a Anti-diuretic hormone (ADH) is produced in the kidneys.
   b Insulin is produced in the liver.
   c Testosterone thickens the uterus in preparation for pregnancy.
   d Thyroid hormone influences body weight and metabolic rate.

Further practice questions and examples can be found on the accompanying CD.

UNIT 7: Short answer questions

1 a i Name the parts of the central nervous system and the peripheral nervous system. *(2)*

   ii Distinguish between a nerve and a neurone. *(3)*

   b Four students investigated their reaction times. They did this by using a computer program which has traffic lights. The program measures the time between the change from red to green by clicking on an icon. Each student took the test three times, without any rest between the tests.

Person	Time taken to click on an icon when the 'traffic light' changes to green/s			
	1st test	2nd test	3rd test	Mean
A	0.234	0.234	0.218	0.229
B	0.298	0.315	0.286	0.300
C	0.200	0.198	0.197	0.198
D	0.259	0.254	0.214	

   i State the stimulus and the response in this test. *(2)*

   ii Calculate the mean reaction time for Person D. *(1)*

   iii State how the reaction times of Person B differ from the other students. *(2)*

   iv Explain why the responses of drivers to real traffic lights changing from red to green would be longer than the times given in the table. *(2)*

   v Make one criticism of the way the students did this test. *(1)*

   c The eye is a major sense organ. List two other sense organs and state the stimulus which the sensory receptors in each detect. *(2)*

Total 15 marks

2 Figure 1 shows the components of the reflex arc that controls the movement of the hand away from a painful stimulus.

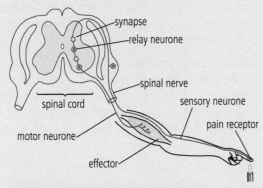

Figure 1

a Explain how all the named parts of the reflex arc coordinate the response. *(8)*

b When moving from darkness into bright light, the diameter of the pupils decreases. Describe in detail how the change in size of the pupils is controlled when this happens. *(7)*

Total 15 marks

3 People living in the Caribbean are at high risk of developing several progressive eye diseases that can lead to blindness. One reason for this is the high prevalence of diabetes; it is estimated that as many as 25% of the population in the region has this disease. People with diabetes are twice as likely to suffer from cataracts or glaucoma than the rest of the population.

Keratoconus. There is an increase in the curve of the cornea resulting in it becoming thin with progressive astigmatism. It is often seen in teenagers and tends to progress until they reach 30 or 40 years of age. The cause is unknown, but it can be treated by surgery.

Retinopathy is closely linked to diabetes and involves a breakdown of the blood vessels in the retina. Blood leaks into the vitreous humour; new blood vessels and fibrous tissue also grows into this region causing blindness. Laser treatment is used to breakdown and disperse the blood vessels.

Glaucoma is an eye disease that has no symptoms, is easily treatable and can cause blindness if untreated. In the Caribbean it is often found in adults as young as their mid 20s. Glaucoma is treated with eye drops if diagnosed early. Left untreated, it eventually causes blindness, which is irreversible.

Life-long exposure to ultraviolet light increases the chances of developing cataracts. Due to their location, people in the Caribbean have a high exposure to UV light.

a Explain what is meant by *progressive eye disease*. *(2)*

b It is suggested that some people may have a genetic predisposition to keratoconus. Suggest how researchers might investigate this claim. *(4)*

c Explain how astigmatism affects vision. *(2)*

d Explain why the loss of central vision is more important than the loss of peripheral vision. *(2)*

e Explain why blindness caused by cataracts is reversible whereas that caused by glaucoma is not. *(3)*

f In some countries cataracts are treated by surgical removal of the lens without any replacement. Explain why this partial treatment is successful at restoring eyesight. *(2)*

g Discuss the ways in which health authorities throughout the region could reduce the prevalence of blindness as a result of eye disorders, such as glaucoma and cataracts. *(5)*

Total 20 marks

Adapted from http://www.ehow.com/way_5492588_common-caribbean-eye-diseases-remedies.html

Further short answer questions can be found on the CD.

The female reproductive system

Sexual reproduction involves the fusion of male and female nuclei to form a **zygote**, producing offspring that are genetically different from each other and their parents. The cells that contain these nuclei are the male and female **gametes**.

In **asexual reproduction** there is only **one** parent. All the offspring are genetically identical to the parent as they inherit exactly the same genetic information. This means that there is little variation amongst the offspring. Any variation is due to the effect of the environment, for example the availability of nutrients and water determine how well organisms grow.

The diagrams (Figures 8.1.1 and 8.1.2) show the structure of the female reproductive system. The **ovaries** are the **gonads** where female gametes are produced and where the hormones **oestrogen** and **progesterone** are secreted. Eggs are fertilised in the oviducts and **embryos** develop within the wall of the uterus.

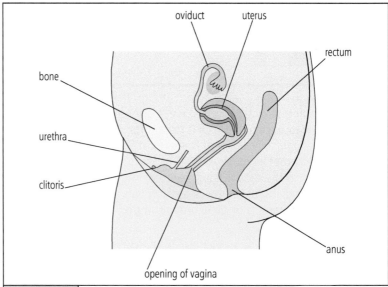

Figure 8.1.2 | The female reproductive system viewed from the side

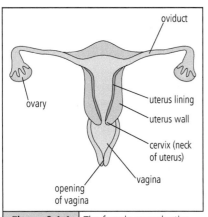

Figure 8.1.1 | The female reproductive system viewed from the front

The functions of the organs labelled in the two diagrams of the reproductive system are summarised in the table opposite.

Female gametes

Every girl is born with a large number of potential eggs in her ovaries. At **puberty**, some of these start to develop. One, or sometimes several, eggs are released from her ovaries each month during her reproductive life.

Organ	Functions
Ovary	• Produces and releases eggs (female gametes) • Secretes oestrogen that stimulates development of secondary sexual characteristics • Secretes progesterone that maintains the soft lining of the uterus during the second half of the **menstrual cycle** and during pregnancy
Oviduct	• Moves eggs from ovary to uterus using cilia and peristalsis • Site of **fertilisation**
Uterus	• Lining provides site for **implantation** and early development of the embryo • **Foetus** develops within the uterus • The muscle in the outer layer contracts during birth
Cervix	• A ring of muscular and glandular tissue at the base of the uterus • Secretes different forms of mucus at certain times during the menstrual cycle • Retains contents of uterus during pregnancy
Vagina	• Lining secretes mucus • Sperm are deposited in the vagina • Widens to form the birth canal
Clitoris	• Sensitive region at the entry to vagina with many sensory receptors that are stimulated during intercourse

Potential egg cells divide by **meiosis** so that they have 23 chromosomes each (Figure 8.1.3). They develop inside a follicle which provides the egg with food that is stored in the cytoplasm. When ready, the follicle fills with fluid and swells. It then bursts releasing the egg surrounded by follicle cells into the oviduct – a process known as **ovulation**.

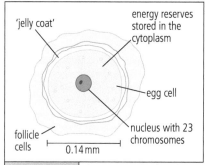

Figure 8.1.3 The ovum – the female gamete

LINK

See 9.2 for information about the role of meiosis in the production of gametes.

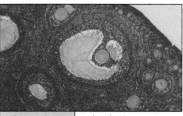

Figure 8.1.4 A developing ovum within a follicle in an ovary just before ovulation

Figure 8.1.5 A follicle just before it bursts to release an egg and some follicle cells

SUMMARY QUESTIONS

1 Make a table to compare asexual and sexual reproduction.

2 Make a large labelled diagram of the female reproductive system. Annotate the diagram with the functions of the organs that you have labelled.

3 State where the female gamete develops and where it is fertilised.

KEY POINTS

1 Eggs and sperm are specialised cells known as gametes. Fusion of gametes occurs in sexual reproduction, but not in asexual reproduction.

2 Sexual reproduction produces genetic variation in the offspring; asexual reproduction does not.

3 Human ovaries produce eggs that are released at ovulation into the oviduct where fertilisation occurs. The uterus is the site of internal development.

The male reproductive system and cancers of the reproductive systems

At the end of this topic you should be able to:

• describe the structure of the human male reproductive system and the function of the different organs

• describe the structure and function of the male gamete.

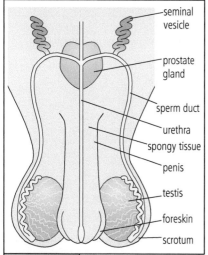

Figure 8.2.1 The male reproductive system viewed from the front

(labels: seminal vesicle, prostate gland, sperm duct, urethra, spongy tissue, penis, testis, foreskin, scrotum)

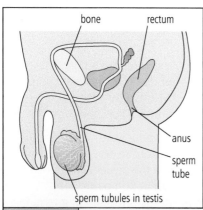

Figure 8.2.2 The male reproductive system viewed from the side

(labels: bone, rectum, anus, sperm tube, sperm tubules in testis)

The male reproductive system

The male sex organs are the **testes**. They produce the male gametes or **spermatozoa**, sperm for short, and secrete the male hormone **testosterone**.

The functions of the organs labelled in the two diagrams of the reproductive system (Figures 8.2.1 and 8.2.2) are summarised in the table below.

Organ	Function
Testis	• Produces sperm (male gametes) in huge numbers from puberty throughout the rest of life • Secretes testosterone that stimulates sperm production and development of secondary sexual characteristics
Scrotum	• Holds the testes at a temperature slightly lower than body temperature
Sperm duct	• Transfers sperm from the testes to the **urethra** in the penis
Cowper's gland	• Secretes an alkaline fluid to neutralise any acid in the urethra before ejaculation
Prostate gland	• Secretes seminal fluid containing sugars as food for the sperm. This fluid and the sperm are called **semen**
Seminal vesicle	• Secretes an alkaline fluid that neutralises the acidity of the vagina
Penis	• Inserted into vagina, releases semen that contains sperm • Has many sensory cells that are stimulated during intercourse

Male gamete

At puberty the testes start to produce sperm. Within each testis are many coiled tubes that are the site of sperm production. Stem cells at the base of each tube divide continuously to provide cells that change to become specialised to deliver 23 chromosomes to an egg at fertilisation.

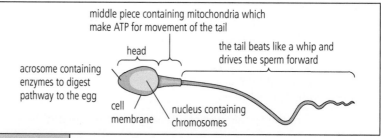

Figure 8.2.3 The sperm cell – the male gamete

(labels: middle piece containing mitochondria which make ATP for movement of the tail; head; the tail beats like a whip and drives the sperm forward; acrosome containing enzymes to digest pathway to the egg; cell membrane; nucleus containing chromosomes)

During intercourse the sperm ducts contract by peristalsis to move the sperm from the testes to the urethra. The muscles of the urethra in the penis contract and as a result semen is ejaculated from the penis into the vagina.

Male cancers

Diseases of the male reproductive system include cancers of the testis and **prostate gland**. **Testicular cancer** is more common in young and middle-aged men and often first detected as a hard swelling on the side of a testis. It is usually painless. Treatment often involves surgical removal of the testis and treatment by radiotherapy or chemotherapy.

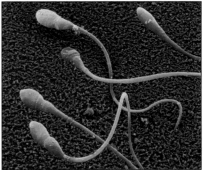

Figure 8.2.4 Human sperm cells

DID YOU KNOW?

Cancer is often thought to be 'a disease' of old age, which in the case of testicular and cervical cancer is not the case.

The prostate gland tends to enlarge with age and interrupt the flow of urine. Men over the age of 60 years often have to urinate more frequently as a result. **Prostate cancer** may be the cause. Treatment is by removal of the prostate gland. Testosterone promotes the growth of the cancer, so often the testes are removed and oestrogen is given.

It is important that men check their testes regularly and that men aged 60 and over report any symptoms about urination to their doctor. With early detection and treatment these cancers can be cured.

Female cancers

Diseases of the female reproductive system include cancers of the ovary and the cervix.

Many growths in the ovaries are cysts that are not harmful. Some growths are cancerous but there are no symptoms until the **ovarian cancer** is large and has spread into the uterus, causing pain. The cancer may be removed in an operation, followed by treatment with drugs (chemotherapy). This cancer is more common in older women who have not had children.

Cancerous cells can develop in the cervix. There are no symptoms until the cancer has spread. However, it is easy to detect in its early stages by taking cervical smears and looking for precancerous cells. **Cervical cancer** is more common in younger women who are sexually active, have had sexually transmitted infections (STIs) or an early pregnancy. Treatment with radiation (radiotherapy) is used if the cancer is not far advanced.

Young women should have cervical smear (pap) tests to check for precancerous cells. With early detection and treatment this disease can be cured.

LINK

There is more information about these and other cancers in 10.1.

KEY POINTS

1 Human testes produce sperm continually. The sperm are released during intercourse to travel through the sperm ducts to the urethra.

2 The prostate gland produces seminal fluid.

3 Testicular cancer and prostate cancer are diseases of the male reproductive system.

4 Ovarian cancer and cervical cancer are diseases of the female reproductive system.

SUMMARY QUESTIONS

1 Make a large labelled diagram of the male reproductive system. Annotate the diagram with the functions of the organs that you have labelled.

2 State where the male gamete develops and describe the pathway it follows before ejaculation.

3 Make a table to compare the human gametes. Use these row headings for your table: size, number produced, movement, food store.

4 Explain why early detection of cancers of the reproductive organs of men and women is important.

The menstrual cycle

At the end of this topic you should be able to:

- define the terms *menstrual cycle* and *ovulation*
- describe the changes that occur in the ovary and the uterus during the menstrual cycle
- explain how the menstrual cycle is controlled by hormones.

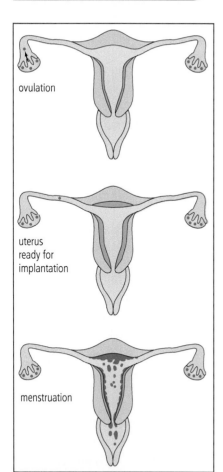

ovulation

uterus ready for implantation

menstruation

Figure 8.3.1 During the menstrual cycle the activities of the ovaries and the uterus are synchronised

The monthly changes in the ovary and the uterus are synchronised so that the lining of the uterus is ready to receive an embryo if fertilisation has occurred. This monthly cycle of changes is the **menstrual cycle**. During puberty girls start to have periods where the linings of the uterus and the vagina break down and blood and cells are passed out. When this **menstruation** happens for the first time it shows that a girl has had her first menstrual cycle.

Girls are born with a very large number of potential egg cells in their ovaries and they do not produce any more during their lifetime. Each potential egg is surrounded by a small group of cells and together they form a **follicle**. Each month one or two follicles develop by dividing by meiosis and increasing in size as the cytoplasm fills with stored food.

As the follicle grows it enlarges and fills with fluid and moves towards the edge of the ovary (see Figures 8.1.4 and 8.1.5). About two weeks after menstruation (day 14 of the menstrual cycle), the pressure inside the follicle is so great that it bursts releasing the egg, some follicle cells and the fluid into the oviduct. This is **ovulation**. Some follicle cells remain in the ovary to form the **yellow body** (corpus luteum). If fertilisation occurs, the egg will grow and remain in the ovary throughout **pregnancy**.

Following menstruation the lining of the uterus repairs itself and starts to thicken. In the week after ovulation it is thick and full of glands and blood vessels with the potential to nourish and protect the embryo. If fertilisation occurs, the embryo arrives in the uterus and sinks into this lining. This stage of reproduction is known as **implantation**.

If fertilisation does not occur, the egg dies and passes out of the vagina and the yellow body in the ovary breaks down. The thick lining of the uterus breaks down and is lost during menstruation. The cycle then begins again.

If a pregnancy does occur, the embryo releases a hormone that stimulates the yellow body to remain active and produce progesterone and oestrogen. This in turn stimulates the lining of the uterus to continue to thicken, supplying the embryo with nutrients and oxygen as it continues its development. This also ensures that menstruation will not occur.

Control of the menstrual cycle

There are four hormones that control the menstrual cycle. The **pituitary gland** secretes follicle stimulating hormone (FSH) and luteinising hormone (LH). The ovary secretes oestrogen and progesterone.

FSH starts the cycle by stimulating a follicle to develop and the follicle cells to secrete oestrogen into the bloodstream.

The role of oestrogen is to stimulate the lining of the uterus to thicken in readiness for the arrival of a fertilised egg and to prevent any more eggs maturing in the ovary. Oestrogen passes in the blood to the pituitary gland and stops it releasing any more FSH. Instead it stimulates the release of LH which stimulates ovulation to occur and the remaining follicle cells to form the yellow body.

The yellow body secretes progesterone which stimulates the further thickening of the uterus lining and prevents it breaking down. Both oestrogen and progesterone are needed to prepare the lining of the uterus for implantation of the embryo.

If implantation occurs so that pregnancy begins, oestrogen and progesterone continue to be released. They ensure that the uterus lining stays thick. They also stop a new menstrual cycle from starting.

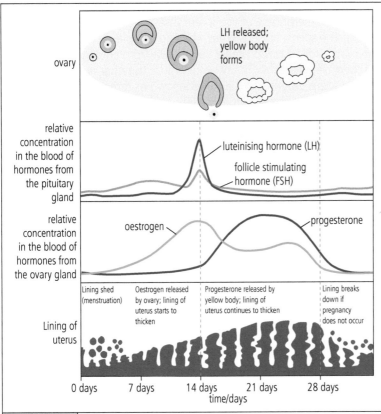

Figure 8.3.2 | Control of the menstrual cycle by hormones from the pituitary gland.
Reproduced by permission of Cambridge International Examinations

KEY POINTS

1 The menstrual cycle is the monthly changes that take place in the uterus. Following fertilisation an embryo can develop.

2 Associated with the menstrual cycle is the ovarian cycle in which changes occur resulting in the production of a mature egg.

3 The pituitary gland secretes FSH and LH that stimulate changes in the ovary and the secretion of oestrogen and progesterone.

4 Oestrogen stimulates the thickening of the uterus lining and the release of LH by the pituitary gland. It stops the release of FSH.

5 LH stimulates ovulation and the formation of the yellow body from the remains of the follicle. The yellow body secretes progesterone to maintain the uterine lining.

SUMMARY QUESTIONS

1 Define the following terms: *menstruation*, *ovulation* and *implantation*.

2 Draw a timeline to show the changes that occur in the ovary and in the uterus during a menstrual cycle.

   a Name four hormones involved in coordinating the menstrual cycle and state where they are secreted.

   b Describe the roles of these hormones in controlling the menstrual cycle.

3 Make a timeline for the human gametes from production until fertilisation.

LEARNING OUTCOMES

At the end of this topic you should be able to:

- distinguish between an embryo and a foetus
- state what happens at fertilisation and implantation
- describe in outline how the embryo and foetus develop
- describe the roles of the placenta, umbilical cord and amniotic sac
- describe what happens at birth.

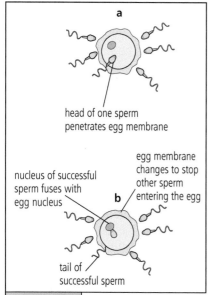

head of one sperm penetrates egg membrane

egg membrane changes to stop other sperm entering the egg

nucleus of successful sperm fuses with egg nucleus

tail of successful sperm

Figure 8.4.1 Fertilisation

LINK

Look at the structure of the sperm in Figure 8.2.3 to see how it is specialised to deliver 23 chromosomes to the egg.

Human fertilisation

Millions of sperm are deposited in the vagina; some sperm swim through the mucus in the cervix into the uterus and then to the oviduct. Many sperm cells do not survive this journey. This is why so many are produced to increase the chances of success.

If there is an egg in the oviduct, a sperm cell may fertilise it. First, the acrosome on the head of the sperm releases enzymes. These digest a pathway through the jelly coat around the egg.

Next, the cell membrane of the sperm fuses with the membrane around the egg. The sperm nucleus enters the egg cytoplasm. A membrane immediately forms to stop other sperm cells from entering so that only **one** sperm is successful. The two nuclei fuse together to form the zygote nucleus. Sperm can stay alive for two or three days so if intercourse happens just before ovulation the sperm can fertilise an egg.

Implantation

After fertilisation the zygote divides by mitosis to form a two-celled embryo. This continues dividing to form four cells and then eight. After a while some cells continue dividing while others stop, so the increase in cells is not regular. After a few hours the embryo is a hollow ball of cells, which moves down the oviduct. The embryo is moved by muscular contractions and the beating of the cilia on the epithelial cells that line the oviduct.

It may take several days for the embryo to reach the uterus. The embryo embeds into the soft lining of the uterus. This is called implantation. The uterus lining is thick with many glands and blood vessels which provide nutrients and oxygen to the embryo by diffusion. Carbon dioxide and chemical wastes diffuse out of the embryo.

The functions of the structures labelled in Figure 8.4.2 are explained in the table.

Organ	Structure	Function
Amniotic sac	Thin layer of cells and fibrous tissue	Encloses foetus in a watery fluid – the **amniotic fluid** – which provides protection against mechanical damage
Placenta	Disc of tissue that has many villi giving a large surface area	Exchange of substances between foetal blood and maternal blood
Umbilical cord	Rubbery cord containing an artery and two veins	Deoxygenated blood flows to the placenta Oxygenated blood returns to the foetus

Birth

A normal pregnancy takes about nine months. Sometimes babies are born early or prematurely. This might be because there has been a problem during pregnancy, usually because the **amniotic sac** breaks early.

The foetus usually turns inside the uterus a few weeks before birth, so that its head lies above the cervix as shown in Figure 8.4.2. Hormones released by the foetus and the build-up of pressure in the uterus trigger the mother to secrete hormones. These hormones stimulate the muscles of the uterus to contract and so the process of **labour** begins. The three stages of labour are summarised in the table below.

Stage	Events
1	The cervix dilates and contractions of the uterus push the baby into the vagina
2	The baby passes through the **pelvis** and enters the vagina
3	This stage begins after the baby is born. The placenta comes away from the uterus and passes out of the vagina

When the contractions become stronger and more frequent the opening of the cervix stretches. The amniotic sac breaks and amniotic fluid escapes.

The muscles of the uterus wall now contract very strongly. They push the baby towards the cervix. The cervix dilates and the contractions push the baby's head through the vagina. This part of the birth takes place quite quickly. When it is born the baby starts to breathe. It is important that the baby has airways clear of mucus and can breathe easily.

The umbilical cord is tied and cut. The remains of the cord heal to form the baby's navel. After a few minutes the placenta comes away from the uterus wall and is expelled as the **afterbirth**.

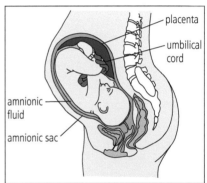

Figure 8.4.2 A full-term foetus in the uterus. *Reproduced by permission of Cambridge International Examinations*

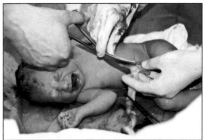

Figure 8.4.3 A newborn baby just before the umbilical cord is cut

DID YOU KNOW?

Once the embryo has organs and is recognisably human it is called a foetus.

KEY POINTS

1 Male and female gametes fuse together at fertilisation to form a zygote.
2 After fertilisation the zygote divides by mitosis to form a ball of cells known as an embryo. After further development the embryo develops organs. It is called a foetus.
3 The amniotic sac holds fluid to protect the foetus which is connected to the placenta by the umbilical cord.
4 The placenta is the site of exchange of substances between maternal blood and foetal blood.
5 During birth the uterine muscles contract to expel the foetus through the vagina

SUMMARY QUESTIONS

1 State what happens at fertilisation and at implantation.

2 Distinguish between the following: ovum and sperm, zygote and embryo, embryo and foetus.

3 Describe the events that occur during birth.

4 Describe the roles of the amniotic sac, placenta and umbilical cord during the development of a foetus.

5 Draw a timeline to show the changes that occur between fertilisation and birth. You may have to research some secondary sources to do this.

Prenatal and post-natal care

At the end of this topic you should be able to:

- distinguish between prenatal and post-natal care
- explain the importance of both types of care for mother and foetus/baby
- outline the advantages of breastfeeding.

| Figure 8.5.1 | A balanced diet is an important part of prenatal care |

| Figure 8.5.2 | A prenatal class is just as important for fathers as for mothers preparing them for birth and how to care for the baby after the birth |

Prenatal care

Prenatal care (also called antenatal), or care before birth, is important for the successful development of the foetus while in the womb and for the mother as well. Women need to know that their pregnancy is progressing well. They need advice about nutrition and how to prepare for birth and take care of the baby.

DID YOU KNOW?

Women who are planning to become pregnant are advised to take folic acid supplements. This is required for the development of the nervous system so reducing the chances of spina bifida.

Diet: The mother needs a balanced diet so the foetus obtains all the nutrients to grow and develop. Vitamins and minerals, such as iron and calcium, are particularly important. A pregnant woman should ensure that she gets adequate quantities of:

- **calcium** for the growing bones of the foetus
- **iron** to make haemoglobin for red blood cells that develop in the foetus and for the extra red blood cells that the mother needs to transport oxygen
- **carbohydrate** so that the pregnant mother has enough energy to move as she gets heavier
- **protein** to provide the amino acids that both mother and baby need to make new tissues; protein is needed for making the placenta and extra muscle tissue in the uterus in preparation for birth.

The quality of food is far more important than the quantity. Pregnant women do not need to increase their energy intake until the last three months of pregnancy.

Smoking: Nicotine and carbon monoxide cross the placenta, resulting in premature or underweight babies. Carbon monoxide in tobacco smoke combines permanently with haemoglobin so that the blood carries less oxygen. Oxygen is crucial for the development of the foetus, which may not grow sufficiently if there is a lack of it.

Alcohol: Alcohol also crosses the placenta to cause a variety of problems including birth defects and mental retardation.

Other drugs: Drugs, such as heroin, cross the placenta and some babies have been born with an addiction to heroin. Smoking marijuana (ganga) is also dangerous, resulting in the birth of underweight babies and children who develop more slowly.

Protection against infectious diseases: Mothers should be vaccinated against diseases that can infect the foetus. An example is **rubella**, which causes serious birth defects. They should also be vaccinated against tetanus which is a major cause of maternal deaths after childbirth. There are no vaccines for some diseases that can infect babies, e.g. HIV/AIDS (see 10.5 for more information on this).

Post-natal care

At birth: The umbilical cord is clamped and then cut. The baby is cleaned and any mucus removed from the nose and mouth. The baby is then checked for any health problems. With a large surface area : volume ratio babies will lose heat easily and so must be kept warm. Premature babies are often kept in incubators.

Care for the mother: Mothers need support, both practical and emotional, after the birth and during the first few years of the child's life. Some women suffer from post-natal depression which, in some cases, can be very severe.

Care for the baby: Newborn babies, apart from constant feeding and cleaning, need protection against childhood diseases. This is provided by vaccination programmes (see 10.8). Plenty of interaction with adults and their surroundings stimulate their physical and mental development.

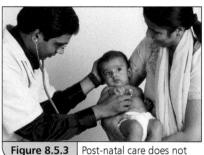

Figure 8.5.3 Post-natal care does not just involve checking on the growth and development of babies, but also the health of the heart and other organs

Breastfeeding

During her pregnancy the glands in the mother's breasts will enlarge. After the birth she is able to secrete milk. This is a 'complete food' with all the nutrients that the baby needs in the right proportions.

Breast milk contains **antibodies** which give the baby **passive immunity** to the diseases that the mother has had recently.

Some women are not able to breastfeed their babies or they find it difficult or embarrassing. Instead they use formula milk and bottle feed. This comes in powdered form and needs to be mixed with water under sterile conditions. In some places women may not be able to do this. Their babies are at risk of infections from non-sterile milk or bottles. Formula milk also costs money whereas breast milk is free.

Figure 8.5.4 Breastfeeding brings many advantages, not least developing a strong bond between baby and mother

LINK

See 10.8 for more on immunity.

KEY POINTS

1 Prenatal care involves eating a balanced diet and reducing risks to the health of unborn babies from infectious diseases, smoking, drinking alcohol and taking drugs.

2 Post-natal care involves proper care of the babies, checking their growth, development and general health. The health of mothers is also important.

3 Breastfeeding provides all the requirements that babies need, including antibodies. It also has psychological benefits for mother and baby.

SUMMARY QUESTIONS

1 Explain the advice that should be given to pregnant women about diet.

2 Explain how a pregnant woman can safeguard the health of her foetus in ways other than eating carefully.

3 Make a table to compare the advantages and disadvantages of breastfeeding.

Family planning and birth control

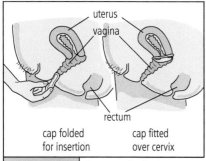

uterus

vagina

rectum

cap folded for insertion

cap fitted over cervix

Figure 8.6.1 A cap or diaphragm

LINK

There is more about sexually transmitted infections in 10.4.

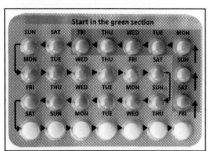

Figure 8.6.3 Contraceptive pills are taken every day during each menstrual cycle to prevent the release of eggs from the ovary

Family planning

Family planning is deciding when to have children and how and when to use contraceptives and other **birth control** methods. Family planning also includes information about limiting the number of children and controlling when to have them. It is the advice given to women and couples who have an unplanned pregnancy and who wish to terminate it and to those who are having difficulties in conceiving.

Birth control

Birth control is any method that prevents the birth of a baby. Methods may prevent fertilisation or implantation or remove the embryo or foetus at some stage during pregnancy. Methods that prevent fertilisation are methods of **contraception**. If conception and implantation have occurred and the embryo/foetus has started to develop then the destruction of this is an **abortion**. It is **not** a method of contraception.

- **Barrier methods**

  A **cap** or **diaphragm** is a rubber dome. The woman places it over her cervix before intercourse. It prevents the man's sperm from entering the uterus. It should be used with sperm-killing cream or foam. It does **not** protect against **sexually transmitted infections (STIs)**.

  A **condom** is a thin rubber tube which is rolled over the man's erect penis before intercourse. It stops the sperm from entering the woman's body. It also gives protection against STIs. It is the most common form of birth control.

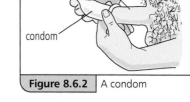

penis

condom

Figure 8.6.2 A condom

  A **femidom** is the female equivalent of a condom and is inserted into the vagina. Femidoms provide protection against the transmission of STIs.

- **Hormonal methods** – The oral contraceptive or pill is taken by mouth. Some pills contain the hormones oestrogen and progesterone and others contain only progesterone. They prevent the ovary releasing eggs by inhibiting the production of FSH by the pituitary. Eggs do not mature and are not released by the ovaries so pregnancy cannot occur. The woman has to take a pill every day.

  The pill is a very reliable and convenient method of contraception. Drawbacks are that failure to take the pill regularly can result in a pregnancy. The side effects are sore breasts, weight gain, depression and painful periods – each type of pill has its own set of side effects. In a very small number of women, the pill can be the cause of heart and circulation problems.

- **Surgical methods** – A sperm duct is also known as a vas deferens. The operation to cut them is a **vasectomy** and is a minor operation for a man. His sperm tubes are cut and tied. The man can still ejaculate but there are no sperm in the semen, just fluid.

  Sterilisation is a minor operation for a woman. Her oviducts are cut and blocked. Sterilisation is not usually reversible so the man or woman must be sure that he or she does not want any more children.

- **Natural methods** – Some couples may have religious or moral objections to using contraception. They may use the rhythm method and abstain from having sex in the days just before and just after ovulation. The woman keeps a record of when she has her periods and predicts when ovulation should occur. This is not a reliable method, especially for women who do not have regular periods. Another method is to follow changes in symptoms associated with ovulation – the increase in body temperature and changes in cervical mucus which becomes wetter and less sticky just before ovulation.

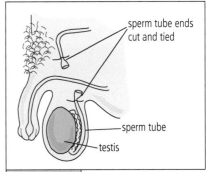

Figure 8.6.4 | A vasectomy

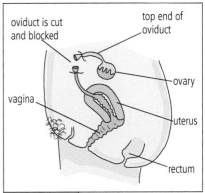

Figure 8.6.5 | Sterilisation in women involves ligaturing the oviducts

> **STUDY FOCUS**
>
> This symptoms-based natural method is proving effective and is useful for people who do not have access to family planning clinics and contraception.

Abortion

Abortion is the termination of a pregnancy. When this occurs naturally it is known as a miscarriage. The term abortion is used when the embryo or foetus is removed either medically by using hormones or surgically. Issues surrounding induced abortion include the right of the child to life and the right of women to choose whether or not they terminate their pregnancy. Some abortions take place because there is a risk to the life of the child or the mother but others occur because the child has or will develop a serious medical condition.

SUMMARY QUESTIONS

1 Define the terms *family planning*, *birth control*, *contraception* and *abortion*.

2 Explain the biological principles involved in the following methods of birth control: barrier, hormonal, surgical and natural.

3 Explain the importance of family planning in countries with high and low birth rates.

4 Find out about laws governing abortion in different countries, for example Cuba, South Korea and Chile. Discuss this with friends and present the case for and against abortion as a method of birth control.

5 Find out about the family planning advice offered in your country and summarise your findings in a presentation.

KEY POINTS

1 Family planning is deciding when to have a child and how many to have.

2 There are barrier, chemical and surgical methods of contraception.

3 Abortion is not a method of contraception. It is the removal of a foetus by surgical or chemical methods and is extremely controversial.

UNIT 8: Multiple-choice questions

1 The fusion of a sperm and an egg to form a zygote is referred to as:

  a fertilisation

  b implantation

  c labour

  d ovulation.

2 Which organ secretes the hormones FSH and LH?

  a Ovary

  b Pituitary gland

  c Placenta

  d Testis

3 Which of the following hormones stimulates ovulation?

  a FSH

  b LH

  c Oestrogen

  d Progesterone

4 The World Health Organization recommends that all babies, as far as possible, are breastfed. Which of the following statements about breastfeeding is NOT true?

  a The baby is given breast milk with the ideal quantities of nutrients for growth and metabolism.

  b Antibodies are present in breast milk to give immunity to the baby.

  c Breastfeeding helps to develop bonding between a mother and her baby.

  d Breast milk provides protection against all infectious diseases.

5 The function of the umbilical cord is to:

  a allow exchange of substances between maternal blood and foetal blood

  b connect the foetus to the placenta

  c contract during birth

  d cushion the foetus against blows to the mother's abdomen.

> Further practice questions and examples can be found on the accompanying CD.

UNIT 8: Short answer questions

1 Figure 1 shows the male reproductive system.

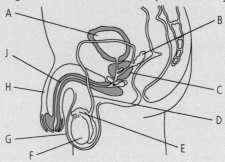

Figure 1 *Reproduced by permission of Cambridge International Examinations*

  a **i** State the letters used to identify the following parts of the male reproductive system:

      scrotum, testis, vas deferens, prostate gland. (4)

    ii Describe the functions of each of the structures named in part **i**. (6)

  b Condoms are used as one form of birth control.

    i What term is used to describe this method of birth control? (1)

    ii Explain how a condom acts as a method of birth control. (2)

  c A vasectomy is another method of birth control. Explain how this prevents pregnancy. (2)

Total 15 marks

2 a Copy and complete the following table comparing human gametes.

Feature	Ovum (egg)	Sperm cells
Size		
Relative numbers produced during reproductive life		
Number of chromosomes in the nucleus		
Mobility (ability to move)		

(4)

b   Describe the events that occur at
    fertilisation. *(3)*

c   Explain the importance of having a
    balanced diet during pregnancy. *(4)*

d   Describe the process of birth. *(4)*

Total 15 marks

3   International organisations, such as the
    United Nations, use a variety of indicators to
    compare the health of populations in different
    countries. Three of these are:

    • birth rate as the number of live births per
      1000 people
    • infant mortality rate, which is the number of
      deaths of children in the first year of life
    • 5-year mortality rate, which is the number
      of deaths of children less than five years old.

    The table shows such data for eight Caribbean
    countries for the period 2005–2010.

Country	Birth rate/ live births per 1000 people	Mortality rate/ number of deaths per 1000 live births	
		Children < 1 year old	Children < 5 years old
Belize	25	17	22
Cuba	10	5	7
Grenada	19	15	17
Guyana	19	42	53
Haiti	28	63	83
Jamaica	19	24	29
Suriname	19	22	30
Trinidad and Tobago	15	27	34

a   Suggest why the data is expressed in terms
    of 'per 1000 live births' rather than the
    total number of births per country. *(2)*

b   Suggest TWO other indicators that the
    United Nations could use to compare the
    health of nations. *(2)*

c   Researchers often state that there is a
    correlation between high birth rates and
    high rates of child mortality.

    Explain whether the data in the table
    supports this idea or not. You may use a
    graph to illustrate your answer. *(4)*

d   Abortion is legal in Cuba but not in many
    other Caribbean countries.

    i   Explain why abortion is NOT a method
        of contraception. *(2)*

    ii Outline the arguments for AND against
        abortion as a method of birth control.
        (5)

e   Medical experts state that breastfeeding
    reduces the infant mortality rate. Explain
    the reasons for this. *(5)*

Total 20 marks

United Nations, Department of Economic
and Social Affairs, Population Division (2011).
World Population Prospects:
The 2010 Revision, CD-ROM Edition.

4 a   Describe the roles of the placenta,
      amniotic sac and umbilical cord in the
      development of a foetus. *(6)*

  b   Discuss the importance of post-natal care
      of children and their mothers. *(5)*

  c   Discuss the social and economic
      importance of family planning. *(4)*

Total 15 marks

Further short answer
questions can be found
on the CD.

9 Heredity and variation

9.1   Mitosis

Figure 9.1.1 | A research worker studies an image of the chromosomes from a man that have been arranged to show 22 homologous chromosomes and the sex chromosomes, X and Y

A cell, such as a zygote, cannot grow by just getting larger. Its surface area to volume ratio **decreases** and it will not get enough oxygen to sustain itself. Instead it divides into two. Before this can happen, the cell nucleus divides by **mitosis** so that each new cell has the genetic information it needs to function.

Chromosomes

Each **chromosome** consists of a very long molecule of DNA, which is the genetic material of cells, and proteins that provide support. Chromosomes become visible in the light microscope as X-shaped structures when cells divide. When division is complete, the DNA in the chromosomes uncoils so that individual chromosomes are no longer visible.

Each nucleus in a human has 46 chromosomes. Figure 9.1.1 shows that they can be sorted into pairs based on their size and shape. In the photograph a man's chromosomes have been sorted into 22 **homologous pairs**. The chromosomes are copies of those that were in the zygote when he was conceived. One chromosome in each pair was inherited from his father and the other from his mother. The chromosomes in each pair have the same genetic instructions or **genes**.

Before mitosis

Before a cell can divide, new copies of the genetic information in the DNA of each chromosome must be made. This copying process occurs before the nucleus divides. While it is going on, the DNA in the chromosomes is uncoiled and arranged very loosely in the nucleus. When copying is finished, each chromosome has two molecules of DNA. As mitosis begins, the DNA coils up tightly and each chromosome appears as a double-stranded structure. The two genetically identical strands are known as **chromatids**.

During mitosis

The diagram (Figure 9.1.2) shows what happens to four chromosomes as the nucleus divides during mitosis. Human cells have 46 chromosomes so this happens to all 46 each time a cell divides.

As a result of mitosis each daughter cell has the same number of chromosomes as the original parent cell. As the DNA in the chromosomes has been copied by a reliable system, the daughter cells are genetically identical to one another and to the parent cell.

Mitosis occurs in:

- growth – this starts with the first division of the zygote and then throughout the body of an embryo. Later it is restricted to certain places like the growth regions in long bones (see 5.1)
- repair of wounds – stem cells at the base of the epidermis divide to repair wounds (see 6.3)

- replacement of cells that wear out and die, such as red blood cells which only live for a short time as they do not have a nucleus so cannot divide (see 5.1)
- asexual reproduction – this occurs in fungi (see Figure 3.4.4) and in plants, but is rare in the animal kingdom (see 8.1).

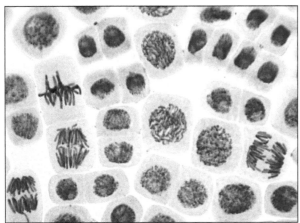

Figure 9.1.3	In this photograph of a growing region of a plant, you can see the different stages of mitosis that are drawn in Figure 9.1.2

KEY POINTS

1 Chromosomes are made of DNA and protein and are located in cell nuclei; DNA is the genetic material.

2 Homologous chromosomes are the same size and shape and have the same genes.

3 Mitosis is a type of division of the nucleus which forms two genetically identical nuclei.

4 The daughter nuclei always have the same chromosome number as the parent nucleus.

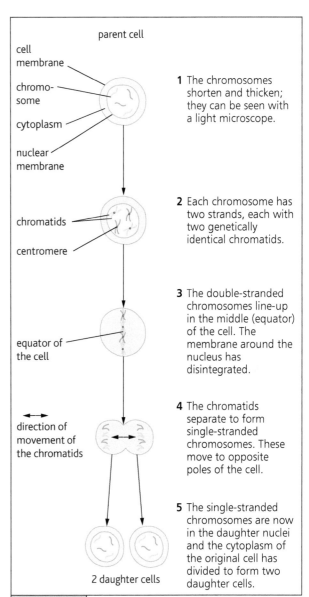

1 The chromosomes shorten and thicken; they can be seen with a light microscope.

2 Each chromosome has two strands, each with two genetically identical chromatids.

3 The double-stranded chromosomes line-up in the middle (equator) of the cell. The membrane around the nucleus has disintegrated.

4 The chromatids separate to form single-stranded chromosomes. These move to opposite poles of the cell.

5 The single-stranded chromosomes are now in the daughter nuclei and the cytoplasm of the original cell has divided to form two daughter cells.

Figure 9.1.2	Mitosis

SUMMARY QUESTIONS

1 Arrange the following in order of size with the largest first: chromosome, nucleus, gene and cell.

2 Explain what is meant by: *chromosome*, *chromatid*, *mitosis* and *cell division*.

3 a Describe what happens inside a cell **before** it can divide by mitosis.

  b Describe what happens to a chromosome **during** mitosis.

  c Describe what happens to a cell **after** mitosis is complete.

4 Make models of chromosomes and use them to show what happens to chromosomes when cells divide by mitosis.

5 Explain why human red blood cells do not live very long and why they cannot divide.

9.2 Meiosis

LEARNING OUTCOMES

At the end of this topic you should be able to:

- define the term *meiosis*
- describe the movement of homologous chromosomes and chromatids during meiosis
- state the importance of meiosis in halving the chromosome number and generating variation
- explain the role of meiosis in human reproduction.

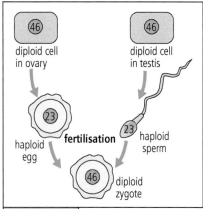

Figure 9.2.1 | The number of chromosomes halves during the formation of gametes and is restored at fertilisation

Sexual reproduction needs gametes. If human gametes were produced by mitosis it would mean that every time they fused together at fertilisation the number of chromosomes would double. However, the number of chromosomes remains the same every generation. **Meiosis** occurs during gamete production to halve the number of chromosomes and to generate variation among the gametes. The nuclei in the daughter cells are genetically different from the parent cell and from each other.

There are two divisions of the nucleus and two divisions of the cell. During the first division, homologous chromosomes pair together and then separate into different nuclei, so halving the chromosome number. During the second division, the chromatids of each chromosome separate.

First division of meiosis

1. Chromosomes shorten and thicken.

2. Each chromosome has two genetically identical chromatids.

3. Homologous chromosomes form pairs in the middle of the cell.

4. Homologous chromosomes separate with each double-stranded chromosome moving to opposite poles of the cell.

5. Nuclear membranes may form around each group of chromosomes. These cells divide again.

Second division of meiosis

6. Chromosomes are in the middle of the cell.

7. The chromatids separate and move to opposite poles of the cells.

8. The cells divide to form four daughter cells.

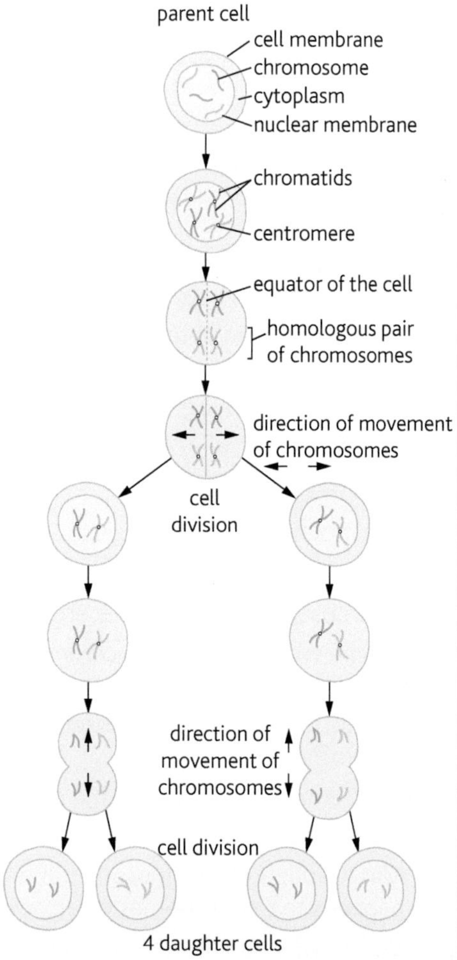

parent cell
cell membrane
chromosome
cytoplasm
nuclear membrane
chromatids
centromere
equator of the cell
homologous pair of chromosomes
direction of movement of chromosomes
cell division
direction of movement of chromosomes
cell division
4 daughter cells

Figure 9.2.2 | Meiosis

The number of chromosomes in the gametes is called the **haploid** number. The number in a zygote and in cells derived from the zygote is the **diploid** number. The diagram (Figure 9.2.3) shows what happens to two pairs of chromosomes during meiosis. Imagine this happening within a cell with 46 chromosomes to give four haploid cells each containing 23 chromosomes. In the testis, each will develop into a sperm cell. In the ovary, three of the cells die to leave one large haploid cell – the egg cell.

In meiosis the daughter cells are not identical. They are genetically different. This contributes to genetic variation and allows organisms to evolve in response to changing environments.

One way in which meiosis generates the variation between gametes is to 'shuffle' the chromosomes that were inherited from mother and father. Figure 9.2.3 shows two ways in which two pairs of homologous chromosomes are arranged during the first division of meiosis. With 23 pairs of chromosomes there are many possible random arrangements of maternal and parental chromosomes to pass on to the next generation. As well as this 'shuffling', further variation is generated by pairs of chromosomes exchanging genetic material between them – a process known as **crossing over**.

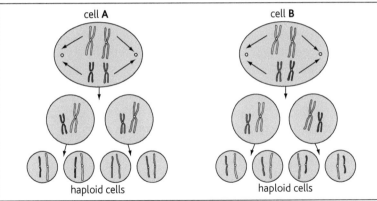

Figure 9.2.3 Meiosis introduces variation into gametes by the random arrangement of homologous chromosomes – see how the nuclei produced from parent cell A differ from those from cell B

STUDY FOCUS

Here is a maths challenge. How many different combinations of maternal and paternal chromosomes are possible in human gametes? The answer is on the CD.

EXAM TIP

Take care when writing mitosis and meiosis as the words are very similar. You must spell them correctly in exam answers. The importance of meiosis is summarised in the answer to question 3(a) on the CD.

KEY POINTS

1. Meiosis produces nuclei that have half the number of chromosomes as the parent nucleus. The number of chromosomes in gametes is the haploid number.

2. Haploid gametes fuse together to form a zygote that has the diploid number.

3. There are two divisions in meiosis. Homologous chromosomes pair in the first division and then separate.

4. Gametes differ from each other as they have different combinations of maternal and paternal chromosomes as a result of the random arrangement of homologous pairs in the first division of meiosis.

SUMMARY QUESTIONS

1. How many chromosomes are there in the following human cells:
   - a cell from the lining of an alveolus
   - b an egg cell
   - c a sperm cell
   - d a zygote and
   - e a red blood cell?

2. Explain why meiosis is necessary in gamete formation.

3. a State three ways in which meiosis differs from mitosis.
   b Explain the advantages of genetic variation among gametes.

4. Use your models of chromosomes to show how variation can be generated in meiosis by the random arrangements of homologous chromosomes in the first division of meiosis

At the end of this topic you should be able to:

- define the terms *variation* and *mutation*
- state the differences between continuous and discontinuous variation
- explain why genetic variation is important to organisms
- state the differences between genetic variation and environmental variation.

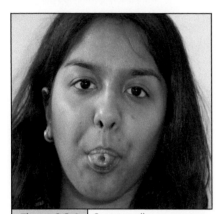

Figure 9.3.1 Can you roll your tongue like this?

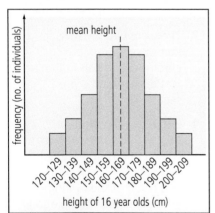

Figure 9.3.2 A histogram showing the normal variation in heights of 16-year-olds

Look around you for examples of ways in which we differ from each other: different sexes, different heights, different hair styles, different skin colours and different fingerprints. These differences are examples of the variation in our species. We also use the term variation for the differences between species but here we are interested in variation among humans.

The variation between us is due to the genes that we inherit and to the effects of the environment. You will learn more about genetic variation in 9.4 to 9.6. The environment influences the way we grow and develop. Environmental variation is not inherited.

Types of variation

DID YOU KNOW?

Some people have very rare blood groups and if they have an accident and need a transfusion it can be difficult to find a match in the blood bank. This is why it is important that everyone should know their blood group – something you will find out if you become a blood donor.

Do you know your blood group? There are many different blood group systems. There are four blood types in this system: A, B, AB and O. There is also the Rhesus system with two blood types: Rhesus positive and Rhesus negative.

Tongue rolling and blood groups are examples of **discontinuous variation**. People can either roll their tongue or not. You have a distinct blood group; there are no intermediates with people having mixtures of the different blood groups. Bar charts are used to present data on this type of variation, e.g. the table below shows the percentages of people with the different blood groups in three places.

Blood group	Percentage of the population with each blood group		
	Jamaica	The Kuna people of Panama (see 9.5)	India
A	25	0	22
B	21	0	33
AB	4	0	7
O	50	100	37

Height and body mass are features that show **continuous variation** as you can see in the histogram. The data does not fit into distinct groups, instead it can be anywhere between the upper and lower values.

Genes and the environment

Variation is influenced by genes and the environment. Blood groups are determined by genes; they do not change during our lifetime because of our environment. This is true for most features that show discontinuous variation. Features that show continuous variation, such as height, are influenced **both** by genes and by the environment. Your final height is determined to some extent by the genes you have inherited and factors such as the quality and quantity of your food. There are some long-term features that are the result of environmental influences alone, such as scars and the effects of diseases such as polio.

There are several causes of genetic variation among people:

- the random arrangement of homologous chromosomes during meiosis
- crossing over between homologous chromosomes during meiosis
- the contribution from two parents who are genetically different
- the random fusion of gametes at fertilisation
- chromosome mutation and gene mutation.

Gene mutation is the only way in which totally new genetic material is formed.

Mutation

A **chromosome mutation** is a change in the number of chromosomes. The girl in the photograph has **Down's syndrome**. Usually in this condition, a pair of homologous chromosomes fails to separate properly during meiosis. Instead of the egg having 23 chromosomes there is an extra chromosome giving a total of 24. When this egg is fertilised by a sperm with 23 chromosomes, the baby will have 47 chromosomes, one more than normal. Down's syndrome affects about 1 in 1000 babies worldwide.

A **gene mutation** is a change to the DNA in a gene that controls a certain feature. This can happen to one of the genes that controls the production of the skin pigment **melanin**. Someone who inherits two copies of the mutant gene cannot make melanin and has the genetic condition **albinism**.

Many gene mutations are harmful, but sometimes they can be useful and help us to survive in certain environments.

Figure 9.3.3 This young girl has Down's syndrome

Monohybrid inheritance

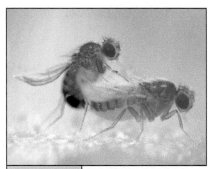

Figure 9.4.1 Fruit flies are small, easy to keep, mate easily, produce many offspring and have short life spans. The only disadvantage for researchers is that they fly!

EXAM TIP

Notice that the dominant allele is always shown as a capital letter and the recessive allele as a small letter. Never use different letters for the alleles of the **same** gene.

Genetics is the study of inheritance of genes. Each gene controls a characteristic of an organism. We have learnt a lot about genetics from studying the fruit fly. **Monohybrid inheritance** concerns the inheritance of a **single** characteristic, such as the wing length of fruit flies that determines their ability to fly.

The **phenotype** is the appearance of an individual. It refers to all the aspects of an organism's biology **except** its genes. It includes features we can see, such as wings, and features that we cannot, such as blood groups in humans. We will use the term for one feature of an organism, for example, wing length in fruit flies.

Figure 9.4.2 shows the inheritance of wing length in fruit flies. Almost all flies have long wings but there are some that have very short wings and are unable to fly. The gene for wings therefore has two forms or **alleles**.

A male with long wings is crossed with a female with short wings and then males and females of the next generation are crossed amongst themselves.

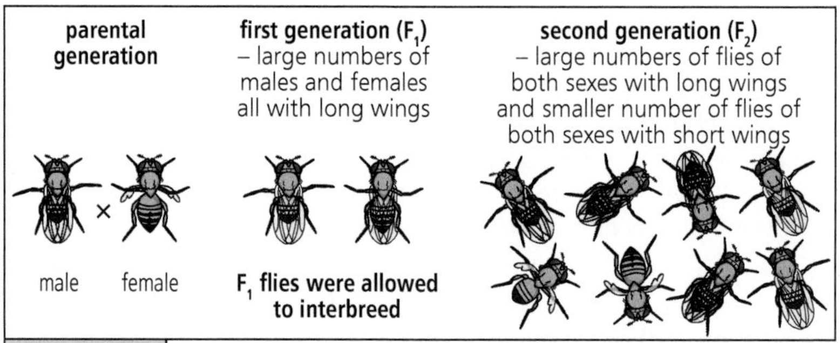

parental generation	first generation (F_1) – large numbers of males and females all with long wings	second generation (F_2) – large numbers of flies of both sexes with long wings and smaller number of flies of both sexes with short wings
male × female	F_1 flies were allowed to interbreed	

Figure 9.4.2 The recessive feature (short wing) does not appear in the first generation

You can see that all the fruit flies in the first generation (F_1) have long wings. This shows that long wing is the **dominant** phenotype and short wing is the **recessive** phenotype. From the results in the second generation (F_2), you can see that the recessive phenotype reappears so the allele for short wing has been passed on but did not affect the wing of the flies in the first generation.

The **genotype** is the genetic composition of an organism. The term usually refers to the alleles of the genes being investigated. In fruit flies there is a gene that controls wing length. There are two alleles of this gene and they are represented in a genotype by letters: **W** for the allele for long wings and **w** for the allele for short wings.

The parental generation in this investigation are 'pure breeding' flies as they come from a stock of fruit flies that had either long wings or short wings for many generations. As a result we know the long-winged flies only have the allele **W** and short-winged flies only have the allele **w**. Genetic diagrams are drawn to explain how the alleles are inherited.

	male	×	female
parental phenotypes	long wing		short wing
parental genotypes	**WW**		**ww**
parental gametes	(W)	+	(w)

F_1 genotype		**Ww**
F_1 phenotype		all long wing

	long wing	×	long wing
F_1 phenotypes			
F_1 genotypes	**Ww**		**Ww**
F_1 gametes	(W), (w)	+	(W), (w)

		male gametes	
		(W)	(w)
female gametes	(W)	**WW**	**Ww**
	(w)	**Ww**	**ww**

F_2 genotypes and phenotypes	**WW** long wing	2**Ww** long wing	**ww** short wing
F_2 phenotypic ratio		3 long wing : 1 short wing	

If an organism has two identical alleles it is **homozygous** for the gene concerned. If the alleles are both dominant, then it is homozygous dominant, if they are recessive then it is homozygous recessive. If the two alleles are different then it is **heterozygous**.

Amongst the F_2 generation $\frac{1}{4}$ (or 25%) are homozygous dominant, $\frac{1}{2}$ (or 50%) are heterozygous, and $\frac{1}{4}$ (or 25%) are homozygous recessive. Since the phenotypes of **WW** and **Ww** are the same, $\frac{3}{4}$ of the F_2 plants have long wings and $\frac{1}{4}$ have short wings. This can also be written as the ratio 3 long wing : 1 short wing.

KEY POINTS

Follow these points when writing genetic diagrams:

1 Genotypes of organisms have two alleles as they are diploid (have two sets of chromosomes).

2 Genotypes of gametes (sperm and eggs) have one allele as they are haploid (have one set of chromosomes). This is because they are produced by meiosis that halves the chromosome number.

3 Always use a grid to show all the possible combinations of alleles that can occur at fertilisation.

4 Write out the genotypes and make sure that you show clearly the phenotypes that they will have.

5 If the males and females in the parental generation are homozygous, then the first generation is known as the F_1 generation, and the second generation is the F_2 generation.

SUMMARY QUESTIONS

1 Fruit flies with grey bodies are crossed with fruit flies with ebony bodies. All the offspring had grey bodies. When these offspring were crossed amongst themselves $\frac{1}{4}$ of the flies in the next generation had ebony bodies and the rest were grey. Draw a genetic diagram like that above to explain these results.

2 A fruit fly with a grey body was crossed with a fruit fly with a black body. Of the offspring, 50% had grey bodies and 50% had black bodies. Use a genetic diagram to explain this result.

3 Define the terms *homozygous*, *heterozygous*, F_1 and F_2.

4 Explain:
   a the terms *gene* and *allele*
   b the difference between *dominant* and *recessive* alleles.

5 Suggest why fruit flies make good animals for studying genetics.

Human genetics

At the end of this topic you should be able to:

- describe in outline how DNA, RNA and endoplasmic reticulum are involved in the production of proteins from amino acids
- describe the inheritance of albinism, sickle cell anaemia and Huntington's disease
- interpret information from family trees/pedigree diagrams.

LINK

There are lots of links for you to follow here. For example, look up the structure of cells in 1.2 and protein structure in 2.1.

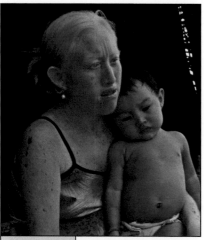

Figure 9.5.1 An albino Kuna Indian woman and her normally pigmented child. The Kuna Indians live along the eastern Caribbean coast of Panama. They have the highest percentage of people with albinism in the World

Genetics is the study of genes and inheritance. Each nucleus in a human cell contains 46 chromosomes with 30 000 genes. A gene is a length of DNA that codes for a specific protein molecule. Each gene is always located in the same place on one of the chromosomes. The nucleus contains the chromosomes within a cell. Proteins are formed as follows:

- Many, short-lived copies of genes are made within the nucleus using **ribonucleic acid** molecules (RNA).
- RNA leaves the nucleus through pores in the **nuclear membrane**.
- In the cytoplasm a RNA molecule attaches to **ribosomes** on the **endoplasmic reticulum**.
- Each ribosome uses a molecule of RNA as a template to assemble amino acids in the required order to make a specific protein, for example insulin.

Mutations affect the way genes code for proteins. In some cases, there is so much change to the gene that it does not code for any protein at all. In others, the change to the DNA is quite small and a protein is produced but it functions in a different way. We have learnt much about the way proteins work in our cells from genetic disorders caused by mutations which are inherited and run in families.

Albinism

People with albinism cannot make the pigment melanin, which is in the skin and the iris of the eye. Several enzymes are needed to make this pigment. It is the mutation in a gene that codes for one of these enzymes that is the cause of the condition. People who are albino are homozygous recessive, **aa**. People who are homozygous dominant, **AA**, or heterozygous, **Aa**, have a normal allele that codes for the enzyme and so melanin is produced. This means that they have normal pigmentation.

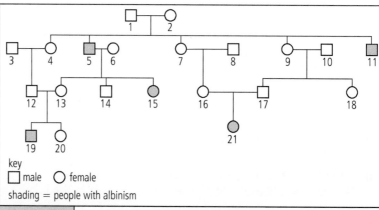

key
□ male ○ female
shading = people with albinism

Figure 9.5.2 Several people in this family have albinism

Sickle cell anaemia (SCA)

The top picture (in Figure 9.5.3) shows normal red blood cells. The blood in the lower picture is from a person with **sickle cell anaemia**. These red blood cells contain abnormal haemoglobin, which makes it difficult for the red blood cells to carry oxygen. SCA is common in West and East Africa, in parts of Asia and in North and South America, including the Caribbean. People who have the genotype **ss** have the symptoms of the disorder. People who are heterozygous, **Ss**, have both the normal and abnormal forms of haemoglobin. They rarely have a problem with transport of oxygen but they are resistant to **malaria**. The allele is common among people from areas where malaria is common.

Huntington's disease

Around the shores of Lake Maracaibo in Venezuela there is a very high proportion of people with **Huntington's disease**. This is a **degenerative disease** that affects the nervous system in later life. It is caused by a dominant allele that interferes with how neurones function. Investigators researched the family trees of these people. They found that they had a common ancestor, Maria Concepción Soto, who moved to the area in the 19th century. She has over 20 000 descendants. Dominant disorders mean that a person only needs one allele to have the disease – not two as with albinism and SCA.

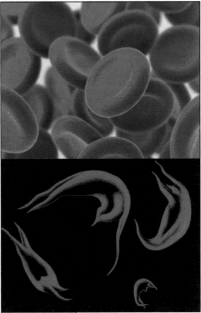

Figure 9.5.3 | Normal and sickle-shaped red blood cells

LINK

There is more information about malaria in 10.6 and you can find out about the inheritance of SCA by writing a genetic diagram in question 5 on the CD.

DID YOU KNOW?

Tongue rolling is often given as an example of a feature that is inherited in a similar way to albinism. It is not! Scientists have produced evidence that shows it is a feature that can be learned and not inherited. Human eye colour is a feature that does not follow the rules of monohybrid inheritance as often given in text books.

SUMMARY QUESTIONS

1 State the health risks of being very fair skinned or an albino.

2 Use the three genetic conditions described here to distinguish between the following pairs of terms: *gene* and *allele*, *genotype* and *phenotype*, *homozygous* and *heterozygous*, *dominant* and *recessive*.

3 State the genotype of the Kuna woman and her child in the photograph. Suggest the two possible genotypes of the child's father.

4 a State the genotypes of the people in the family tree (if you cannot be absolutely sure whether someone's genotype is homozygous dominant or heterozygous, then you can write A- where the dash stands for a dominant allele **or** a recessive allele).

  b What is the probability that the next child of 16 and 17 will have albinism? Draw a genetic diagram to explain your answer.

KEY POINTS

1 Genes are made of DNA and code for the assembly of amino acids to make proteins.

2 Genes determine the sequence of amino acids in each protein. If the sequence changes then the protein does not function or functions in a different way.

3 Albinism is the result of a mutation in one of the genes for the production of skin pigment.

4 Albinism and SCA are recessive conditions and are present from birth; Huntington's disease is a dominant mutation and affects people in later life.

Sex inheritance and sex linkage

At the end of this topic you should be able to:

- describe the inheritance of sex based on the X and Y chromosomes
- explain what is meant by the term *sex linkage*
- state that haemophilia and colour blindness are examples of sex linkage
- use genetic diagrams to explain sex linkage.

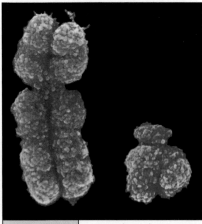

Figure 9.6.1 | An X and a Y chromosome viewed in an electron microscope

EXAM TIP

The diagram shows only the inheritance of the sex chromosomes, X and Y. Do not forget that each of the gametes (egg and sperm) contain 22 other chromosomes to give the haploid number of 23.

Sex inheritance

Your chromosomes determine whether you are male or female. Humans have 46 chromosomes that occur in 23 pairs. Images of the 46 chromosomes in females can all be matched into pairs. Males have two chromosomes that are not alike. They are called the X and Y chromosomes. Females have two X chromosomes and males have an X chromosome and a Y chromosome.

The diagram shows how the X and Y chromosomes in the gametes determine the sex of individuals.

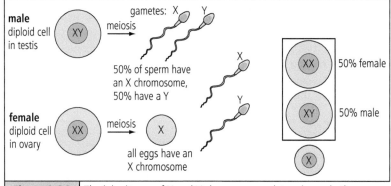

Figure 9.6.2 | The inheritance of X and Y chromosomes determines whether we are male or female

All egg cells contain an X chromosome. Half of the sperm contain an X chromosome and half of the sperm contain a Y chromosome. At fertilisation an egg may fuse with either an X-bearing sperm or a Y-bearing sperm. There is an equal chance of the zygote inheriting XX or XY and the child being female or male because there are equal numbers of X-bearing sperm and Y-bearing sperm.

The Y chromosome has far fewer genes than the X chromosome. The Y chromosome has a gene that stimulates the development of testes in the embryo. If this gene is not present or if it has mutated then the body that develops is female.

Sex linkage

Genes located on the X chromosome are sex linked.

The X chromosome is a large chromosome with many genes. Most have nothing to do with determining gender. There are genes involved with controlling vision and blood clotting. Males only have one copy of the genes that are on X chromosomes; if any of them are recessive then the effect will be seen. Because women have two X chromosomes they are less affected by sex-linked recessive alleles and this is why sex-linked conditions are more common in boys than in girls. Two examples are discussed here.

Colour blindness

One of the genes on the X chromosome controls the ability to see red and green colours. In colour blindness, there is a mutant allele of this gene which does not produce a protein necessary for colour vision. The allele is recessive, so any girl or woman who is heterozygous, **Rr**, has normal colour vision. Males only have one X chromosome, so if they have inherited the allele **r** they will be colour blind.

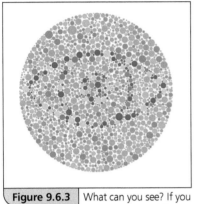

Figure 9.6.3	What can you see? If you cannot see something familiar then you must have red-green colour blindness

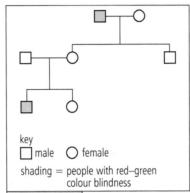

key
☐ male   ◯ female
shading = people with red–green colour blindness

Figure 9.6.4	Note that the boy who is colour blind has parents who both have normal vision

Father's genotype X^RY × X^RX^r *Mother's genotype*

Gametes $(X^R), (Y)$ + $(X^R), (X^r)$

		Female gametes	
		X^R	X^r
Male gametes	X^R	X^RX^R	X^RX^r
	Y	X^RY	X^rY

Children's genotypes X^RX^R X^RX^r X^RY X^rY

Children's phenotypes

| Girl with normal colour vision | Girl who has normal vision, but is a carrier | Boy with normal colour vision | Boy with red–green colour blindness |

Haemophilia

Haemophilia is a disease in which the blood clots very slowly. It is a result of a mutation of the gene that codes for a blood clotting protein that is on the X chromosome. The mutant allele is recessive. A **carrier** of haemophilia is a woman who has the recessive allele, **h**. Her blood clots normally because she also has the dominant allele, **H**. It is rare for a woman to have haemophilia. This is because she would have to inherit the mutant allele from her father as well as from her mother. Historically, many haemophiliac men did not live long enough to have children. Successful treatment is now available, so a haemophiliac man may have a daughter with the genotype **HH**.

SUMMARY QUESTIONS

1 The ratio of males to females is about 1 : 1 with slightly more females than males in the population. Draw a genetic diagram to show why the ratio is 1 : 1 and suggest why there are slightly more females.

2 What is the probability of a woman who is a carrier of haemophilia having a child with the disease if her husband has normal blood clotting time? Draw a genetic diagram to explain your answer.

3 None of the conditions described in 9.5 are sex linked. How can you tell the difference between a genetic condition that is sex linked and one that isn't?

LINK

Now try question 2 on page 135 to test your understanding of sex linkage.

Genetic engineering

At the end of this topic you should be able to:

- define the term *genetic engineering*
- explain the principles behind the process of genetic modification of organisms
- discuss the advantages and disadvantages of genetic engineering
- explain how medicines, such as insulin, are produced by genetic modification of bacteria and mammalian cells.

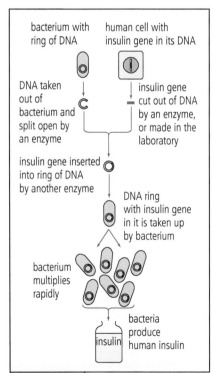

bacterium with ring of DNA

human cell with insulin gene in its DNA

DNA taken out of bacterium and split open by an enzyme

insulin gene cut out of DNA by an enzyme, or made in the laboratory

insulin gene inserted into ring of DNA by another enzyme

DNA ring with insulin gene in it is taken up by bacterium

bacterium multiplies rapidly

bacteria produce human insulin

insulin

Figure 9.7.1 This process was carried out in the 1970s to make genetically modified bacteria that could produce human insulin

Genetic engineering involves moving genes from one organism to another. Genes can be transferred from one species to a completely different species, such as from bacteria to plants and from an individual of one species to another individual of the same species. This can be done by simply firing a gene into a cell or the gene can be placed into a **vector** that 'carries' it into a cell. Examples of vectors are viruses and small loops of DNA known as plasmids. DNA produced by joining up DNA from two or more different organisms is called **recombinant DNA**. Organisms containing recombinant DNA have been **genetically modified** (GM).

Insulin

All people with diabetes used to be treated with insulin obtained from pigs and cattle that were slaughtered for the meat trade. There was a concern that people with diabetes might get diseases from using animal-derived insulin and that the demand for insulin would exceed supply. In the 1970s, scientists identified the gene that codes for insulin in humans. They transferred the piece of DNA (gene) responsible for coding insulin to bacteria. Figure 9.7.1 shows how this is done. Bacteria with recombinant DNA divide to produce many more bacteria. The insulin-producing bacteria are given the nutrients and conditions they need to produce human insulin.

Human insulin produced like this became available in 1982. The advantages of producing insulin this way are:

- no risk of diseases from animals
- a reliable and consistent supply, not dependent on the meat trade
- supply can be increased to meet the huge global demand for insulin (see 10.2)
- the structure of the insulin molecule can be modified so it is more effective for different groups of people with diabetes.

Other medicines

Many other medicines and chemicals for research into human diseases are made using genetically modified bacteria. However, bacteria are not always very good at producing human proteins, so yeasts and certain mammalian cells are also modified in similar ways for industrial production of medicines and other substances.

Examples of these medicines are:

- a protein that prevents thrombin from forming blood clots (see 4.5)
- a drug to treat emphysema (see 3.5)
- vaccines for influenza (see 10.8) and for protection from cervical cancer (see 8.2)
- factor 8 to treat haemophiliacs (see 9.6).

Gene therapy

Genetic engineering is also used in **gene therapy**. This involves putting a dominant allele into cells which then divide within the body. Gene therapy has been used to treat forms of leukaemia and a disorder of the retina. There are medical trials in progress to use gene therapy to treat or cure other genetic disorders, such as **cystic fibrosis**.

Genetic modification

Many crops are genetically modified. Examples of features that have been put into crops, such as soya, cotton, maize and tobacco, are:

- herbicide resistance, so weed killers can be used while the crop is growing
- pest resistance, so insect pests are killed when they eat the crop
- drought resistance, so crops will grow where there is little rainfall
- improved nutritional qualities, such as increasing the vitamin A content of rice to reduce the number of children with blindness (see 2.2).

Figure 9.7.2 Many people are concerned about the effects on human health of herbicides that are sprayed on herbicide-resistant crops, such as this maize

Domesticated animals have also been genetically modified – for example, sheep and goats that produce human proteins in their milk and a type of fish that grows very quickly.

Advantages and disadvantages

The advantages of genetic modification are:

- it is much faster than using traditional methods, such as selective breeding
- it is possible to move genes from one species to another, which is not possible by other methods
- chemicals available in tiny quantities can be produced in much larger quantities – for example, a genetically modified (GM) goat can produce the same quantity of a human plasma protein in its milk in a year as can be collected from 90 000 blood donations.

The disadvantages are:

- herbicide resistance could pass from crops to weeds so that they become 'superweeds' that farmers cannot control
- GM microbes could escape from laboratories and factories and become dangerous
- GM technology gives a huge advantage to the companies that develop and market GM crops – this discriminates against small farmers who cannot afford it
- consumers are resistant to GM foods because of the fear of the new and the unknown.

KEY POINTS

1 Genetic engineering is the process of moving genetic material from one organism and putting it in another.

2 This may happen by taking a gene from one species and placing it into another as happened with the production of human insulin in bacteria.

3 Genes are cut from DNA or they are produced from RNA. They are inserted into vectors, such as plasmids, that carry the gene into bacteria.

4 GM bacteria, yeasts and mammalian cells produce useful chemicals such as insulin.

5 GM crops and livestock with different features are available or in development.

6 There are advantages and disadvantages of genetic engineering.

SUMMARY QUESTIONS

1 Define the following terms: *genetic engineering*, *vector* and *plasmid*.

2 Explain how human insulin is made by genetic engineering.

3 Some people are very much against genetic engineering. Find out the reasons for this.

4 Discuss the advantages and disadvantages of genetic engineering.

UNIT 9: Multiple-choice questions

1 If an organism possesses two different alleles of a gene, it is said to be:

  a dominant

  b heterozygous

  c homozygous

  d recessive.

2 Which of the following is NOT a source of variation in humans?

  a Chromosome mutation

  b Fusion of gametes at fertilisation

  c Gene mutation

  d Mitosis

3 How many chromosomes are present in a liver cell and a gamete of a human?

	Liver cell	Gamete
a	46	46
b	23	23
c	46	23
d	23	46

4 A couple discover that they are both carriers of albinism. What is the probability that their first child will have albinism?

  a 0%

  b 25%

  c 50%

  d 100%

5 A man has normal colour vision. His wife does not have colour blindness but her father is colour blind. What is the probability that their sons will be colour blind?

  a 25%

  b 50%

  c 75%

  d 100%

Further practice questions and examples can be found on the accompanying CD.

UNIT 9: Short answer questions

1 Each female Indian muntjac deer has a diploid number of 6. Figure 1 shows the chromosomes of this species, labelled A to F, in a cell dividing by mitosis.

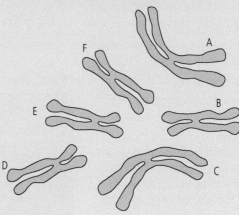

Figure 1

  a i   Use the letters to identify the homologous pairs of chromosomes. *(1)*

     ii Describe in outline what will happen to the chromosomes AFTER the stage visible in Figure 1. *(3)*

     iii State the number of chromosomes in the gametes of female Indian muntjac deer. *(1)*

  b Figure 2 shows a diploid cell with four chromosomes. Copy and complete the diagram in Figure 2 to show the possible combinations of chromosomes in the gametes of this organism.

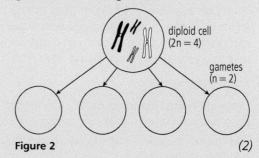

diploid cell (2n = 4)

gametes (n = 2)

Figure 2   *(2)*

c Copy and complete the table to compare mitosis and meiosis in humans.

Feature	Mitosis	Meiosis
Number of divisions of the nucleus	1	
Pairing of homologous chromosomes	No	
Genotypes of daughter nuclei		All are different
Role in humans		Production of gametes

(4)

A gene in fruit flies controls eye colour. The allele **R** gives red eyes and the allele **r** gives purple eyes. A researcher crossed homozygous red-eyed flies with homozygous purple-eyed flies (cross 1).

d State the genotypes of the fruit flies used in cross 1. (1)

The offspring of cross 1 were allowed to interbreed (cross 2). Further crosses (3 and 4) were carried out with the offspring of cross 2.

Cross		Phenotype of the fruit flies		Ratio of red-eyed flies to purple-eyed flies
		Red eyes	Purple eyes	
1	red-eyed × purple-eyed	✓	✗	1:0
2	red-eyed × red-eyed			
3	red-eyed × purple-eyed	✓	✓	
4	purple-eyed × purple-eyed			

e Complete the table above by indicating
- the type of flies present in the offspring with a tick (✓) or a cross (✗)
- the ratio of red-eyed to purple-eyed flies. (3)

Total 15 marks

2 a In humans the ratio of males to females at birth is about 1 : 1.

Use a genetic diagram to show how the inheritance of the sex chromosomes, X and Y, is responsible for this. (4)

A gene on the X chromosome codes for a blood clotting factor known as factor 8. People without factor 8 have the disease haemophilia.

b Explain the dangers to health for someone who has haemophilia. (2)

Aleksei, the last Tsarevitch of Russia, had haemophilia which he inherited from his great grandmother Queen Victoria. Figure 3 is part of his family tree.

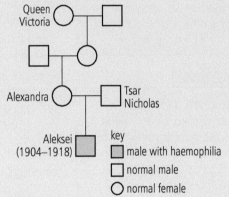

Figure 3

c Use genetic diagrams to help explain the following:
  i Aleksei inherited haemophilia even though his father and grandfather did not have the disease.
  ii A boy can inherit haemophilia from his grandfather but never from his father.
  iii There are very few women with haemophilia. (8)

d In a third of cases of haemophilia there is no known family history. Suggest an explanation for this. (1)

Total 15 marks

Further short answer questions can be found on the CD.

LINK

See 3.1 to remind yourself about the structure of the airways and 3.2 to revise the factors that influence the rate of breathing.

Definitions

In 1946, the World Health Organization (WHO) defined health as:

a state of complete physical, mental and social well-being and not merely the absence of disease and infirmity.

Physical health refers to the proper functioning of all the systems of the body. If we are in good physical health we are able to live an active life without any problems.

Mental health refers to the functioning of the mind. People who have good mental health are generally free of disorders, such as anxiety or depression, and cope adequately with the stresses and strains of life.

Social health refers to the way we interact with others. People with good social health have good relationships with family, friends, work or school colleagues and cope well when meeting strangers.

Good health is the sum of all these aspects and is not just the absence of disease.

Disease is any change from normal health where part of the body is not functioning efficiently. Diseases give certain **symptoms** that we feel and can report to medical professionals. They look for certain **signs** that indicate which disease we may have. Doctors may also carry out diagnostic tests to identify the disease. There are many causes of disease, including the invasion of the body by disease-causing organisms or **pathogens**.

Classification of disease

Diseases are classified in a variety of different ways. Two large categories of disease are:

- **communicable diseases** – diseases caused by pathogens and often known as infectious diseases
- **non-communicable diseases** – diseases **not** caused by organisms. There are many different types, some of which are given in the table below.

Category of disease	Cause	Example
Communicable (infectious)	Pathogen (disease-causing organism)	Malaria caused by the protozoan *Plasmodium* (see 10.7)
Non-communicable (non-infectious)		
Cancer	Various causes, e.g. exposure to tobacco smoke, viruses and some environmental pollutants	Cervical cancer (see 8.2)
Degenerative	A gradual decline in bodily functions	Coronary heart disease (see 4.5)
Nutritional deficiency	A lack of a nutrient or nutrients in the diet	Rickets (deficiency of vitamin D) (see 2.2)
Inherited (genetic)	A mutant allele	Sickle cell anaemia (see 9.5)

Asthma

Asthma is a very common condition and the number of people with it has increased in recent years. Asthma is a disease with many causes. Asthma symptoms can be:

- breathlessness – often gasping for breath and having difficulty breathing out
- a tight chest
- wheezing
- coughing, particularly in the evening and early morning.

An asthmatic 'attack' occurs when these symptoms are at their worst. People can often identify what triggers these attacks.

When diagnosing asthma a doctor would measure the forced vital capacity (see 3.1) and use a peak flow meter to measure the expiratory flow rate to see how quickly air is breathed out.

The lining of the respiratory tract is irritated by a variety of factors:

- smoke, for example from cigarettes
- **allergens**, such as dust mites
- feeling anxious
- exercise
- fungal spores.

People may inherit a susceptibility to develop asthma. It is a debilitating disease and if not treated may be fatal.

During an asthmatic attack muscles in the walls of the bronchi and bronchioles are stimulated to contract. The mucus-secreting cells in the lining become more active and secrete more mucus into the airways. This makes breathing very difficult as the resistance to air flow in and out of the lungs increases.

- People can avoid asthmatic attacks if they know what triggers them. Sometimes this is not possible, for example when fungal spores are brought in the wind to the Caribbean. If they need treatment people can take **steroid** drugs by inhaler.

Figure 10.1.1 A peak flow meter

Figure 10.1.2 This inhaler contains the drug salbutamol that relaxes the walls of the airways

KEY POINTS

1 Good health is defined as physical, mental and social well-being. Disease is the poor functioning of the body as a result of a number of different causes.
2 Diseases are classified into many different categories. Two important categories are communicable (infectious) and non-communicable.
3 Asthma is a non-communicable disease that results in contraction and inflammation of the airways making it difficult to breathe.

SUMMARY QUESTIONS

1 Write definitions of good health, disease and signs and symptoms of disease.
2 Make a table to show the differences between communicable and non-communicable diseases.
3 Explain the effects of asthma.
4 Make a poster for a school or health clinic to show the dangers of asthma.

Chronic diseases

At the end of this topic you should be able to:

- define the term *chronic*
- discuss the causes of obesity, diabetes types I and II and cardiovascular diseases
- discuss the importance of diet and exercise in maintaining good health
- discuss the impact of chronic diseases on populations.

LINK

Obesity is described in 2.3, lung cancer in 3.5. Chronic bronchitis and smoking was considered in 3.5.

Humans now live much longer. The life expectancy has increased considerably since 1900 as you can see in question 5 of the short answer questions on the CD. This means that we are more susceptible to long-term or **chronic** diseases. These are **degenerative diseases**, such as arthritis, that get worse with age.

STUDY FOCUS

Arthritis is a disease of the joints. Chronic diseases are not all diseases of old age. As we saw in 8.2, young people are particularly at risk of cervical and testicular cancer.

People who are overweight or obese are at risk of a variety of chronic conditions:

- arthritis
- **diabetes type II**
- high blood pressure and coronary heart disease
- cancers of the colon, rectum, prostate gland in men and uterus, cervix and breast in women
- hernias, varicose veins and **gall stones**.

Diabetes

Diabetes mellitus (most often just called diabetes) occurs when the body stops producing insulin or the target cells stop responding to it. People with diabetes cannot control the concentration of glucose in their blood. The symptoms are:

- urinating a lot, especially at night and feeling very thirsty
- increased appetite and eating more
- extreme tiredness and weight loss with loss of muscle tissue
- itchiness around the vagina or penis
- recurring infections of the fungal disease thrush – the growth of this yeast-like fungus is promoted by glucose in the urine
- blurred vision caused by the lenses in the eyes becoming very dry.

A medical professional will look for **signs** of diabetes. One sign is glucose in the urine. Test strips are used to detect glucose. A diagnosis can be confirmed by carrying out a glucose tolerance test – see question **1** page 90.

Diabetes type I usually starts in childhood or adolescence. The cells that make insulin in the pancreas are often destroyed so no insulin is produced at all. Treatment involves injecting insulin.

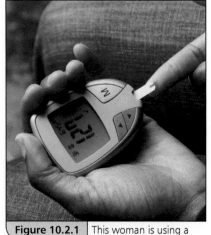

Figure 10.2.1 This woman is using a glucose biosensor to measure the glucose concentration of her blood

Diabetes type II usually starts later in life. There is a very high risk of developing this form of diabetes if there is genetic predisposition, a diet high in fat and refined sugar and not enough fibre. Obesity, high blood pressure and high blood cholesterol concentration are also factors that increase the risk of developing this disease.

Treatment may not involve taking insulin until the disease has progressed a lot. Instead, careful diet and exercise may be sufficient.

Many complications follow diabetes, for example damage to the retina that can lead to blindness.

A study in six Latin American countries found that people who had lived with diabetes for 20 years suffered from damage to the retina, nervous system and kidneys. Some had become blind and some had had amputations.

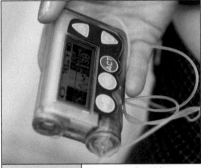

Figure 10.2.2 Some people with diabetes use pumps like this one to deliver insulin as and when they need it

Prevention and control of chronic diseases

Most chronic diseases cannot be cured but they can be treated to reduce the symptoms. The cost of medical services and the drugs involved for treating these conditions are often very high and represent a huge proportion of health budgets in most countries. It is much better to prevent these diseases developing in the first place. Eating a balanced diet, taking exercise, not smoking and drinking alcohol in moderation (if at all) are simple ways in which people can avoid developing many of these chronic diseases.

A balanced diet provides all the nutrients needed for good health and the prevention of deficiency diseases. It also means that people do not have more energy in their diet than they expend in daily activities. This reduces the risk of storing excess fat and developing obesity.

Figure 10.2.3 This man is injecting himself with insulin to control his diabetes – a common consequence of being overweight or obese

LINK

See 8.5 for information about the protective role of folic acid.

There are many health benefits of exercise. The circulatory system, skeletal system and muscle system are improved and often people's mental health improves as well because they feel better about themselves.

SUMMARY QUESTIONS

1 Define the terms *chronic* and *degenerative* as applied to diseases.

2 Make a table to show the causes, signs and symptoms, treatment and methods of prevention for the chronic diseases mentioned in this topic.

3 Discuss the impact of chronic diseases in the Caribbean.

4 Discuss the benefits of eating a balanced diet and taking regular exercise on health.

5 What steps can health authorities and governments take to reduce the prevalence of chronic diseases?

KEY POINTS

1 Chronic diseases are long-term diseases.

2 Cancers and degenerative diseases, such as arthritis and coronary heart disease, are chronic diseases.

3 Type II diabetes is an increasing health problem throughout the world as the prevalence of obesity increases.

4 A balanced diet and plenty of exercise reduces the chances of developing chronic diseases, such as heart disease and diabetes type II.

At the end of this topic you should be able to:

- define the term *infectious disease*
- for each of seven infectious diseases, state the causative agent, method of transmission, the signs and symptoms, treatment and methods of control.

Infectious (or communicable) diseases are caused by pathogens that invade the body. Many of them are viruses and bacteria, but some protozoans, worms and fungi are also pathogenic.

Pathogens enter the body through a variety of routes. **Infectious diseases** can be classified into those that enter the digestive system in food and water, the respiratory system in the air, the reproductive system during sexual activity and the blood by insects that puncture the skin. Some pathogens live on the skin and do not enter the body. You can find examples of diseases caused by pathogens that enter by all these routes on the next few pages.

Type of pathogen	Disease	Method of transmission	Signs and symptoms	Treatment
Virus	Influenza	Air droplets	Chills, fever, sore throat, muscle pain, headache, coughing, and fatigue	Bed rest, high fluid intake, paracetamol for muscle pain, Antiviral drugs
Virus or bacterium	Acute bronchitis	Air droplets	Coughing, shortness of breath, chest pain	Bed rest, **antibiotics** should only be used if bacteria are in sputum
Virus or bacterium	Pneumonia	Air droplets; Pathogens live in the nose and may spread to the lungs as a consequence of another disease	Coughing, chest pain, fever, breathing difficulty	Bed rest, high fluid intake, painkillers, antibiotics for bacterial form and Antiviral drugs for viral form
Bacterium	**Tuberculosis** (TB)	Air droplets	Persistent coughing that brings up **phlegm** (which may be bloody), breathlessness, lack of appetite and weight loss, a high temperature, night sweats, fatigue	Several antibiotics and other drugs often taken for up to six months or more
Fungus	**Ringworm** (tinea)	Direct skin contact with infected person or with shared towels, flannels, bedding, hair brushes, etc.	Ring-like red rash on the skin	Antifungal creams (tablets are taken if it is on the scalp)
Bacterium	Typhoid	Faecal contamination of drinking water or food	Fever, headache, cough, delirium, painful abdomen	**Oral rehydration therapy**, antibiotics
Bacterium	Cholera	Faecal contamination of drinking water or food	Lots of watery diarrhoea leading to rapid dehydration	Oral rehydration therapy, antibiotics

Gastroenteritis is inflammation of the stomach and/or intestine that occurs in several infectious diseases, such as **cholera** and typhoid, and in non-infectious disorders, such as food intolerance.

Diarrhoea is one of the main symptoms of gastroenteritis.

Methods of prevention and control

We can control infectious diseases if we can break the transmission between hosts.

Diseases that are transmitted through the air can be controlled by advising people to cover the mouth and nose when coughing or sneezing. Good ventilation in the home and public places is also effective. People who sleep close together are at special risk of becoming infected with TB.

Ringworm and other diseases passed by direct contact can be controlled by avoiding sharing towels and taking suitable precautions in public places, such as swimming pools.

Waterborne diseases can be controlled by ensuring there is a good sanitation system that keeps human wastes separate from drinking water. In many countries, sewage is carried by a drainage system to sewage works (see 11.3 and 11.4). The water supply is treated to kill potential pathogens and is distributed in a network of pipes.

STUDY FOCUS

Influenza, bronchitis and pneumonia are acute infections of the respiratory system because they have a sudden onset and do not usually last very long. Contrast with chronic bronchitis described in 3.5.

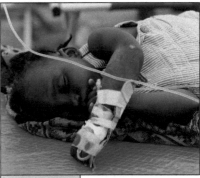

Figure 10.3.1 Treatment for a victim of the cholera epidemic in Haiti in 2010. For serious cases intravenous rehydration is given using lactated Ringer's solution which contains lactic acid and salts (mostly sodium chloride)

LINK

See 2.2 for more about diarrhoea. See 10.1 for categories of disease. Diseases may be categorised according to the part of the body affected – gastroenteritis is a category that includes those diseases that cause inflammation of the stomach and intestines.

KEY POINTS

1. Infectious diseases are caused by pathogens and are transmitted when the pathogen passes from an infected person to an uninfected person.

2. Details of seven infectious diseases are shown in the table opposite.

3. Gastroenteritis is the category of disease that includes all those (including infectious diseases) that cause inflammation of the digestive system.

SUMMARY QUESTIONS

1. Describe the key features of infectious diseases.

2. Outline the different ways in which pathogens enter the body.

3. State the pathogens and describe the methods of transmission of influenza, acute bronchitis, pneumonia, TB, ringworm, typhoid and cholera.

4. What is gastroenteritis?

5. How can infectious diseases be controlled?

STUDY FOCUS

Some people are carriers of infectious diseases. They transmit the pathogen without having any symptoms. This is a different use of the word carrier to that for **inherited diseases**. See 9.6 and the glossary.

Sexually transmitted infections

At the end of this topic you should be able to:

- state four examples of *sexually transmitted infections (STIs)*

- state the causative agent, the signs and symptoms and treatment of genital herpes, gonorrhoea, syphilis and HIV/AIDS

- explain how STIs can be controlled.

The pathogens that cause sexually-transmitted infections (STIs) pass from one person to another during sexual activity.

Pathogen	Disease	Signs and symptoms		Treatment
		Males	**Females**	
Virus	**Genital herpes**	Painful sores on penis and scrotum	Painful sores and blisters around genitals	(No cure) Antiviral drugs taken orally and applied as creams
Virus	**HIV/AIDS**	No symptoms for some time; collapse of immune system leading to cancers and variety of infectious diseases		(No cure) Antiviral drugs for HIV; antibiotics for secondary bacterial infections
Bacterium	**Gonorrhoea**	Pain when urinating Yellow discharge from penis	There are unlikely to be any symptoms	Antibiotics
Bacterium	**Syphilis**	Sores on the genitals	Sores on the genitals	Antibiotics

The pathogens in the table above cannot survive for very long outside the human body, which explains why they are transmitted from person to person during intimate contact.

STIs are particularly dangerous for pregnant women. The pathogens can infect the foetus during pregnancy and this increases the chances of miscarriage. Babies may become infected during birth. The eyes are particularly at risk of infection with the bacteria (see Figure 10.4.1). If left untreated the disease can lead to serious blood or joint infections and meningitis in the baby.

Syphilis also increases chances of having a miscarriage, stillbirth or premature birth. Some babies show a variety of symptoms at or just after birth. Left untreated these may develop into serious health problems later in life, especially with poor eyesight, poor mental health and weak bones and teeth.

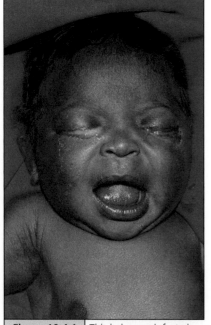

Figure 10.4.1 This baby was infected with gonorrhoea bacteria as it passed through the vagina during birth. The eyes are oozing pus as they are infected by the bacteria. If left untreated, this baby would go blind

LINK

There is more about HIV/AIDS in 10.5.

Prevention and control

STIs are transmitted when an infected person has sex with an uninfected person. This is more likely to happen when people have more than one sexual partner. The spread of STIs can be prevented if people change their sexual behaviour. Health awareness campaigns are organised by government health departments, non-governmental agencies, schools and charities.

Contact tracing is an important part of control. Medical personnel interview people who attend STI clinics for treatment to find out who they may have infected. All sexual contacts should be screened and if found to be infected given appropriate treatment.

Impact of disease

The impact of diseases on a population is recorded in a number of ways. There are many diseases that have a quick onset and then people recover quite quickly. Influenza is a disease like this. The **incidence** of influenza is the number of people who have it within a certain time period, for example a week, month or year. Other diseases, such as HIV/AIDS and diabetes last a long time – often a lifetime. In this case it is the **prevalence** that is often recorded as well as the number of new cases. This is the number of people living with the disease over a suitable period, usually a year. **Mortality** refers to the number of deaths and the mortality rate is the number of deaths over a certain time period, often a year.

SUMMARY QUESTIONS

1 Describe the effect of the following diseases on the body: genital herpes, gonorrhoea and syphilis.

2 Describe the likely effects on a foetus and or baby if its mother has an STI.

3 Explain how the spread of STIs can be controlled.

4 Explain the following terms that are used to measure the impact of disease on the human population: *prevalence*, *incidence* and *mortality*.

5 Explain how you might compare the impact of disease on different countries, such as Cuba, Jamaica and Haiti.

EXAM TIP

You will see these three ways of measuring the impact of disease used throughout this unit. They are also used in examination questions; see 10.12 and pages 160–161 for examples.

HIV/AIDS

At the end of this topic you should be able to:

- state that HIV is the causative agent of AIDS
- explain how HIV is transmitted
- explain the difference between HIV and AIDS
- describe the effect of HIV/AIDS on the body and how it is treated
- explain how the spread of HIV can be controlled.

Figure 10.5.1 Across the world there are many children like these who have been orphaned by HIV/AIDS

DID YOU KNOW?

The infectious diseases that infect people with HIV are known as **opportunistic infections**. TB is one of the most common and infects a large proportion of people who have HIV/AIDS.

The impact of HIV/AIDS

In 1982, doctors in North America and in Africa began to see patients with rare conditions, especially a rare cancer and a rare form of pneumonia. Scientists discovered that these conditions were the result of immune systems that did not function efficiently. This condition was called **acquired immunodeficiency syndrome** or AIDS. The agent that caused this collapse in the immune system is a virus – **human immunodeficiency virus** or HIV. AIDS is not a single disease, like those listed in 10.2 to 10.4, it is a syndrome. This means it is a collection of different diseases, some cancers and some infectious diseases. People who have AIDS do not always have the same collection of diseases. The condition is generally known as HIV/AIDS. Since the early 1980s about 30 million people have died of AIDS.

Since the 1980s the number of people with HIV/AIDS has increased steeply and it occurs all over the world. Diseases that affect large areas of the world are known as pandemics. Regions with the largest proportion of the population with HIV/AIDS are sub-Saharan Africa and the Caribbean (see 10.12).

Transmission of HIV

HIV does not survive for long outside the human body. It is passed from an infected person to an uninfected person in body fluids:

- in semen and vaginal fluids during unprotected (unsafe) sexual intercourse
- in blood if there is blood-to-blood contact between two people. For example, intravenous drug users sharing needles to inject drugs, such as heroin, and by 'needle stick' accidents in hospitals, if surgical instruments are not sterilised thoroughly
- in blood that is used in transfusion, if it is not heat treated to kill HIV
- from mother to baby during birth and in breast milk.

Treatment of HIV/AIDS

Early in the HIV/AIDS pandemic, doctors could do little to treat the condition. Now there are Antiviral drugs to control the spread of HIV in the body. Other drugs, such as antibiotics, control infections caused by fungi and bacteria. The life expectancy for people living with HIV/AIDS has increased. Some doctors think that people who are newly infected now will live a normal life span. There is still no cure for the condition. Research work on developing a vaccine has yet to prove successful (as of 2013).

When HIV enters the body it infects certain types of lymphocyte. The genetic material of the virus is in the form of RNA. An enzyme in the virus uses the RNA to make DNA. This DNA combines with the DNA in the chromosomes of the host cells. Later the host makes many new virus particles by using this DNA to make many RNA copies. The lymphocyte also makes the protein coats and assembles the new virus particles. These virus particles 'bud' off from the surface to infect other cells.

Anti-retroviral drugs used to treat HIV interfere with how the genetic material of the virus is copied from RNA to DNA shortly after infection of the host cells. However, these drugs have side effects, such as **nausea**, fever, diarrhoea, skin rashes and mood swings.

Treatment of mothers who test positive for HIV has reduced the transmission of the virus to babies. If this is not done, babies are often born with the infection and need a lifetime of treatment.

Controlling the spread of HIV

The only effective way to control the spread of HIV is to use condoms during sex. Other barrier methods of contraception, such as the diaphragm, are not effective as there is still contact between semen and vaginal fluids. There are many programmes to try to reduce the spread of HIV and the infection rate appears to have peaked and may be decreasing.

Avoiding sexual intercourse with infected people is difficult since they may have no symptoms – sometimes for about ten years following the initial infection. Tests for HIV infection are readily available. Most of these tests detect the protein antibodies produced by lymphocytes to protect against HIV. These antibody tests cannot be taken immediately after someone suspects that they might be infected since it takes time for the antibodies to HIV to appear in the blood (see 10.8). Some tests detect HIV itself.

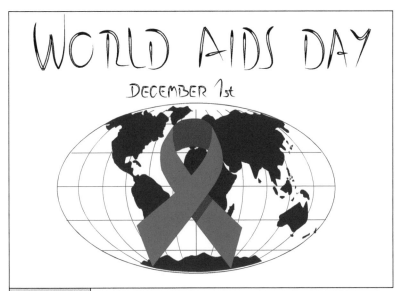

Figure 10.5.3 World Aids Day, which is on 1 December each year, maintains the profile of HIV/AIDS

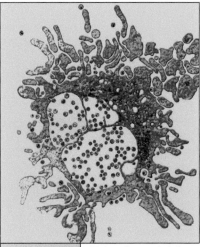

Figure 10.5.2 This lymphocyte is full of HIV particles that are released to infect many other lymphocytes

KEY POINTS

1 HIV causes a decrease in the number of lymphocytes so those infected are at high risk of opportunistic infections, such as TB, and cancers.

2 HIV is transmitted through unprotected sex, blood-to-blood contact, breastfeeding and at birth.

3 Anti-retroviral drugs are used to treat HIV.

4 Preventing the spread of HIV is by health awareness campaigns, especially promoting the use of condoms.

SUMMARY QUESTIONS

1 Distinguish between HIV and AIDS.

2 Describe three different ways in which HIV is transmitted.

3 Explain the steps that can be taken to reduce the number of new cases of HIV infection.

EXAM TIP

The term vector is used for viruses and plasmids that are used to carry genes into an organism. See 9.7 for more about the use of vectors in genetic engineering. Do not confuse these two uses of the term.

Leptospirosis, also known as Weil's disease, is a bacterial disease that is passed from animals to humans. Many animals can act as the host of the bacteria. The bacteria pass out in the urine and if they come in contact with breaks in the skin, the membranes of the eyes or into the nose they can infect us. People also become infected by drinking infected water or eating food that is contaminated by the bacteria.

DID YOU KNOW?

People who work in the water industry, are involved with water sports or work with animals, such as vets and slaughterhouse workers, are especially at risk of catching leptospirosis, as are children who play in water.

The chances of catching leptospirosis can be reduced by controlling the number of rodents (rats and mice). Signs are often put up to warn people of swimming in water that is likely to be contaminated.

Rats carry the bacteria that cause leptospirosis. An animal that carries a disease which can be passed on to humans is a **vector**.

Houseflies

Houseflies are important vectors of disease as they feed on human waste and on human foods. Human pathogens can be carried on their hairs, feet and the proboscis that they use for feeding. If they ingest pathogens then they can be passed out in their faeces. Houseflies can transmit a variety of human diseases, such as typhoid, cholera and other diarrhoeal diseases. These are discussed in 10.3.

Figure 10.6.1 This housefly is feeding using its proboscis and leaving bacteria behind that could cause disease

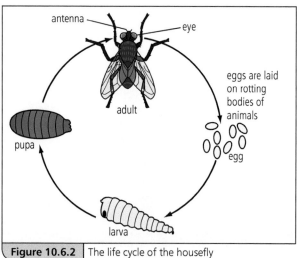

Figure 10.6.2 The life cycle of the housefly

Mosquitoes

Some species of mosquito are vectors of human diseases as they feed directly on human blood. The *Anopheles* mosquito transmits the pathogen that causes **malaria** and *Aedes aegypti* is the vector for the virus that causes **dengue fever**.

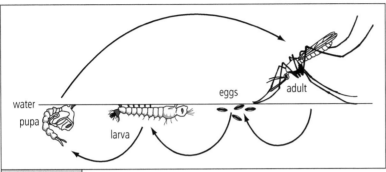

Figure 10.6.4 | The life cycle of the mosquito, *Anopheles*

The control of diseases transmitted by vectors often centres on control of the vectors. Keeping houseflies away from waste, protecting food and using flytraps are effective measures. The control of *Anopheles* is described in 10.7.

Figure 10.6.3 | These *Aedes* mosquitoes are mating; the female will lay her eggs in water

KEY POINTS

1. A vector is an animal that transmits an infectious disease to humans.

2. Rats are vectors of leptospirosis, *Aedes aegypti* of dengue fever, *Anopheles* of malaria and houseflies of diarrhoeal diseases, such as typhoid and cholera.

SUMMARY QUESTIONS

1. Define the term *vector*.

2. Describe the roles of rats, houseflies and mosquitoes as vectors.

3. Redraw the life cycle diagrams of houseflies and mosquitoes as flow chart diagrams (without pictures).

EXAM TIP

How to remember which mosquito is the vector of which disease: *Aedes* is the shorter name and transmits dengue, which has six letters. *Anopheles* is a longer word and it transmits malaria, which has seven letters.

Malaria and dengue fever

Figure 10.7.1 Technicians searching slides of blood to find malarial parasites inside red blood cells

Tropical diseases

Malaria and dengue fever are two tropical diseases that are transmitted by mosquitoes. They are found throughout the tropics, although malaria has been eliminated from many countries. Dengue fever is often described as an emerging disease as the numbers of people infected is on the increase. The transmission depends on the reproduction of the pathogens in their vector.

Malaria is caused by pathogens of the group of protozoans known as *Plasmodium*. The parasite goes through part of its life cycle in humans and the other part of its life cycle within the body of the female *Anopheles* mosquito. At temperatures lower than 20 °C the parasite does not complete its life cycle, so it is not transmitted by mosquitoes in temperate countries.

Dengue fever is caused by four strains of a virus; the strains are known as DENV-1 to DENV-4. The disease is found across the tropics and in recent years there have been epidemics in parts of the Caribbean. Dengue fever is transmitted by *Aedes aegypti,* which is found within the tropics.

Both diseases are extremely debilitating. Malaria is a major cause of death of children under the age of five. Epidemics of these diseases affect the economic activity of countries where they are **endemic**. People cannot work or cannot work efficiently if they have these diseases.

The only countries in the Caribbean region with malaria are Belize, Guyana, Haiti and the Dominican Republic. It is also found in Central and South America. Dengue is found throughout the Caribbean and there were epidemics in 2010 and 2012.

Malaria

The table summarises facts about malaria.

Causative agent	Parasitic protozoan – different species of *Plasmodium* The most severe is *Plasmodium falciparum*
Method of transmission	The female *Anopheles* mosquito takes a blood meal from an infected person; the parasite completes its life cycle inside the gut of the mosquito and the parasites transfer to her salivary glands. Transmission is complete when she takes a blood meal from an uninfected person, injecting her saliva to stop the blood clotting
Symptoms and signs	Fever, **nausea**, headache, muscle pain, shivering, sweating (often mistaken for influenza in countries where malaria is rare)
Treatment	Various antimalarial drugs that are also taken to prevent developing the disease

Dengue fever

The table summarises facts about dengue fever.

Causative agent	Four strains of a virus: DENV-1 – DENV-4
Method of transmission	Transmitted in the saliva of the mosquito *Aedes aegypti*
Symptoms and signs	High fever, nausea, painful body aches, severe headaches, skin rash. A period with no symptoms is followed by a second attack of severe symptoms
Treatment	(No cure) Bed rest, high intake of fluids, paracetamol as painkiller

Figure 10.7.2 The mosquito, *Aedes aegypti* feeding on human blood

Methods of prevention and control for the two diseases are very similar as they are directed against the vector. People can avoid mosquito bites by:

- wearing long clothes to avoid exposing the skin
- putting up screens on doors and windows to prevent mosquitoes entering houses
- keeping areas around houses tidy and free of possible breeding places for mosquitoes
- using mosquito coils and insect repellents; repellents with DEET as the active ingredient tend to be the most effective. DEET is an insecticide with an odour that mosquitoes dislike actively.

Mosquito breeding sites can be cleared of bush. They can also be sprayed with insecticides. Permanent bodies of water can be covered in oils to stop the larvae breathing air. They can also be stocked with fish that eat mosquito larvae.

Figure 10.7.3 Fogging with insecticide is one way to control mosquito vectors

STUDY FOCUS

There are no vaccines to protect people against these two diseases. There is much active research and in a few years vaccines may be available.

SUMMARY QUESTIONS

1 What causes malaria?

2 Explain why malaria and dengue are distributed throughout the tropics, but not in temperate areas of the world.

3 Make a table to show the similarities and differences between malaria and dengue fever.

4 Outline the different ways in which the spread of malaria and dengue fever are controlled.

5 Explain the impact of these two diseases

KEY POINTS

1 *Plasmodium* is the causative agent of malaria. There are four different strains of a virus that cause dengue fever.

2 The signs and symptoms of the two diseases are similar. Antimalarial drugs can cure malaria but there is no cure for dengue fever.

3 Control methods for the two diseases are directed at the mosquito. There are no vaccines yet available for these diseases.

10.8

Immunity

At the end of this topic you should be able to:

- define the terms *immunity* and *immune system*
- outline how the immune system provides defences against pathogens
- explain how immunity is acquired.

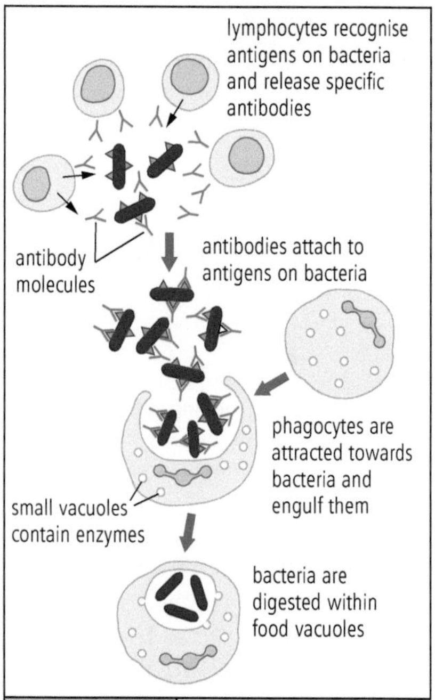

Figure 10.8.1 Lymphocytes secrete antibodies that make it easier for phagocytes to ingest bacteria and destroy them

Immunity is our protection from infectious diseases. You have body defences that reduce the chances of a pathogen entering the body:

- the epidermis of the skin provides a barrier to entry (see 6.3)
- sebum secreted by sebaceous glands in the skin acts as an **antiseptic** (see 6.3 and 10.9)
- hydrochloric acid in the stomach (see 2.9) and lactic acid in the vagina provide acidic conditions that prevent the growth of bacteria
- mucus is secreted by cells in the respiratory tract and cilia move mucus away from the lungs (see 3.5)
- the enzyme **lysozyme** is in many body secretions, e.g. tears, to breakdown the cell walls of bacteria.

When pathogens get through these defences, phagocytes in the blood may engulf and destroy them. When viruses, like those that cause flu and common colds, enter cells then the infected cells secrete chemicals to 'warn' other cells about this invasion. These **non-specific defences** may defeat the invasion. However, the body has an **immune system** that consists of tissues, cells and molecules that are dispersed throughout the body. This system is able to produce responses **specific** to the type of pathogen.

When you have an infection, such as the common cold, you will be ill for a while and have a variety of symptoms. You will then begin to feel better and within two weeks you will be healthy again. If the same strain of the common cold virus invades again, you will not get the same symptoms. You will not be ill. Lymphocytes are responsible for this.

You are born with a very large number of different types of lymphocytes. These cells are specific to different surface chemicals, known as **antigens**, found on bacteria, viruses and other pathogens. Lymphocytes fight infection in the following way:

- When a pathogen enters the body, phagocytes 'cut up' and 'show' these antigens to lymphocytes.
- Those lymphocytes that recognise the antigens divide by mitosis and multiply.
- Some of these lymphocytes become bigger and fill with endoplasmic reticulum and ribosomes. They secrete protein molecules into lymph and in the blood. These proteins are **antibodies**.
- Some antibodies stick to the surface of pathogens and cause them to clump together as in Figure 10.8.1.
- **Antitoxins** are antibodies that combine with the toxic waste products of bacteria, such as those that cause tetanus and diphtheria, and neutralise them so that they have no effect.

Other lymphocytes are activated to patrol the body looking for infected cells. They destroy infected cells to stop them producing more pathogens. HIV is a serious infection because it destroys the body's lymphocytes that are responsible for much of our defence against infectious diseases.

The response to the first infection is very slow. This is why you have fallen ill. The response to the second infection by the same pathogen is so much faster that you are unlikely to have any symptoms. This is the role of the **specific immune system**.

Vaccination

If you fall ill and respond by developing immunity to the disease you have gained **natural active immunity**. It is possible to promote the same immunity without having to be ill. This is done by injecting a **vaccine** that contains live pathogens, dead pathogens or antigens taken from the surface of pathogens. Each vaccine stimulates immunity to a specific disease and sometimes to a strain of that disease. Vaccination is **artificial active immunity**.

If protection is required in a hurry, then antibodies may be given by injection. This only provides temporary immunity, but should be sufficient. Immunity gained in this way is **artificial passive immunity**. Antibodies pass across the placenta and are present in breast milk. This gives a baby protection against diseases that his/her mother has immunity against and which are in the environment. This form of immunity is **natural passive immunity**.

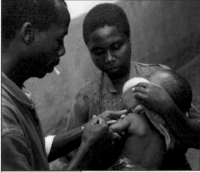

Figure 10.8.2 | Vaccination is a key part of protecting populations against disease

STUDY FOCUS

Immunisation is provided in two ways: long-term immunity by **vaccination** and short-term immunity by injecting antibodies prepared from the plasma of blood isolated from blood donations.

KEY POINTS

1 There are a variety of ways to stop pathogens entering the body, e.g. the epidermis of the skin, mucus, sebum and stomach acid.

2 Phagocytes are part of the body's non-specific defences. During an infection, lymphocytes are activated to produce antibodies that act against specific pathogens.

3 Immunity is our protection from infectious diseases.

4 Active immunity is the production of antibodies by lymphocytes in response to a natural infection or by introducing a vaccine.

5 Passive immunity is gaining antibodies from another source naturally as in mother to child and artificially by injection.

SUMMARY QUESTIONS

1 Define the terms *immunity*, *immune system*, *vaccine* and *vaccination*.

2 Distinguish between specific and non-specific immunity.

3 Explain the differences between the following: active and passive immunity; natural and artificial immunity.

4 State **one** way in which each of the following types of immunity may be gained: natural passive; natural active; artificial passive; artificial active.

5 Discuss the importance of vaccinating young children.

10.9

Controlling growth of microorganisms

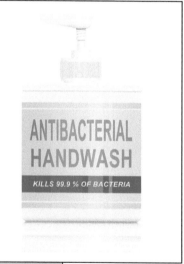

LEARNING OUTCOMES

At the end of this topic you should be able to:

- discuss the ways in which people can maintain personal hygiene
- define the terms *sterilisation* and *pasteurisation*
- describe the ways in which high temperatures, disinfectants and antiseptics are used to control microorganisms.

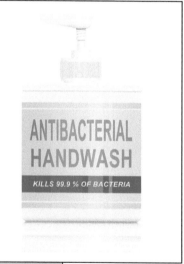

Figure 10.9.1

LINK

See 2.5 to remind yourself of the ways in which people can prevent tooth decay (dental caries).

Personal hygiene

Our bodies are covered in bacteria. Sebum is a substance that prevents the growth of bacteria. Although we produce sebum, bacteria still grow and produce volatile substances that contribute to our body odour. In many places body odour is not socially acceptable. You can prevent body odour by washing frequently and using antiperspirants to reduce the quantity of sweat produced and deodorants to mask body odours.

After washing, careful drying prevents the spread of the fungal infection known as ringworm or tinea. This starts to grow in places which remain damp, such as the feet and between the toes (see 10.3).

Using antibacterial handwashes and gels can reduce the chances of infection via the hands after using the toilet. They are also used in hospitals to try to reduce the cases of hospital acquired infections.

DID YOU KNOW?

Sweat itself has no smell and if it is lost efficiently it will evaporate as soon as it reaches the body's surface. However, it tends to accumulate providing a suitable environment for bacteria that produce unpleasant odours.

Particular care should be taken over the genitalia as they are likely sources of infection. Females should take particular care to prevent bacteria feeding on vaginal secretions and during their period. This reduces the risk of diseases such as cystitis and thrush. In males, secretions of the foreskin accumulate. Bacteria feed on these and this gives rise to a bad odour. Circumcision removes the foreskin so this build-up does not happen. Uncircumcised men should draw back the foreskin and clean thoroughly underneath.

Oral hygiene is also very important, not only to reduce the smells of bad breath, but also to prevent **dental caries**.

STUDY FOCUS

Do not become confused between all the words that begin with 'anti-' in this unit. An antigen is a chemical that stimulates lymphocytes to produce antibodies. Antibodies are proteins that help to destroy pathogens. Some antibodies neutralise the toxins (poisonous chemicals) that bacteria produce – they are antitoxins. The skin makes antiseptics in sebum (see 6.3) to stop bacteria growing. We also manufacture antiseptics for doing the same job. Antibiotics are medicines that can be taken orally, injected or applied to the skin to kill bacteria or stop them growing.

Preventing the spread of microorganisms

Exposing microorganisms to high temperatures usually kills them. Proteins, such as enzymes, are denatured at high temperatures and without enzymes the cells of bacteria and fungi cannot respire, grow or reproduce. The protein coats and genetic material of viruses are also destroyed by heating.

The table summarises the use of high temperatures in preventing the spread of microorganisms.

Method of control	Uses	Procedure
Sterilisation	Medical equipment Laboratory equipment	Place in an **autoclave** that uses steam under pressure; e.g. 121 °C at 100 kPa for around 15–20 minutes
Ultra high temperatures	Long-term preservation of milk and other foodstuffs	Food is heated for 1–2 seconds, at a temperature greater than 135 °C
Boiling	Foods for immediate consumption	Water is heated to 100 °C and boiling is maintained for a short while
Canning	Long-term food preservation, e.g. fruit, vegetables, processed foods	Following preservation with another technique, food is sealed in an airtight container
Pasteurisation	Short-term food preservation, especially for milk as it does not alter the taste too much	Food is raised to 71.7 °C for 15 seconds, then cooled; this kills potential pathogens (e.g. TB bacteria) but not all bacteria

Disinfectants are chemicals that are used to kill bacteria. They are used within the home and work place. Chlorine is a very effective disinfectant that is added to the drinking water supply when it leaves water treatment plants (see 11.2).

Antiseptics are chemicals that can be rubbed on the skin to stop microorganisms growing; antiseptics do not kill bacteria and other microbes.

SUMMARY QUESTIONS

1 Describe how people should control body odours, so they are not offensive to others.

2 Discuss the precautions that people can take to prevent the spread of infections in the home and the workplace.

3 Define the terms *sterilisation* and *pasteurisation*.

4 Explain what an autoclave is used for.

5 Describe the effect of high temperatures on microorganisms.

Figure 10.9.2 A medical technician puts surgical instruments into an autoclave for sterilisation

KEY POINTS

1 Personal hygiene is achieved by regular washing and use of products that reduce or hide body odours.

2 Regular brushing and use of mouthwashes and dental floss help to maintain good oral health.

3 The spread of microorganisms is prevented by using methods that employ high temperatures that denature enzymes, killing bacteria and fungi and destroying viruses.

4 Disinfectants are applied to surfaces and kill bacteria; antiseptics are applied to the skin and stop bacteria growing, but do not kill them.

10.10 Antibiotics and prescription drugs

The term drug is used for many different types of chemical substance. In its widest sense it refers to any substance that is taken into the body or applied to the skin that alters a chemical reaction in the body or interferes with any pathogen.

Drugs can be divided into those that are for medical use and those that are not. Most medical drugs are available only on prescription from a doctor. Others are freely available 'over the counter' from pharmacies, shops and supermarkets. **Non-medicinal drugs** are often known as recreational drugs as people use them for the pleasure that they are supposed to give. In most countries, these recreational drugs are illegal and people found in possession of drugs or involved in their production, trafficking and supply are prosecuted by law enforcement agencies.

The distinction between legal and illegal drugs varies from country to country. Alcohol, for example, is legal in many countries but is banned for general consumption in countries such as Saudi Arabia.

LINK

See 10.2 to find out why insulin is prescribed for a person's lifetime.

Prescription drugs

There are **medicinal drugs** for treating many conditions. Some are prescribed for short periods of time and some for much longer, in some cases for a lifetime. The table below shows drugs taken for relieving pain and anxiety.

Type of drug	Examples (trade names)	Effects on the body	Effects of abuse
Sedative or tranquilliser	Valium, Librium	Slows down bodily functions to relieve anxiety; induces sleep	Overdose of some sedatives may be fatal especially if taken with alcohol
Antidepressant	Prozac	Relieves depression; also taken for many other conditions, including pain relief	Even without taking more than the prescribed dose these can have severe side effects, such as untypical violent behaviour
Painkillers	Paracetamol Aspirin Ibuprofen	Relieve pain by interfering with production of chemicals that cause inflammation	Aspirin causes bleeding of the stomach; an overdose of paracetamol can lead to liver failure and may be fatal

Antimicrobial drugs are used to treat infectious diseases caused by bacteria, viruses and fungi. Antibiotics were originally prepared from microorganisms and were chemically treated. They are now manufactured. They are used to treat bacterial diseases.

Type of drug	Uses	Effects on the pathogen
Antibiotics	Control spread of bacterial diseases in the body	Kill bacteria or stop them reproducing Interfere with protein synthesis and cell wall synthesis
Anti-fungal drugs	Controls the growth of fungi, e.g. those that cause thrush and ringworm	Interfere with enzymes that are only found in fungi, not in human cells
Antiviral drugs	Control the spread of viral diseases, e.g. genital herpes	Prevent the production of viral genetic material Interfere with viral protease enzymes

STUDY FOCUS

Antibiotics are not effective against viruses. Antibiotics target processes such as cell wall synthesis, movement of substances across membranes and protein synthesis at ribosomes. Viruses do not have any of these targets. There are antiviral drugs, such as the anti-retroviral drugs used to treat HIV infection – see 10.5.

DID YOU KNOW?

In 1998 the UK government introduced a law limiting the number of tablets of paracetamol that could be sold to each person. Between 1993 and 2009 the number of paracetamol-related deaths decreased by 43%.

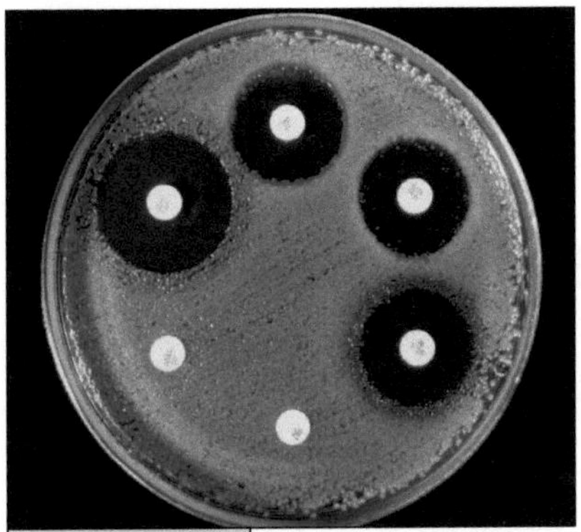

Figure 10.10.1 Before prescribing antibiotics a doctor can ask for an antibiotic sensitivity test to find out which antibiotic will be most effective. The clear area around each disc indicates that bacteria are sensitive to that antibiotic. Where there is no clear area, the antibiotic is not effective

One major problem with antibiotics is their overuse. Antibiotics are chosen to treat certain diseases. For example, tetracycline can be used to treat serious cases of cholera, but penicillin would not be chosen because it has no effect on the bacteria that cause cholera. The antibiotic streptomycin was introduced to treat TB in the 1950s. It was very successful, but after a short period it did not kill the TB bacteria anymore as they had become resistant. Resistant bacteria have a mutation that changes them, so that a specific antibiotic has no effect.

Many bacteria have become resistant to 'front-line' antibiotics. Some have even become resistant to those kept in reserve for difficult cases. Some strains of bacteria that cause TB are resistant to many drugs used to control the disease. This is why it is important not to prescribe antibiotics for less serious cases, to rotate them so they are not used all the time and to keep some for only the most serious cases.

Eventually antibiotics may become useless and we will have to devise some other way to treat infectious diseases.

KEY POINTS

1 A drug is any substance taken into the body or applied to the skin that interferes with body processes or those of pathogens.

2 Drugs are categorised as medicinal and non-medicinal drugs. Many medicinal drugs are available only on prescription. Some, such as aspirin, are available without a prescription.

3 Antimicrobial drugs are taken to control viral, bacterial and fungal pathogens. The drugs interfere with processes that occur in the pathogens but not in human cells.

SUMMARY QUESTIONS

1 Define the terms *drug* and *antibiotic*.

2 Explain what the following drugs are used for: sedatives, pain killers and antibiotics.

3 What is the danger of overusing antibiotics?

4 Explain what precautions should be taken to avoid misuse of prescription and non-prescription drugs.

Misuse of drugs

At the end of this topic you should be able to:

- define the term *drug dependence*
- list some types of non-prescription illegal drugs that are misused
- discuss the physical and psychological effects of the misuse of drugs.

Figure 10.11.1 One of the most addictive drugs is the legal drug nicotine. A few puffs and she is addicted

STUDY FOCUS

The boundary between categories of drugs is blurred. For example, other substances obtained from the opium poppy are morphine and codeine. Although both are addictive they are used in medicine for pain control.

People take recreational drugs for a variety of reasons, initially possibly because other people are taking them or because they are curious about their effects. The initial effects can be pleasurable, giving a sense of well-being known as euphoria. Some drugs have a stimulant effect and help people keep up with whatever they have to do. After the experience of taking recreational drugs, some people become **addicted**.

Continued use of a drug can reduce its effect. The user increases the dose to regain the same effect as when they started taking it. **Drug tolerance** develops because the body 'gets used' to the drug and this reduces its effect. The drug interferes with the body's metabolism and has physiological effects. Eventually, users feel they cannot live without the drug. They become dependent.

Physical dependence occurs when the drug becomes part of the body's metabolism. When they are not taking the drug, users have **withdrawal symptoms** that are only relieved by taking the drug again.

Psychological dependence is a craving for the drug. Drug-taking becomes a habit and the rituals surrounding drug-taking often help to reinforce the dependence.

For most people who are dependent, it is likely that there are elements of both forms of dependence. A gradual reduction in the use of a drug may reduce physical dependence but any underlying psychological problems may make it difficult to 'kick the habit'.

Table 1 summarises some of the effects of some recreational drugs.

Table 1

Type of drug	Example	Effects on the body
Stimulant	• Cocaine • Amphetamines, e.g. ecstasy	• Greater alertness and wakefulness • Cocaine is highly addictive
Hallucinogen	• LSD • Marijuana (ganga)	• Causes changes in consciousness that users compare to having dreams or going into trances
Depressant	• Heroin (obtained from opium poppies) • Alcohol	• Reduces feelings of anxiety, provides relief from pain and may induce sleep • Lowers blood pressure, heart rate and breathing rate

The effects of drug misuse on society

People dependent on illegal drugs can find it hard to maintain normal social behaviour. The withdrawal effects of drugs often involve mood swings and violent behaviour. They may lose their friends, become distant from their family and join a drug sub-culture. They may lose their means of obtaining an income and resort to crime to buy drugs. Many crimes are associated with drug misuse. Some women turn to prostitution to gain enough money to buy drugs.

The cost to society of drugs is very high. Communities have to provide the facilities to treat drug addiction, cope with drug-related criminal offences and rehabilitate drug users. Resources are devoted to apprehending drug traffickers and suppliers. However, the social cost of alcohol is much higher than the costs of dealing with illegal drugs, as a greater proportion of the population misuse alcohol. Alcohol misuse can result in serious medical and social effects, such as physical abuse and family breakdown.

Figure 10.11.2 Alcohol misuse is the cause of many social problems, including homelessness

Table 2 Admissions to the psychiatric unit of the University Hospital of the West Indies in Jamaica between March and September 2010

Substance	No. of people	Average no. of days spent in the psychiatric unit
Alcohol	65	17.22
Marijuana	37	18.62
Crack/cocaine	6	15.62
Any combination of the drugs above	4	12.50
Total cost (J$)	2 322 282	

Data from Table 4 Page 15. An assessment of the economic costs of substance abuse in Caricom Member States: Jamaica. May 2012. Prepared by UWI Consulting.

STUDY FOCUS

The impact of alcohol misuse is evident in the admissions to the psychiatric unit of the University Hospital of the West Indies in Jamaica between March and September 2010.

KEY POINTS

1 Drug tolerance occurs when a drug has become part of the body's metabolism. This can lead to physical dependence when withdrawal symptoms are only alleviated by taking the drug.

2 Psychological dependence occurs because drug-taking has become a ritual.

3 Drug misuse has many adverse effects on individuals, families and the wider community that has to find the resources to cope with drug-related crime, violence and family breakdown.

SUMMARY QUESTIONS

1 Define the following terms: *drug tolerance*, *physical dependence* and *psychological dependence*.

2 Outline the effects of cocaine, ecstasy, LSD, marijuana, heroin and alcohol on the body.

3 a Use the data in the table to calculate:
  i the percentage of admissions to the psychiatric unit for each type of substance
  ii the total number of days of treatment in the psychiatric unit for each substance
  b Present the results of your calculations in suitable charts or graphs.

4 Discuss the effects of drug misuse on the individual, the family and the community.

Disease and its impact: Data analysis

At the end of this topic you should be able to:

* discuss the impact of diseases on human populations

* make and use tables to summarise data on health, disease and the impact on human populations

* carry out calculations to analyse data on health and disease

* present information on health and disease using bar charts, pie charts and line graphs.

EXAM TIP

Do not confuse bar charts with histograms. See 2.4 to remind yourself about how to draw line graphs and bar charts. Histograms are not appropriate for any of the information in these tables. Do you know why? If you are not sure, look at 3.6.

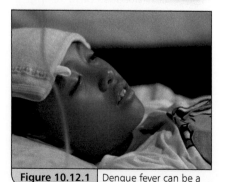

Figure 10.12.1 | Dengue fever can be a very serious disease requiring hospital treatment

The impact of diseases on human populations extends from the inconvenience of short-term infections, such as the common cold, to long-term chronic diseases and diseases, such as malaria, that kill about half a million people worldwide each year. Throughout human history there have been plagues that have killed huge numbers of people. Currently we are living through the HIV pandemic. People who are sick are unable to work, effectively reducing family and national incomes. The provision of health services to prevent, treat and cure diseases is a huge expense for governments. Many around the world can only afford a basic health service.

Read through the following tables of data and then answer the summary questions on page 160. The questions will help you to analyse data on diseases and the impact that they have on populations.

Table 1 shows the number of cases of dengue fever in Trinidad and Tobago between 1978 and 2003.

Table 1

Year	No. of cases of dengue fever	Year	No. of cases of dengue fever
1978	373	1991	36
1979	0	1992	116
1980	15	1993	268
1981	16	1994	48
1982	117	1995	312
1983	31	1996	3983
1984	5	1997	1396
1985	145	1998	2981
1986	125	1999	1330
1987	80	2000	2066
1988	80	2001	564
1989	11	2002	6246
1990	526	2003	120

Data from WHO Denguenet. For information about Denguenet, see http://apps.who.int/globalatlas/default.asp

Table 2

| Country | Mortality rate for heart disease and diabetes/ no. of deaths per 100 000 population | |
	men	women
Japan	118	65
Barbados	293	178
Russian Federation	772	414
United Kingdom	166	102
Spain	140	86
Trinidad and Tobago	545	316

Data from the WHO. http://apps.who.int/gho/data/?vid=2510

Table 3 shows data on HIV in seven Caribbean countries for 2011.

Table 3

Country	Population in thousands	Estimated number of people living with HIV/AIDS	Estimated number of deaths due to AIDS
Barbados	274	1400	<100
Belize	318	4600	500 (2009)
Cuba	11 254	14 100	<200
Dominican Republic	10 056	44 000	1700
Haiti	10 124	120 000	5800
Jamaica	2751	3000	1600
Trinidad and Tobago	1346	13 000	<1000

Population data from Unicef: http://www.unicef.org; HIV/AIDS data from Avert (except deaths from AIDS in Belize): http://www.avert.org; Deaths from AIDS in Belize 2009 from http://www.indexmundi.com/g/g.aspx?c=bh&v=37

Many infectious diseases are preventable by vaccination. Vaccination coverage is a good indicator of the success of governments in protecting their populations. Table 4 shows coverage with measles vaccine for children up to 1 year old in Trinidad and Tobago.

Table 4

Year	Percentage of children vaccinated
1984	10
1989	59
1994	86
1999	88
2004	95
2009	94
2010	92

Data from WHO. http://gamapserver.who.int/gho/interactive_charts/immunization/mcv/atlas.html?filter=filter4,Americas

STUDY FOCUS

A good way to learn about the role of vaccination in controlling disease is to find the schedule used by the health authorities in your country. This lists the vaccines recommended for children and adolescents at different ages.

SUMMARY QUESTIONS

1 a Plot a graph to show the changes in number of cases of dengue fever shown in Table 1.

   b Describe the pattern shown in the graph.

   c Suggest explanations for the incidence of dengue fever over the time period shown by the graph.

2 a Draw bar charts to compare the data shown in Table 2.

   b Explain why the data shown is expressed as 'per 100 000' and not simply as number of deaths.

   c Suggest explanations for the differences between the various countries.

   d Explain how countries could reduce the mortality rates from chronic diseases.

3 a Use the figures in Table 3 to calculate the prevalence of HIV infection and the death rates from AIDS in the seven countries.

   b Show the results in a suitable graphical form.

4 a Plot the data in Table 4 as a graph.

   b Explain why measles is a preventable disease.

   c Suggest how you would determine the success of a government's vaccination programme other than the method used in this example.

UNIT 10: multiple-choice questions

1 Antibiotics are used to treat:
   a   most bacterial diseases
   b   most airborne diseases
   c   most genetically-inherited diseases
   d   most viral diseases.

2 Paul is a lifelong smoker. He complains of pains in his chest and his doctor sends him for an X-ray which shows a white patch on his lungs. The doctor tells Paul that he has:
   a   asthma
   b   chronic bronchitis
   c   coronary heart disease
   d   lung cancer.

3 Felice was diagnosed with an infectious disease which produced hard red ulcers and a rash initially. She was treated with a penicillin injection. Which STI did she have?
   a   Genital herpes
   b   Gonorrhoea
   c   HIV infection
   d   Syphilis

4 Which respiratory infection is caused by a bacterium, affects the lungs, the bones and the lymph glands, and causes a person to lose weight and develop a fever?
   a   The common cold
   b   Influenza
   c   Pneumonia
   d   Tuberculosis

Further practice questions and examples can be found on the accompanying CD.

UNIT 10: Short answer questions

1 a i   State the causative agents of malaria and dengue fever. (2)
     ii Describe how the two diseases are transmitted. (3)

Malaria is a difficult disease to control. Figure 1 shows the change in cases of malaria in Suriname between 1990 and 2011.

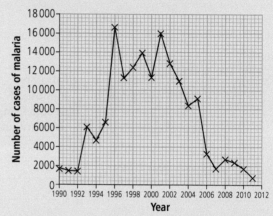

Figure 1

   b i   Describe the changes in the number of cases of malaria in Suriname between 1990 and 2011. (4)
      ii State two ways, OTHER THAN NUMBER OF CASES, in which the impact of malaria on a country can be measured. (2)
   c   Describe four ways in which health authorities can reduce the number of cases of malaria. (4)

Total 15 marks

2 a   State three ways in which HIV is transmitted. (3)
   b   Describe:
      i   the treatments available for people with HIV/AIDS (4)
      ii the methods used by health authorities to limit the spread of HIV. (4)
   c   Discuss the impact of HIV/AIDS on the populations of the Caribbean. (4)

Total 15 marks

3 a Copy and complete the table showing information about four diseases.

Disease	Causative agent	Symptoms	Treatment
Influenza			Bed rest; high fluid intake; painkillers
Cholera	Bacterium		
Tuberculosis			Long-term course of antibiotics
Ringworm		Red rings on the skin	

(4)

b i Explain how houseflies transmit diseases. (3)

  ii Describe THREE ways in which houseflies are controlled. (3)

c Distinguish between disinfectants and antiseptics. (2)

d Explain how surgical instruments are sterilised. (3)

Total 15 marks

4 a Explain the importance of personal hygiene in maintaining good health. (6)

The causative agents of some infectious diseases, such as rubella, gonorrhoea and syphilis, can pass from mother to foetus. All girls should be vaccinated against rubella before they reach reproductive age.

b Describe the effects of gonorrhoea and syphilis on newborn babies. (4)

c Describe how vaccination against rubella provides protection for the foetus. (5)

Total 15 marks

5 a i Define the term *good health*. (3)

  ii State what is meant by the term *chronic* as applied to disease. (1)

The table shows life expectancy and infant mortality for the Caribbean and Latin American region and for five countries in the Caribbean in 1900 and 2009.

Country	Life expectancy at birth		Infant mortality (deaths of children under the age of 1 year per 1000 live births)	
	1900	2009/ 2010	1900 (estimated)	2009
Belize		76.9		17.9
Cuba	32	78.0	136	4.5
Haiti		62.0		57 (2006)
Jamaica	38	73.1	174.3	14.6
Trinidad and Tobago	38	70.3	170	13.2
Caribbean and Latin America	29	74	250	20

Data from Health in the Americas 2012 Edition. PAHO/WHO. http://new.paho.org/saludenlasamericas/. Statistics from UNICEF www.unicef.org/infobycountry/

b i Calculate the PERCENTAGE CHANGE in infant mortality in Jamaica between 1900 and 2009. Show your working. (2)

  ii Summarise the data shown in the table. (4)

c Suggest reasons for the changes in life expectancy and infant mortality shown in the table. (5)

Total 15 marks

Pollutants

LEARNING OUTCOMES

At the end of this topic you should be able to:

• define the terms *pollutant* and *pollution*

• list different sources of pollutants and describe their effects on humans and the environment

• discuss the causes of water and air pollution

• describe methods of controlling pollution.

LINK

For more information about PCBs see question 2 of the short answer questions for Unit 11. There is more about pollution of water by organic wastes in 11.3.

Figure 11.1.1 Water pollution – unsightly, smelly, dangerous, damaging, disgusting and totally unnecessary

A **pollutant** is anything released into the environment as a result of human activity that has the potential to cause harm. We think of most pollutants as being chemical substances, such as fertilisers, oil and carbon monoxide or as biological material, such as human body wastes. However, heat released from power stations and noise from industrial and domestic sources are also forms of pollutant. **Pollution** is the release of substances harmful to the environment from human activities.

The table summarises some of the major pollutants, their sources, the effects that they have on humans and the environment and the ways in which they can be reduced or prevented.

Water pollution

As most rivers are very short in the Caribbean, much of the pollution ends up in the sea. The Caribbean Sea is also prone to pollution by ships and off-shore oil rigs. Oil pollution at sea leads to the formation of oil slicks, which cause environmental damage to coral reefs, sea grass communities and beaches. The most obvious victims of this pollution are sea birds that become coated in oil. Chemical wastes from industry have devastating effects on natural environments. Polychlorinated biphenyls (PCBs) and heavy metals are absorbed by small organisms, such as plankton. These provide food for slightly larger animals. These pollutants are not excreted and so remain in the bodies of these organisms and become concentrated in food chains. The high concentrations in top predators have effects on the physiology of these animals, often reducing their fertility.

Air pollution

Some air pollutants remain near the ground and have direct effects on the environment and on humans. Dust, dirt, exhaust fumes and smoke cause deposits on buildings and on plants. Deposits on plants can reduce photosynthesis and kill plants. Sulphur dioxide (SO_2) and nitrogen oxides (NO_x) react with water vapour in the atmosphere to form sulphuric and nitric acids. These return to the surface as **acid rain**, which reacts with mineral nutrients in the soil. They are carried away in drainage water. Aluminium is often mobilised in this way and it damages plants and animal life. Where acid rain falls on ground above granite it acidifies ponds, lakes and rivers. This kills much of the animal life that depends on these waters.

Gases such as carbon dioxide and methane in the upper atmosphere prevent infrared radiation being reflected to outer space. This adds to the natural greenhouse effect and is called the **enhanced greenhouse effect**. The effect of this is **global warming**, which may lead to the rise in sea levels and to more unpredictable weather patterns.

Source of pollutant	Effects on *humans* and the environment	Methods of control
Domestic		
Washing powders and household detergents	Contain phosphate which is a plant nutrient, causes **eutrophication**	Development of 'eco-friendly' detergents without phosphate
Sewage	Improper disposal causes eutrophication *Increases risk of diarrhoeal diseases*	Proper sewage disposal – a drainage system and sewage treatment
Industrial		
Carbon dioxide (from combustion of fossil fuels)	A **greenhouse gas** contributing to global warming	Energy efficiency measures; reduce demand for energy
Sulphur dioxide (from combustion of high sulphur fuels)	Damages plants, forms acid rain *Irritates lining of the respiratory system*	Use low sulphur fuels, remove sulphur dioxide from waste gases from factories, use catalytic converters on car exhausts
Heavy metals, e.g. mercury and lead	Accumulates in food chains *Poisons the human nervous system*	Prevent release from factories
PCBs	Accumulates in food chains	Use alternatives, e.g. for electrical insulation
Agricultural		
Herbicides	Kills non-target species so reducing biodiversity	Apply more carefully or not at all
Pesticides		
Fertilisers	Runoff into water where they cause eutrophication	Only apply when plants require fertilisers most
Farmyard manure	Eutrophication *Increases risk of diarrhoeal diseases*	Collect into pits where manure can decay in controlled conditions (as in sewage works)
Methane	Emitted by anaerobic bacteria in flooded rice fields and by cattle	Grow strains of rice that do not need to be flooded

SUMMARY QUESTIONS

1 Define the terms *pollutant* and *pollution*.

2 Explain why heat from power stations and noise from industrial and domestic sources are pollutants.

3 List pollutants from domestic, industrial and agricultural sources.

4 Explain how water and air pollution occurs and explain how they may be controlled.

5 Describe the effects of **named** pollutants on humans.

KEY POINTS

1 A pollutant is any substance produced by human activity that may cause harm in the environment. Pollution is the release of any such substance or its presence in the environment.

2 Examples of pollution from domestic, industrial and agricultural sources are listed in the table.

3 Pollution is controlled by taking steps to find alternative processes that do not release pollutants or capturing the pollutants before they reach the environment.

11.2 The water cycle

LEARNING OUTCOMES

At the end of this topic you should be able to:

- describe the processes that occur in the water cycle
- explain how to test water for bacteria
- describe how to purify water for domestic use
- describe the processes that occur in a water purification plant
- discuss the impact of humans on water supplies.

STUDY FOCUS

Agar is a powder to which nutrients, such as glucose and minerals, are added. Nutrient agar is dissolved in water and sterilised in an autoclave (see 10.9) and then poured into sterile plastic Petri dishes. A known volume of water for testing is mixed with it just before it sets as a jelly-like substance. The dish is sealed with transparent sticky tape, turned upside down and incubated in a warm place for 24 hours.

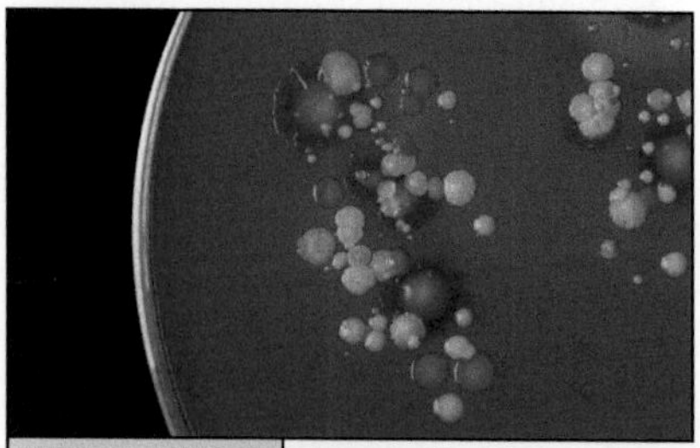

Figure 11.2.2 If a sample of water gave results like these it would be very dangerous to drink it!

Water is one of our most precious resources and also the easiest to abuse by polluting it, taking too much of it and wasting it.

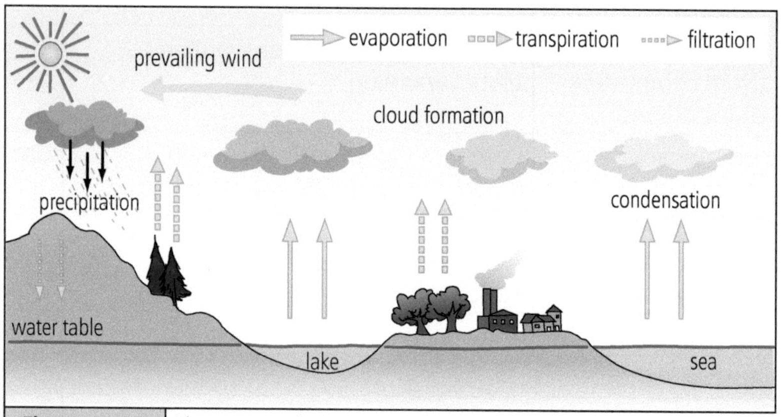

Figure 11.2.1 The water cycle

Precipitation: water falls from the air as rain, sleet, snow or hail stones.

Filtration: water soaks into the ground passing between the soil particles to reach the **water table** – this is where the ground is fully saturated with water.

Much water runs off artifical surfaces into streams, lakes, rivers and drains.

Evaporation: water in the oceans, rivers, lakes and in soils changes state from liquid to a gas – water vapour.

Transpiration: much of the water absorbed by plants travels to the leaves where it evaporates. The water vapour diffuses out of the leaves through stomata – small holes in the surfaces of the leaves.

Respiration by organisms: produces water, some of which is excreted from plants and animals.

Condensation: water vapour rises in the atmosphere and changes state to form liquid water in the clouds.

Testing drinking water for bacteria

Water samples can be taken from different water sources – household taps, wells and stand pipes. The bacteria may be present in such low numbers that they cannot be detected without doing some form of biological or chemical test. Bacteria are grown on **agar plates** that are prepared with a known volume of the water to be tested. If bacteria are present colonies will grow on the agar as in the photograph. These can be counted and the number of bacteria per cm^3 of water can be calculated.

If water is found to be, or thought to be, unsafe to drink it can be boiled or treated with water purification tablets. These tablets contain chlorine that forms hypochlorous acid (HClO) and oxygen that kill bacteria. One teaspoon of household bleach added to a litre of water does the job as well.

LINK

See 12.2 for a structured question on water testing.

DID YOU KNOW?

Scientists are developing test strips to detect bacteria in drinking water. These already exist for testing water in swimming pools, but they need to be much more sensitive to detect the very low levels of bacteria that make water unsafe to drink.

Large-scale purification of water

Water is taken from rivers, lakes and boreholes. Water passes into the water purification plant through screens (A in Figure 11.2.3) that remove any debris, such as leaves, twigs and plastic bottles. The water flows into **sedimentation** tanks (B) where particles of soil fall to the base and are removed. Water then passes through filtration tanks (C) filled with sand. In some sand filters, microorganisms on the particles remove much of the fine organic material. The water is then treated with chlorine or ozone (D) to kill bacteria and then flows through pipes to water storage tanks (E) and on to domestic and commercial customers.

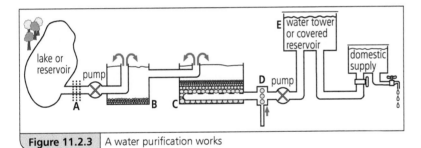

| **Figure 11.2.3** | A water purification works |

The impact of human activities on water supplies

- Humans take too much water from the environment for domestic, industrial and agricultural use. Much of this is wasted.
- Pollutants enter water supplies and it is expensive to treat the water to remove them.
- Drainage from farmland and from built-up areas reduces water that percolates through the soil to the water table.
- Runoff from artificial surfaces, such as roads, contributes to flooding.
- Deforestation reduces the amount of water absorbed by plants, so contributing to flooding and reducing the volume of water transpired into the atmosphere.
- Dams and reservoirs secure water supplies for people, although they can cause environmental problems, such as providing breeding grounds for disease vectors.
- Development, especially for housing and tourist accommodation, causes destruction of wetlands, which are a valuable source of water.

KEY POINTS

1 Water passes from soils, oceans, lakes and rivers by evaporation. Transpiration is the loss of water vapour from plants.

2 Water vapour condenses in the air and returns to the earth as precipitation. The passage of water through soils known as filtration.

3 Water purification works use filtration and chlorination to produce safe drinking water.

4 Humans use dams and reservoirs to increase the water supply, but many activities have polluted those supplies and wastage of water has depleted them.

SUMMARY QUESTIONS

1 Explain how the following contribute to the cycling of water: evaporation, transpiration, respiration, condensation, precipitation and filtration.

2 Describe how to test drinking water for the presence of bacteria.

3 Draw a flow chart diagram to show how water is purified in a water purification works.

4 Discuss the effects, good and bad, that humans have on the water supply for homes, industry and agriculture.

11.3
Sewage disposal

LEARNING OUTCOMES

At the end of this topic you should be able to:

- distinguish between proper and improper sewage disposal practices
- explain why contaminated water is harmful to humans
- explain the impact of improper sewage disposal practices.

Figure 11.3.1 Improper sewage disposal encourages rats, which are vectors of diseases such as leptospirosis (see 10.6)

Figure 11.3.3 A lack of oxygen in polluted rivers often kills many fish

Improper sewage disposal practices occur when human wastes are not collected and treated but just enter the environment in an uncontrolled fashion. In places without proper sanitation in the form of flush toilets or latrines and no drainage system, raw sewage is put into watercourses or into gullies. This attracts flies and rodents which spread disease.

There are numerous problems and dangers to health with improper sewage disposal.

- Sewage provides food for vectors of disease.
- Sewage leaks into water supplies and contaminates them – for example, water from wells, standpipes and water pipes that are cracked.
- Water polluted with sewage is unsightly and smelly.
- Sewage floats on water and blocks out the light.
- Sewage covers the bottom of rivers and lakes, killing many bottom-dwelling animals and plants.
- Water can become anaerobic and this leads to the death of many organisms.
- Sensitive natural environments, such as the coral reefs and sea grass communities in the Caribbean, have been badly damaged by the effects of untreated sewage.

There are risks to human health from waterborne diseases, such as cholera, typhoid and other diarrhoeal diseases.

Raw sewage is often dumped, improperly, into rivers. The organic compounds in sewage change the nature of rivers considerably. Figure 11.3.2 shows what happens as the sewage moves downstream.

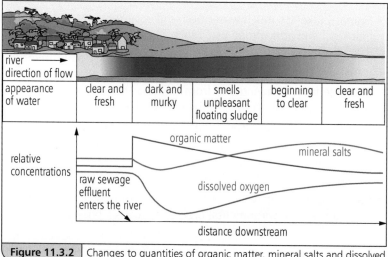

Figure 11.3.2 Changes to quantities of organic matter, mineral salts and dissolved oxygen downstream of raw (untreated) sewage entering a river

The release of organic material, such as sewage, into a river provides the decomposers (bacteria and fungi) with a huge supply of food. The numbers of decomposers increase and they use up much of the dissolved oxygen in the water. Most small animals and fish cannot survive in water with a low oxygen concentration. Some invertebrate animals can survive in anaerobic conditions and their numbers increase as they now have few predators or competitors.

As you can see in the diagram (Figure 11.3.2), the river improves as it flows away from the source of the sewage. This is because the organic material is broken down. However, bacteria release ammonium ions which are converted into nitrate ions by nitrifying bacteria. The nitrate ions are used by plants in the water and this helps the recovery as plants photosynthesise and release oxygen.

Proper sewage disposal practice involves providing houses with an organised water supply, flush toilets and a drainage system to take the wastes to a sewage treatment works. Where there is no drainage system, the wastes are collected in a septic tank which is emptied at regular intervals and the wastes transported away and treated.

Eutrophication

Eutrophication occurs if the concentration of minerals, such as nitrate ions and phosphate ions, is increased. This happens when waterways are polluted by fertilisers and detergents. When they enter waterways the following chain of events may occur:

- Algae grow rapidly over the surface of the water.
- Many of these algae produce toxic substances that kill plants and poison fish.
- Small animals that feed on algae do not reproduce fast enough to prevent the increase in the numbers of algae.
- The green coating on the surface of the water cuts out light for other plants.
- These plants die and are decomposed.
- Decomposers reduce the concentration of oxygen.
- Many fish and invertebrate animals die through lack of oxygen.

KEY POINTS

1 Improper sewage disposal occurs when human wastes enter the environment in an uncontrolled fashion. This causes numerous environmental problems and is a serious risk to human health.

2 Proper sewage treatment involves transferring human wastes to sewage treatment works.

3 If raw sewage mixes with the water supply or contaminates human food, people are at risk of gastroenteritis, diarrhoeal diseases, such as cholera and typhoid, and worm infestations.

SUMMARY QUESTIONS

1 Explain what is meant by the terms: improper sewage disposal and proper sewage disposal.

2 Explain the dangers of water supplies that are contaminated by sewage.

3 Describe and explain the changes that occur in the river after the entry of the sewage.

4 Describe the impact of improper sewage disposal on the environment.

11.4 Sewage treatment

LEARNING OUTCOMES

At the end of this topic you should be able to:

- state that sewage is treated by the biological filter and the activated sludge methods
- describe how these two methods are used in sewage treatment
- explain the roles of microorganisms in sewage treatment.

Figure 11.4.1 Aerobic digesters are in the foreground of this aerial view of a modern sewage works; sedimentation tanks are in the background

Proper sewage disposal involves collecting raw sewage and transporting it in enclosed sewer pipes to a sewage treatment works. During the sewage treatment there may be as many as six different processes as shown in the diagram opposite.

The role of microorganisms

The effluent from domestic sources contains the following wastes:

- urine – that contains urea and mineral salts, such as sodium chloride
- cellulose (fibre) – that we are unable to digest
- proteins – from the many dead cells and dead bacteria from our guts.

Sewage also contains waste food (fats, carbohydrates, such as starch, and proteins) that goes down the drain.

Domestic waste water also contains many chemicals, such as cleaning agents and hair products. The water that enters sewage treatment works also contains water from the streets and storm drains. Therefore it also contains pollutants, such as oils, heavy metals and poisons.

The most important parts of the sewage works are the parts in which microorganisms break down the organic compounds in sewage. Other slightly larger organisms feed on these microorganisms so helping to keep their populations under control and reduce the numbers that leave the sewage works.

Bacteria and fungi in **biological trickle filters** and **aerobic sludge digesters** secrete enzymes that digest urea, proteins, fats and carbohydrates. They absorb the soluble products and respire them, and use them for their growth and reproduction. These microorganisms require oxygen for their respiration. Biological trickle filters are made of clinkers or large stones that provide a large surface area for the growth of microorganisms. The large air spaces between the stones allow air to circulate so the organisms can respire aerobically.

Compressed air is pumped into aerobic sludge digesters. This mixes the microorganisms with the sewage, increasing the rate at which they digest the organic compounds. In some sewage works the sludge that is not broken down is removed to an anaerobic digester in which bacteria breakdown material to form methane. The methane is burnt as a fuel to provide energy to run the sewage works.

Water may flow through fields of reeds that absorb minerals, such as nitrate ions and phosphate ions, so reducing the effect that they can have on waterways (see eutrophication in 11.3).

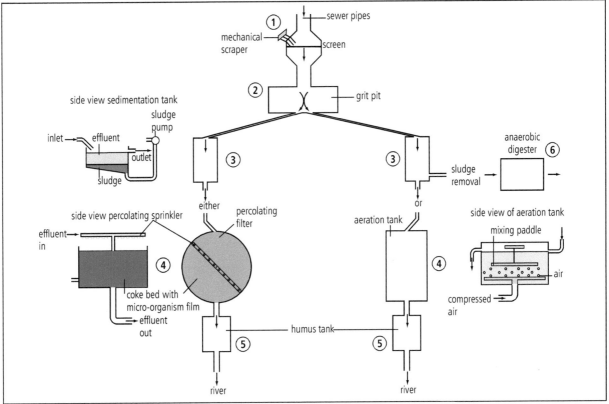

Figure 11.4.2 This diagram shows the processes that occur as sewage is treated in a modern sewage treatment plant

1 Screens remove any non-biodegradable debris, such as plastic bottles, cans and used condoms.
2 Grit tank: to allow large particles of grit and sand to sediment and be removed.
3 Sedimentation tank: to allow smaller particles of sand to settle. Compounds, such as aluminium sulphate, are added to cause tiny particles to collect together and deposit on the base of the tank.

4 Breakdown of organic material by microorganisms.
5 Humus tank: to allow small particles to sediment.
6 Anaerobic digester for production of methane.

SUMMARY QUESTIONS

1 Describe the role of microorganisms in sewage treatment.

2 Distinguish between the biological trickle filter and the activated sludge methods of waste water treatment.

3 Explain how reed beds are used to improve the quality of water leaving a sewage treatment works.

KEY POINTS

1 Microorganisms, such as bacteria and fungi, breakdown the organic compounds present in sewage, such as cellulose, fat and protein.

2 Aerobic conditions are provided for the microorganisms in activated sludge tanks and biological trickle filters.

3 Treated sewage may be chlorinated to kill bacteria or allowed to flow through reed beds to remove minerals such as nitrate ions.

Pit latrines

At the end of this topic you should be able to:

• explain why the careful siting of pit latrines is important

• explain how the parts of a pit latrine ensure their proper functioning

• discuss the use of pit latrines in the Caribbean.

People who do not have access to a drainage system can dispose of their body wastes safely using a latrine. **Pit latrines** are built over holes in the ground. They are temporary structures and after a while the pits need to be filled and the latrines moved to a new location.

The siting of a pit latrine is important. If the base of the pit is in ground that is too porous, the wastes will soak away before they are broken down by the microorganisms. The pits should not be placed in places where they can contaminate water courses or groundwater, especially if it is used as a source of drinking water.

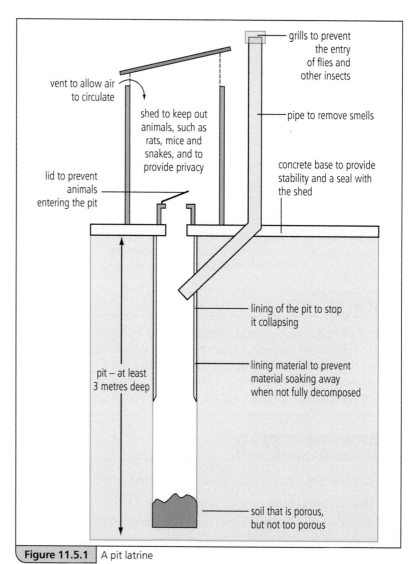

Figure 11.5.1 | A pit latrine

Figure 11.5.2 | Children and staff at a school in Zimbabwe put the finishing touches to a Blair toilet they have built themselves

Advantages and disadvantages

Pit latrines provide basic sanitation to people who live in remote rural areas or indeed anywhere that does not have a drainage system and sewage treatment works. If properly constructed, they should allow for the disposal and breakdown of human wastes in a hygienic way. They can also be constructed so that urine is separated to use as a fertiliser. The solid waste can also be used as a fertiliser.

The disadvantages are that pit latrines become less suitable as the population increases, as there is a limited amount of land where they can be sited. They often have to be moved and eventually there is no suitable space. There are still health risks associated with them, especially if they are not maintained properly. For these reasons they are being phased out in many regions in the Caribbean.

KEY POINTS

1 Pit latrines are sited in places where decomposed wastes can seep slowly into the soil without contaminating water sources.

2 The design of pit latrines excludes rodents and insects and permits good ventilation.

3 Pit latrines provide sanitation in rural areas that do not have access to a drainage system. They are less efficient as the population increases.

Figure 11.5.3 A Blair toilet from rural Zimbabwe

SUMMARY QUESTIONS

1 Explain why the siting of pit latrines should be carried out with care.

2 Make an annotated diagram of a pit latrine to show how it is designed to avoid pollution of the surroundings.

3 Discuss the advantages and disadvantages of pit latrines.

Figure 11.6.1 | Garbage collection the right way!

Collection of domestic and commercial wastes

In almost all parts of the world garbage trucks visit households and commercial premises on a regular (often a weekly) basis to collect solid wastes. These wastes consist of paper and packaging, tins, bottles, household dust and unwanted food. They should be kept in bins with lids to keep nasty smells in the bin and rodents and insects out. Properly maintained bins also prevent items, such as tins, filling with water and becoming breeding places for the insects that act as vectors of disease. Garbage trucks collect and compress the waste and take it to a refuse collection centre. Here it may be sorted so that some material can be recycled. It may be incinerated or loaded onto trucks or containers and shipped elsewhere.

STUDY FOCUS

What happens to solid domestic waste in your local area? How often is it collected and where does it go? Carrying out an evaluation of local waste disposal and preparing a report of your findings will provide you with useful material for answers on this topic.

Landfill

A sanitary **landfill site** should be dug out of the ground and lined to prevent toxic liquid wastes leaching away into the soil and entering waterways or groundwater. The top soil, removed when the site is dug, should be stored and used to cover the site at regular intervals. Refuse that is not sent for recycling or incinerated is put into landfill and then compacted to exclude vermin, such as rats and mice. When full, these sites should be covered over with soil and vented to allow any methane that is formed inside to escape or be burnt.

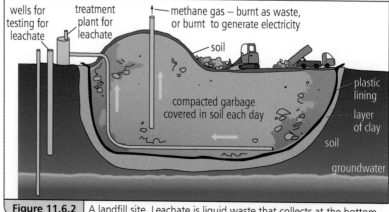

Figure 11.6.2 | A landfill site. Leachate is liquid waste that collects at the bottom of the site and can drain into the soil and groundwater

Many such sites in the Caribbean and elsewhere are not operated like this, but instead are just refuse dumps where garbage is added and left exposed to the elements. They may also provide a source of living for some of the poorest in society who pick through the refuse and sell it for recycling or for reuse. Among the reasons for poor solid waste management in the Caribbean are:

- lack of space for developing proper sanitary landfill sites
- not enough finance to purchase and develop suitable sites for waste management
- objections by local people to incinerators
- populations that are too small to provide enough waste to support new technologies, such as incinerating waste for generating power.

Less garbage

The quantity of refuse that is thrown away into landfill or incinerated can be reduced significantly. This can be achieved by reducing the quantity of material that needs to be thrown away, reusing materials and **recycling** them.

- Glass bottles can be returned to the manufacturer and reused.
- Glass can be collected in bottle banks and recycled.
- Tin and aluminium cans can be collected and recycled.
- Some plastics can be collected and recycled into objects, such as park benches and insulation material.
- Organic garden and food wastes can be shredded, composted and turned into fertilisers.
- Paper and cardboard can be collected and recycled as newsprint.
- Packaging from manufactured products and processed food can be recycled.

LINK

There is more about the impact of solid waste on the environment in 11.7.

Figure 11.6.3 Bales of paper about to be recycled as newsprint

KEY POINTS

1 Domestic refuse should be kept in bins with lids until collected and taken to landfill.

2 Landfill sites should be dug out of the ground and restored and managed carefully once they are full.

3 Pollution from poorly managed landfill sites releases methane from the anaerobic breakdown of organic wastes into the air and toxic effluent that may run into water courses.

4 The quantity of refuse can be reduced by using less material, such as packaging, reusing bottles and recycling glass, paper and plastic.

SUMMARY QUESTIONS

1 Name two vectors of disease that may breed in water that collects in items of household refuse.

2 State what is meant by the term *landfill*.

3 Explain how landfill sites should be operated.

4 Assess the difficulties of refuse disposal in the Caribbean.

5 Explain how the volume of solid domestic wastes can be reduced.

Table 1

Biodegradable wastes	Non-biodegradable wastes
Discarded food	Most plastics
Green waste from parks, gardens and farms	Metals
	Glass
Human wastes	Polystyrene
Animal manure	
Waste from slaughterhouses	

Figure 11.7.1 A large sanitary landfill site in Quito, Ecuador

Biodegradable wastes are those that can be broken down by decomposers. **Non-biodegradable** wastes cannot be acted on by decomposers and so persist in the environment. Table 1 gives examples of these different types of wastes. This topic includes information and data about waste disposal in three countries in the Caribbean.

The problem

The quantity of solid wastes in the Caribbean has doubled over the past 30 years.

Over time the composition of wastes has changed to become more non-biodegradable and hazardous. In Jamaica, 1.2 million tonnes of wastes are generated each year. Approximately 828 000 tonnes are taken to legal disposal sites, none of which are properly managed sanitary landfills. Almost 300 000 tonnes of wastes are illegally dumped causing severe environmental problems.

Riverton disposal site receives 60% of the wastes produced on the island. It has an area of 119 hectares and is adjacent to mangroves and the Duhaney River. As the site is not managed properly it has a huge negative environmental effect on the surrounding area and on the health of the local population.

Public health risks from unmanaged dumps like Riverton are:

- water pollution (e.g. of the Duhaney River, which is used for drinking and bathing by people living nearby)
- pollution (of Hunt's Bay, which scientists call 'The Dead Zone')
- heavy metal contamination from cadmium, manganese, lead and pesticides.

A wide range of air pollutants are produced when the dump burns. Amongst these are particulates, such as dust, carbon monoxide, hydrogen cyanide, nitrogen oxides (NOx), sulphur dioxide and dioxins.

The air pollution from dump fires increases the risk of:

- death among elderly people and those with pre-existing respiratory and cardiac illnesses
- infant mortality and low birth weight of babies
- onset of childhood asthma, coughs, wheezing, chest tightness, shortness of breath, burning in eyes, nose and throat, dizziness, weakness, confusion, nausea, disorientation
- exposure to known carcinogens.

The seriousness of these risks depends on how close people are to the fires.

The impacts of raising animals on the dump include the **bioaccumulation** of heavy metals, such as lead and mercury which move up the food chain into the bodies of humans.

Table 2 shows the various types of solid wastes sent to landfill sites in Trinidad and Tobago in 2010.

All the organic wastes in the list in Table 2 are biodegradable wastes as they contain material which decomposers, such as bacteria and fungi, are able to break down. The material in the wastes is respired so that carbon dioxide is released into the atmosphere. Nitrogen compounds are broken down into ammonia and then recycled to nitrate ions by the action of nitrifying bacteria (see 1.8).

Decomposers cannot break down non-biodegradable wastes and so these accumulate unless they can be collected and used in the manufacture of new materials, as is the case with glass, some plastics and paper (see 11.6).

The solution

The waste management authority of St Lucia operates an integrated waste management system, which comprises one sanitary landfill site at Deglos in the north of the island, and an upgraded disposal site at Vieux Fort in the south. The Deglos sanitary landfill is a 9-ha purpose-engineered facility with clay lining, piping and two ponds that prevent toxic substances leaching from the site and contaminating the groundwater. The site also has an industrial autoclave and a tyre shredder. Waste collection services are provided for both kerbside collection and communal bins and are organised into eleven collection zones, which are run by private contractors, thereby providing garbage collection to 100% of the island.

Table 3 shows the quantities of waste taken to the two sites in St Lucia from the years 2004–2005 to 2007–2008.

Table 2

Waste category	Percentage of solid waste
Organics	27
Paper	19
Old corrugated cardboard	4
Plastics	19
Textiles	8
Beverage containers	1
Household hazardous	5
Construction and demolition	1
Metals (ferrous)	2
Metals (non-ferrous)	1
Glass	10
Other	3

From Table 7 http://www.eclac.org/ publicaciones/xml/3/45473/LCARL.349.pdf

Table 3

Year	Waste quantity/tonnes		
	Deglos sanitary landfill	Veux Fort waste disposal facility	Total
2004–2005	49 885	23 130	73 015
2005–2006	59 426	22 191	81 617
2006–2007	58 663	20 173	78 836
2007–2008	64 691	19 836	84 527

Data from table on p. 15 of Waste Characterization Study 2008; St Lucia Solid Waste Management Authority.

KEY POINTS

1 Biodegradable wastes can be broken down by decomposers (bacteria and fungi) into carbon dioxide, ammonia and other simple compounds.

2 Non-biodegradable wastes cannot be broken down and will persist in the environment indefinitely.

3 The Caribbean has seen a huge increase in solid wastes and rarely has the facilities to reduce this quantity and bury it safely in landfill sites.

4 St Lucia has an integrated waste management system which is a model that other countries could follow.

SUMMARY QUESTIONS

1 Explain the difference between biodegradable wastes and non-biodegradable wastes.

2 Outline the environmental impact of a poorly maintained waste-disposal site, such as Riverton in Jamaica.

3 What do scientists mean by a 'dead zone'? Suggest how the one in Hunt's Bay has been formed.

4 Discuss how the quantity of solid wastes sent to landfill in Trinidad and Tobago could be reduced.

5 Discuss the benefits of an integrated waste management system as operated in St Lucia.

The information in this spread comes from: The Jamaica Environment Trust and St Lucia Solid Waste Management Authority: Waste Characterization Study 2008.

UNIT 11: Multiple-choice questions

1 Pollution from agricultural sources usually leads to:

  a a decrease in dissolved carbon dioxide in rainwater

  b a decrease in dissolved nitrogen compounds in streams and rivers

  c an increase in the coral population in the ocean

  d an increase in the population of algae in rivers.

2 Which of the following statements about atmospheric pollutants is NOT true?

  a They can cause an increase in the number of people with asthma.

  b They can include smoke and dust.

  c They can increase the concentration of carbon monoxide in the blood.

  d They can increase people's vital capacity.

3 Deforestation in the Caribbean:

  a decreases the organic material in the soil

  b increases atmospheric oxygen

  c increases rainfall

  d provides fertile land for agriculture.

4 Biodegradable waste materials:

  a break down when left in the soil

  b persist indefinitely in the environment

  c dissolve easily in water

  d melt in sunlight.

5 Pit latrines should:

  a be as close as possible to rivers or streams

  b have a window with a mesh cover

  c be no more than two to three feet deep

  d be located on clay soils.

Further practice questions and examples can be found on the accompanying CD.

UNIT 11: Short answer questions

1 a Copy and complete the table to show the sources of three different pollutants and the effects that they have on the environment.

Pollutant	Source	Effect on the environment
Carbon dioxide		
Sulphur dioxide		
Fertilisers		
Heavy metals		

(4)

b The Beetham Landfill in Trinidad is the country's largest disposal site and has been in operation for over 30 years. The table shows the solid wastes delivered there in 1993 and 2004.

	1993	2004
Solid wastes delivered per day/Mt	396	777
Annual solid wastes/ Mt	144 554	283 456
No. of vehicles entering the landfill per year	80 749	154 661
No. of vehicles entering the landfill per day	221	424

  i Use the data in the table to plot two suitable graphs to compare the activity at the landfill site in 1993 and 2004.(5)

  ii Calculate the percentage change in the solid wastes delivered per day to the landfill site between 1993 and 2004. Show your working. (2)

  iii Discuss the possible reasons for the increase in activity at the landfill site.(4)

Total 15 marks

2 a State two causes of air pollution. (2)

Polychlorinated biphenyls (PCBs) are very persistent pollutants which are not metabolised or excreted by organisms. PCBs were used in the manufacture of insulation material and deposited in rivers such as the Hudson River in the USA. Research in the USA measured the concentrations of PCBs in the body tissues of organism in a marine food chain. The results are shown in the table.

Organism	Concentration of PCBs in body tissues/ parts per billion
Phytoplankton	2.85
Zooplankton	1.56
Herring (a fish)	6–45
Porpoise (a marine mammal)	11 400–17 300

b i Use the information in the table to draw a food chain and indicate the concentration next to each trophic level. (4)

ii Suggest how the effects of PCBs on fish and marine mammals might be investigated. (2)

c Use the data in the table to explain the reasons for controlling the release of non-biodegradable wastes into the environment. (3)

d Discuss the advantages of producing packaging materials that are biodegradable. (4)

Total 15 marks

3 Figure 1 shows the main stages in a water treatment works.

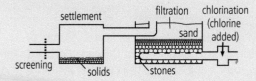

Figure 1

a Use the diagram to explain what happens in a water treatment plant. (6)

b Water supplies are often disrupted following natural disasters such as earthquakes, floods and hurricanes. Explain what people should do to ensure that their drinking water is safe. (3)

c Discuss the effects that human activities have had on the supply of water for domestic consumption and agriculture. (6)

Total 15 marks

4 Raw sewage contains substances, such as cellulose, starch, proteins and fats. Sewage works use the biological filter and activated sludge methods.

a Explain the roles of microorganisms in sewage treatment. (5)

b Explain how a biological filter and an activated sludge tank provide the conditions necessary for microorganisms. (4)

c Discuss how the quantity of solid waste matter in island states in the Caribbean can be reduced. (6)

Total 15 marks

5 a Explain, with the use of examples, how biodegradable wastes differ from non-biodegradable wastes. (4)

b Outline the environmental problems caused by both types of wastes in the Caribbean. (6)

c Discuss the reasons for phasing out pit latrines in the Caribbean. (5)

Total 15 marks

12 How to take the exam

12.1   Paper 1

Paper 1 consists of 60 multiple-choice questions. The paper lasts for 75 minutes, which means you have 75 seconds to answer each question. That's not long if you need thinking time.

In this topic you will see what these types of questions look like, based on topics in the whole syllabus. There are many more MCQs in the 'Test yourself' sections on the CD.

Multiple-choice questions (MCQs)

The MCQs in paper 1 test your recall of knowledge and your skill at comprehension.

Each question has four possible answers and you must choose one. In the examination you put your answers on a special answer sheet.

1 Which substances produced during photosynthesis are essential for the survival of humans?

    a   Carbon dioxide and water

    b   Glucose and carbon dioxide

    c   Glucose and oxygen

    d   Oxygen and water

Read the question very carefully and then read the four answers. Before you make your choice, read the question again to be sure you have chosen the right answer. If you are not sure of the answer, put an asterisk (*) by the side of the question and come back to it later. When you are sure of the answer, shade the appropriate space on the answer sheet. Do not shade more than one. If you change your mind make sure that you erase your first answer thoroughly.

2 Which of the following changes cause inspiration (breathing in) to occur?

	Diaphragm muscle	Internal intercostal muscles	Volume of thorax	Pressure in thorax
a	contracts	contracts	decreases	increases
b	contracts	relaxes	increases	decreases
c	relaxes	contracts	decreases	increases
d	relaxes	relaxes	increases	decreases

Questions like this can be confusing because there is so much information to sift through. It is best to read the question first. The key word here is *inspiration*. Next look at the column headings and try to remember what happens to these four items when you breathe in. Then look for the row that matches your answer. Always read all the possible answers even if you are certain that **a** is the correct answer.

3 The diagram below shows the inheritance of albinism in a family.

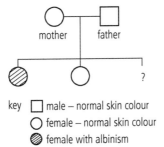

key   ☐ male – normal skin colour
       ○ female – normal skin colour
       ◉ female with albinism

The family is expecting their third child. What is the probability that this child will inherit albinism?

a 0% (none)   **c** 50% (1 in 2)

b 25% (1 in 4)   **d** 100% (all)

This question requires you to work out the genotypes of the parents. Do not guess; work it out logically by writing out a genetic diagram on the exam paper so you can be sure of the answer.

4 Immediately after natural disasters, such as hurricanes and earthquakes, epidemics of diarrhoeal diseases can occur.

What is the best action to take FIRST to stop the spread of these diseases?

a Control the breeding of houseflies

b Restore the piped water supply

c Restore the sewage treatment works

d Supply water purification tablets

All of these actions may need to be taken after a natural disaster. Often the answers to MCQs are all correct statements but you are asked to select the best answer. Look critically at all four answers and in this case try to put yourself in the position of someone living in an area devastated by a natural disaster. What would be your immediate need?

5 Which of the following CANNOT be prevented by a good diet and exercise?

a Influenza   **c** Obesity

b Coronary heart disease   **d** Diabetes type II

Look very carefully for MCQs with 'not' in the question. These are quite common and require careful reading. In this case **a** is the right answer – but always double check if this happens. Do not choose **a** straight away without reading and considering the other possibilities.

If you are not 100% certain of an answer then find what you think is the best answer based on what you can remember. After making your choice, you could look at the other answers and decide why you think that they are not correct.

EXAM TIP

When you have decided which answer is the right one, ask yourself why the others are incorrect. In question 3, what would be the genotypes of the parents if each of the other answers was correct?

STUDY FOCUS

Write out the genetic diagram starting with the phenotypes of the parents and ending with the phenotypes of the children. If you draw a square to show all the possible genotypes of any children, you will see the probabilities. Why are the answers probabilities and not ratios? See 9.4 and 9.5.

EXAM TIP

In questions 4 and 5, a key word is highlighted. This may be done in bold type or in capital letters

Paper 2: Section A – structured questions

Paper 2 lasts for 2 hours. **Section A** in Paper 2 consists of four compulsory structured questions. Each question has a total of 15 marks with six marks for Knowledge and Comprehension (KC) and nine for Use of Knowledge (UK). The total mark for this section is 60. You should spend about 70–80 minutes on this section. The questions in this section of the paper are usually on several different topics, not just one.

First of all, read the whole of each question before you start writing any answers. This will help you understand what the question is about and gives you time to think about your answers. Then, read the question again slowly and highlight any words or terms that you think are important in understanding what you are being told.

Structured question on practical work

Practical work is an important part of your course. One of the structured questions in the paper is always based on an investigation of a practical nature. Here is an investigation that some students carried out using the technique described in 11.2 for testing water quality. Read it through and try imagining yourself carrying out the investigation.

1 A river flows past a school. Students at the school were concerned that it was polluted and should not be used by local children for swimming.

The students took samples of water from five different places (**A** to **E**) along the river. They diluted each sample by a factor of 1000 by adding 1 cm³ of river water to 999 cm³ of sterile water. They then added 0.1 cm³ of each diluted sample to molten agar in a Petri dish and allowed it to set. After incubation for 24 hours the students counted the number of bacterial colonies on each agar plate.

Three agar plates were set up to test the water from each sampling place. The results are shown in the table.

Sampling place	Number of bacterial colonies on each plate of nutrient agar				Number of bacteria in 1.0 cm³ of undiluted river water
	1	**2**	**3**	**mean**	
A	65	84	79	76	760 000
B	68	76	71	72	720 000
C	45	60	55	53	530 000
D	29	43	38	37	370 000
E	15	23	28		

   a i   Suggest how the students sterilised the water. *(1)*

      ii Explain why they prepared three agar plates for each sample. *(2)*

b Explain why the students
   i diluted the sample of river water by a factor of 1000; *(2)*
   ii used sterile water to make the dilutions. *(2)*

c Calculate for sampling place **E**:
   i the mean number of bacteria in 0.1 cm^3 of the diluted river water;
   ii the number of bacteria in 1 cm^3 of undiluted river water. *(2)*

EXAM TIPS

Tables of data can be difficult to understand. Read the column headings first. Then read what is in the left-hand column. Ask yourself questions, e.g. why have the mean numbers been multiplied by 10 000? Look for patterns or trends – here the numbers decrease from **A** to **E**.

EXAM TIPS

The structured question based on practical work may require you to present data as a graph or chart. What type of graph or chart would you use to present the data collected by the students in question 1?

Hint: You do not know anything about the distances along the river. You should also have a calculator in the exam room so you can answer questions like part **c**.

d The students spoke to an environmental protection officer who said that raw sewage often leaked into the river and that there had been cases of leptospirosis in the area.
   i Explain why the river water contained such high numbers of bacteria. *(3)*
   ii Explain what steps should be taken to control the spread of leptospirosis. *(3)*

EXAM TIP

Part **d** is where you are being tested on your knowledge.

2 a i Make a large drawing to show a vertical section of the human heart and the four major blood vessels. *(3)*
   ii Label the four chambers of the heart and the four main blood vessels on your drawing. *(6)*

EXAM TIPS

You should have practised this drawing. Before you start answering, make a large drawing with faint outlines in pencil first to get the proportions correct: two upper chambers with thin walls and two lower chambers, one with thicker walls than the other. Indicate the four blood vessels and then go over your outlines with single solid lines in pencil. Do **not** draw in ink.

EXAM TIPS

If you have a question with a graph, you should write some notes on the graph as you analyse it. This will help you prepare your answer. As you analyse the graph, think about what the graph means. This will help you explain the trend or pattern shown.

b One of the most important causes of death in Caribbean countries is diabetes type II. There are many factors that increase the risk of developing this disease.
   i State four risk factors for diabetes type II. *(4)*
   ii Suggest two ways in which health authorities in the Caribbean can try to reduce the number of cases of diabetes in the Caribbean. *(2)*

Answers to these questions are on the CD.

Paper 2: Section B – essay questions

EXAM TIP

When you read the questions always look for clues. In question 1, 'hot object', 'withdraws hand' and 'quickly' are big hints that you should write about a reflex action. See 7.3 for the ideas you should use in your answer.

EXAM TIPS

Remember the reflex arc from 7.3? You could make a simple diagram of the reflex arc and use it in your answer to show how the response to the hot object is coordinated by the nervous system. You could also use a diagram in answering part **b**. You cannot answer the questions with diagrams alone – you should write prose as well.

Section B in Paper 2 consists of two compulsory structured essay questions. Each question has a total of 15 marks with six marks for Knowledge and Comprehension (KC) and nine for Use of Knowledge (UK). You should spend about 20–25 minutes on each question.

LINK

There are plenty of examples of these types of questions in this book and also in the **On your marks** questions on the CD.

It is a good idea to look at the essay titles in Section B of Paper 2 before you start answering Section A. If you read through these questions you will start to think about what you want to include. You may need time to recall the information. Often your subconscious will work on a problem while you are doing something else. When you think of appropriate things to include, write them down.

When you are ready to start Section B, read through the questions again highlighting the command word that usually starts each question and any key words in the rest of the question. Write a brief plan. This could be in the form of a spider diagram (see page 4) or a list of bullet points. When you have decided what you are going to include begin writing in continuous prose. You may want to include a diagram in your answer; if so, make sure it is labelled and annotate it if that helps to convey your ideas.

There are plenty of essay questions in the book, but here are three more annotated with comments that show you the sorts of things to write as you think about and plan your answers.

Essays

1 A girl touches a hot object and withdraws her hand very quickly.
   a   Describe how this action is coordinated.   (6)
   b   Explain how the structure of the elbow joint allows the movement of the hand to occur easily.   (5)

EXAM TIP

Essay questions cover different topics – **a** is from Unit 7, **b** from Unit 5 and **c** from Units 2 and 5.

   c   Discuss how good nutrition can prevent diseases of the skeletal system, such as osteoporosis.   (4)

2 a Describe the changes that occur in the ovary and the uterus during the menstrual cycle. (6)

  b Explain the roles of hormones in controlling the menstrual cycle. (5)

  c Discuss the effects of sexually transmitted infections (STIs) on pregnant women and the risks that these present for their children. (4)

3 Nitrogen is in many biologically important compounds. Plants absorb nitrogen in the form of nitrate ions.

  a Describe how the nitrogen in protein in dead animals is recycled to nitrate ions for plants to absorb. (6)

  b Discuss how humans are dependent on the activities of plants. (5)

EXAM TIP

Activities of plants? Remember to think laterally – this is not just about food. What else should be in this answer?

  c Explain how agriculture is responsible for releasing pollutants rich in nitrogen into the environment. (4)

Here is some advice on writing your answers in Paper 2:

- Make sure that you write legibly so the examiner can read what you have written.

- Look at the mark allocation and the space available and write enough to answer the question and gain the marks available and not too much.

- As you write keep looking back to the question and *stick to the point.*

- Use short sentences.

- Do not repeat yourself; do not say the same idea in two or more different ways.

- Always use the correct scientific terms; remember the words in your revision glossary.

- When you have finished, read your answer and *check that it answers the question.*

Drawing and analysing graphs

The structured questions in Section A of Paper 2 may require you to draw a graph. There is plenty of advice on drawing graphs in this Study Guide. You may have to analyse and interpret a graph that you have drawn or you may be given a graph. There are two things you should be prepared to do if you see a graph: **describe** the pattern or trend and **explain** what the graph shows.

Be prepared to draw sketch graphs in your answers in Paper 2. These can be a good way to convey information that takes many words to describe.

EXAM TIPS

You should make a diagram to help you with your answer; this could be a plan or it could be the basis of your whole answer. There are two clues here – 'dead' and 'plants to absorb'. Dead implies you should write about decomposers and 'plants to absorb' means you can stop your answer at nitrate ions. Nitrification is the key idea to use in this answer. See 1.8.

STUDY FOCUS

Nitrogen is an element present in many compounds. As N_2 it forms much of the atmosphere and is not readily available to organisms except those that carry out nitrogen fixation. A useful way to revise is to link together everything in the syllabus that involves nitrogen: try starting with proteins, enzymes, urea, kidney, urine, fertilisers and pollution.

Answers to these questions are on the CD.

Index

Note: Key terms (glossary terms) are in **bold** type.

Index

Acknowledgements

The author and the publisher would also like to thank the following for permission to reproduce material:

Text extracts

p72, data table about deaths from heart disease sourced from the Caribbean Epidemiology Centre, http://www.paho.org/, Pan American Health Organization; p99, diagram of eye function sourced from Mackean, D.G. (1995) *GCSE Biology*. London: John Murray; p199, data table sourced from United Nations – Population Division Department of Economic and Social Affairs; p157, data table on the economic costs of substance abuse sourced from the National Council on Drug Abuse (NCDA), accessed May 2013; p158, data from WHO Denguenet. For information about Denguenet see http://apps.who.int/globalatlas/default.asp, accessed May 2013; p159, tables 2 and 4: Pan American Health Organiztion, table 3: Global Health Observatory Data Repository, http://apps.who.int/gho/data/node.main, accessed May 2013, table 5: UNICEF, The State of the World's Children 2013, UNICEF, New York, 2013, pp. 100–103, table 6: Immunization surveillance, assessment and monitoring Measles, http://gamapserver.who.int/gho/interactive_charts/immunization/mcv/atlas.html?fi%20lter=fi%20lter4,Americas, accessed May 2013; p161, World Malaria Report 2012, http://www.who.int/malaria/publications/world_malaria_report_2012/en/index.html, accessed May 2013; p175, information on biodegradable wastes (11.7) sourced from the Jamaica Environment Trust and Solid Waste Management Authority: Waste Characterization Study 2008; p175, table 2 on the percentage of solid waste sourced from Willard Phillips and Elizabeth Thorne, "Municipal Solid Waste Management in the Caribbean – a benefit cost Analysis", series Studies and perspectives Nº 22 (LC/L.3543; LC/CAR/L.349), Port of Spain, Economic Commission for Latin America and the Caribbean (ECLAC) Subregional Headquarters for The Caribbean, December 2011; p175, table 3 on quantity of waste taken to two sites in Saint Lucia, sourced from Saint Lucia Solid Waste Management Authority: Waste Characterization Study 2008; p176, table on the Beetham Landfill, Mr. Al Binger (2011), Economic Opportunities in Waste Management in Small Island Developing States (SIDS), Presentation delivered at the CSD-19 Intercessional Conference on Building Partnerships for Moving towards Zero Waste, 16–18 February 2011, Tokyo, Japan, co-organized by the United Nations Department of Economic and Social Affairs (UNDESA), the United Nations Centre for Regional Development (UNCRD), and the Ministry of the Environment of Japan(MOEJ). http://www.uncrd.or.jp/env/csd18_19.htm

Images and diagrams

p6, iStockphoto; p7, iStockphoto; p8, palisade mesophyll cells: Ian Couchman of Cambridge International Examinations, membrane, cytoplasm and nucleus: Ed Reschke/Getty Images; p10, CNRI/SCIENCE PHOTO LIBRARY; p12, Michael Abbey/Science Photo Library; p14, Richard Fosbery; p15, iStockphoto; p16, Richard Bickel/Corbis; p18, dbimages/Alamy; p19, Bruce Watson; p21, top: inga spence/Alamy, bottom: POWER AND SYRED/SCIENCE PHOTO LIBRARY; p26, child with night blindness: Lance Bellers, published in *Community Eye Health Journal* Vol.22 No.71 DECEMBER 2009 www.cehjournal.org, rickets: BSIP SA/Alamy; p27, Bob Krist/Corbis; p28, therapeutic food: Michaël Zumstein / Agence Vu'. These photographs were shot at St-Camille Hospital in Ouagadougou, Burkina Faso, and illustrate the use of Plumpy'nut®, Plumpy'doz® and ZinCfant®, child with marasmus: WESLEY BOCXE/SCIENCE PHOTO LIBRARY, child with kwashiorkor: Christine Osborne Pictures/Alamy; p33, Andersen Ross/Getty Images; p38, MARTYN F. CHILLMAID/SCIENCE PHOTO LIBRARY; p39, Ian Couchman of Cambridge International Examinations; p40, iStockphoto; p42, DR. RICHARD KESSEL & DR. GENE SHIH, VISUALS UNLIMITED /SCIENCE PHOTO LIBRARY; p46, iStockphoto;

p51, Ian Couchman of Cambridge International Examinations; p52, Shutterstock; p53, yeast cells: Science Photo Library/Alamy, brewery: iStockphoto, bread dough: Nelson Thornes; p55, x-ray of lung cancer: iStockphoto, lung cancer: MEDIMAGE/SCIENCE PHOTO LIBRARY; p57, using spirometer: Laurence Wesson and John Luttick (James Allen's Girls' School), athlete on treadmill: SCIENCE PHOTO LIBRARY, Shelley-Anne Fraser Pryce: Shutterstock, Tirunesh Dibaba: AFP/Getty Images; p62, both: Ian Couchman of Cambridge International Examinations; p66, PAUL RAPSON/SCIENCE PHOTO LIBRARY; p67, BIOPHOTO ASSOCIATES/SCIENCE PHOTO LIBRARY; p68, Science Photo Library/Alamy; p76, top: Mark Horn/Getty Images, bottom: Shutterstock; p79, both: iStockphoto; p81, top: iStockphoto, bottom: ZEPHYR/Getty Images; p84, both: Richard Fosberry and Ian Couchman of Cambridge International Examinations; p93, iStockphoto; p94, Science Photo Library/Alamy; p96, Laurence Wesson and John Luttick (James Allen's Girls' School); p97, Ian Couchman of Cambridge International Examinations; p98, SUSUMU NISHINAGA/SCIENCE PHOTO LIBRARY; p99, Shutterstock; p100, Shutterstock; p107, developing ovum: Ian Couchman of Cambridge International Examinations, ovulation: PROF. P. MOTTA/DEPT. OF ANATOMY/UNIVERSITY "LA SAPIENZA", ROME/SCIENCE PHOTO LIBRARY; p109, JUERGEN BERGER/SCIENCE PHOTO LIBRARY; p111, fig. 8.3.2 two separate graphs of the changes in the concentration of oestrogen and progesterone in the blood during a menstrual cycle, adapted from Cambridge IGCSE Biology 0610 Paper 33 Q6 Fig. 6.1 October/November 2010; p113, top: fig. 8.4.2 'a full term foetus in the uterus, adapted from Cambridge IGCSE Biology 0610 Paper 31 Q3 Fig. 3.1 May/June 2011, bottom: iStockphoto; p114, top: Vladimir Pcholkin/Getty Images, bottom: Purestock/Alamy; p115, top: Dinodia Photos/Alamy, bottom: iStockphoto; p116, iStockphoto; p120, BSIP, V & L/SCIENCE PHOTO LIBRARY; p118, a diagram of the human reproductive system, adapted from Cambridge IGCSE Biology 0610 Paper 32 Q5 Fig. 5.1 May/June 2012; p121, Shutterstock; p124, Laurence Wesson and John Luttick (James Allen's Girls' School); p125, iStockphoto; p126, SOLVIN ZANKL/VISUALS UNLIMITED, INC. /SCIENCE PHOTO LIBRARY; p128, Visual & Written SL/Alamy; p129, top: iStockphoto, bottom: FRANCIS LEROY, BIOCOSMOS/SCIENCE PHOTO LIBRARY; p130, SCIENCE PHOTO LIBRARY; p131, DAVID NICHOLLS/SCIENCE PHOTO LIBRARY; p133, iStockphoto; p137, top: Laurence Wesson and John Luttick (James Allen's Girls' School); bottom: SCIENCE PHOTO LIBRARY; p138, iStockphoto; p139, top: iStockphoto, bottom: SAMUEL ASHFIELD/SCIENCE PHOTO LIBRARY; p141, Julie Dermansky/Corbis; p142, DR M.A. ANSARY/SCIENCE PHOTO LIBRARY; p144, Amanda Koster/Corbis; p145, top: DR. HANS GELDERBLOM, VISUALS UNLIMITED /SCIENCE PHOTO LIBRARY, bottom: Shutterstock; p146, iStockphoto; p147, CDC/SCIENCE PHOTO LIBRARY; p148, ANTHONY MARTINET/LOOK AT SCIENCES/SCIENCE PHOTO LIBRARY; p149, top: Nigel Cattlin/Alamy, bottom: Fotolia; p151, Buena Vista Images/Getty Images; p152, Shutterstock; p153, iStockphoto; p155, JOHN DURHAM/SCIENCE PHOTO LIBRARY; p156, iStockphoto; p157, iStockphoto; p158, ZUMA Press, Inc./Alamy; p162, iStockphoto; p164, iStockphoto; p166, both: iStockphoto; p168, iStockphoto; p170–171, Sustainable Sanitation Alliance; p172, Shutterstock; p173, Marcus Clackson/Getty Images; p174, Shutterstock.

Every effort has been made to trace the copyright holders but if any have been inadvertently overlooked the publisher will be pleased to make the necessary arrangements at the first opportunity.